# Work and Leisure

Edited by John T. Haworth
and A. J. Veal

 Routledge
Taylor & Francis Group

LONDON AND NEW YORK

First published 2004
by Routledge
27 Church Road, Hove, East Sussex BN3 2FA

Simultaneously published in the USA and Canada
by Routledge Inc
270 Madison Avenue, New York, NY 10016

Transferred to digital printing 2010

*Routledge is an imprint of the Taylor & Francis Group, an Informa business*

Copyright © 2004 Psychology Press

Typeset in Times by RefineCatch Limited, Bungay, Suffolk
Printed and bound in Great Britain by
TJI Digital, Padstow, Cornwall
Paperback cover design by Hybert Design

Every effort has been made to ensure that the advice and
information in this book is true and accurate at the time of going
to press. However, neither the publisher nor the authors can
accept any legal responsibility or liability for any errors or
omissions that may be made.

This publication has been produced with paper manufactured to
strict environmental standards and with pulp derived from
sustainable forests.

*British Library Cataloguing in Publication Data*
A catalogue record for this book is available from the British Library

*Library of Congress Cataloging-in-Publication Data*
Work and leisure / [edited by] John T. Haworth and A.J. Veal.
    p. cm.
  Includes bibliographical references and index.
  ISBN 0-415-25057-9–ISBN 0-415-25058-7 (pbk.)
  1. Work. 2. Leisure. 3. Voluntarism. 4. Well-being. 5. Quality
of life. 6. Twenty-first century—Forecasts. I. Haworth, John
Trevor. II. Veal, Anthony James.
HD4904.6.W667 2004
306.3'6—dc22                                    2004009692

ISBN 978-0-415-25058-0 (pbk)

Work a... _____

Here is a book that smashes discipline boundaries and addresses one of the twenty-first century's really big issues. The economy is more productive than ever. Leisure and spending are still on the rise. So why are we no happier? This book supplies answers. The chapters, all by specialists in their field, review what is known about how our jobs and how we use the rest of our time affect our well-being, positively and negatively.

Ken Roberts, Professor of Sociology, University of Liverpool

Globalisation, economic development and changes in social environments have put the relationships between work, leisure, social structure and quality of life in the spotlight. Profound transformations in the nature and organisation of work are occurring, with potentially far-reaching social and economic consequences. Increasingly, organisations demand greater flexibility from their workforces and are introducing new technologies and practices in response to global competitive pressures. At the same time many employees are experiencing long working hours, increasing workloads and job insecurity, along with the challenge of balancing work and domestic responsibilities. These changes threaten long-term gains in leisure time while, simultaneously, the leisure environment is also changing radically, through increasing commercialisation and professionalisation of leisure services and experiences, the influence of the Internet, the rise of gambling and the decline of community-based activities.

Exploring all of these issues, *Work and Leisure* brings together specially commissioned chapters from international experts in a wide range of disciplines concerned with work, leisure and well-being. Each author takes stock of the current position, identifies core practical and theoretical issues and discusses possible future trends in order to provide an invaluable resource for all policy-makers, educators, employers and researchers in the field.

**John T. Haworth** is Research Associate, Centre for Social Change and Well-being, and Honorary Research Fellow, Department of Fine Arts, Manchester Metropolitan University, UK.
**A. J. Veal** is Adjunct Professor, School of Leisure, Sport and Tourism, University of Technology, Sydney, Australia.

# Contents

**PART II**
**Quality of life and work and leisure** 121

# Illustrations

## FIGURES

## TABLES

# Notes on contributors

**Alisa M. Ainbinder** is a PhD candidate in the School of Social Service Administration at the University of Chicago, USA. Her major interest is studying stress and coping, particularly in lower-income communities.

**Peter Bramham** is Senior Lecturer in the School of Leisure and Sport Studies at Leeds Metropolitan University, UK. He is author or editor of *Understanding Leisure* (1989); *Leisure and Urban Processes* (1989); *Leisure Policies in Europe* (1993); *Sociology of Leisure: A Reader* (1995); *Leisure Research in Europe* (1996); *Sport and Recreation Development: Policy, Process and Practice* (2001).

**Chas Critcher** is Professor of Communications and Head of the Humanities Research Centre at Sheffield Hallam University, UK. He is author or editor of *The Devil Makes Work* (1985); *Sociology of Leisure: A Reader* (1995); *Out of the Ashes? Decline and Regeneration in Britain's Mining Communities* (2001); *Moral Panics and the Media* (2003).

**Mihaly Csikszentmihalyi** is Professor of Psychology at the Peter F. Drucker School of Management of Claremont Graduate University, California, USA, and Director of the Quality of Life Research Center. His major interests include the study of creativity, of optimal human experiences, and the evolution of culture. He is the author of 18 books; *Flow: The Psychology of Happiness* (1992) has been translated into 19 languages. The latest, *Good Business* (2003), is a best-seller in several languages.

**Chris Gratton** is Professor of Sport Economics and Director of the Sport Industry Research Centre (SIRC) and the Leisure Industries Research Centre (LIRC) at Sheffield Hallam University, UK. He is a specialist in the economic analysis of sport and leisure markets. He has just completed his term as Chair of UoA (Units of Assessment) 69 Sport-related Subjects in Research Assessment Exercise 2001.

**John T. Haworth** is Research Associate (part-time), Centre for Social Change and Well-being, and an Honorary Research Fellow, Department of Fine

Arts, Manchester Metropolitan University, UK. He has published extensively on work, leisure and well-being. Formerly at Manchester University, he co-founded the Leisure Studies Association (LSA), and the international journal *Leisure Studies*. Recent funded projects on well-being, and on creativity and embodied mind, can be seen at www.haworthjt.com.

**Seppo E. Iso-Ahola** is a Professor in the Department of Kinesiology, University of Maryland, USA. He has published extensively on the social psychology of leisure, sports, exercise and health.

**Roger C. Mannell** is a Professor in the Department of Recreation, University of Waterloo, Canada. His numerous publications and studies focus on various social psychological aspects of leisure behaviour.

**Chris Rojek** is Professor of Sociology and Culture in the Theory, Culture and Society Centre at Nottingham Trent University, UK. He is author or editor of *Capitalism and Leisure Theory* (1985); *Leisure for Leisure* (1989); *Sport and Leisure in the Civilizing Process* (1992); *Ways of Escape: Modern Transformations in Leisure and Travel* (1993); *Decentring Leisure: Rethinking Leisure Theory* (1995); *Leisure and Culture* (2000); *Celebrity* (2001).

**Barbara Schneider** is a Professor of Sociology at the University of Chicago, USA, and Co-Director of the Alfred P. Sloan Center on Parents, Children, and Work. She is also the Director of the Data Research and Development Center. Her most recent book, co-authored with Anthony Bryk, is *Trust in Schools: A Core Resource for Improvement*. Her major interests are families and adolescent development.

**Robert A. Stebbins** is Faculty Professor in the Department of Sociology, University of Calgary, Canada. He received his PhD in 1964 from the University of Minnesota. He is author of 29 books and monographs, plus numerous articles and chapters, including *Between Work and Leisure* (2004). He is a Fellow of the Royal Society of Canada.

**Peter Taylor** is a specialist in the economics of sport and leisure markets and organisations. He is Professor of Leisure Management, University of Sheffield, UK; editor of *Managing Leisure: an International Journal*; Companion of the Institute of Sport and Recreation Management; and a director of the English Institute of Sport, Sheffield.

**A. J. Veal** is Adjunct Professor in the School of Leisure, Sport and Tourism at the University of Technology Sydney, Australia. He is author or editor of *Leisure and the Future* (1987); *World Leisure Participation* (1996); *Research Methods for Leisure and Tourism* (1997); *The Olympic Games: A Social Science Perspective* (2000); *Australian Leisure* (2001); *Leisure and Tourism Policy and Planning* (2002).

**Judy White** recently retired from the position of Reader in the University of North London, UK, having previously worked at the University of Birmingham. She has written extensively on leisure and recreation issues, with a recent emphasis on the role of women in leisure management. She is author or editor of *The Future of Leisure Services* (1998); *The Economic and Social Impact of the National Lottery* (1998); *Women's Leisure Experiences* (2001).

**Jiri Zuzanek** is Distinguished Professor Emeritus at the University of Waterloo, Canada. He previously held university appointments in Lund (Sweden), New York and Prague. He is author or editor of *Social Research and Cultural Policy* (1979); *Work and Leisure in the Soviet Union* (1980); *World Leisure Participation* (1996); *The Effects of Time Use and Time Pressure or Child–Parent Relationships* (2000).

# Preface

The year 2000 was the twenty-fifth anniversary of the publication of *Work and Leisure: An Interdisciplinary Study in Theory, Education and Planning* (Haworth and Smith 1975). The book was based on the proceedings of a conference at which the Leisure Studies Association was conceived. Three decades later, global economic and social environments are very different, the mood is more uncertain and forecasting simplistic trends in work and leisure patterns is no longer appropriate. In this transformed environment, the relationship between work, leisure, social structure and well-being have emerged as challenging concerns for researchers, educators and policy-makers. Some commentators argue that profound transformations in the nature and organisation of work are occurring with potentially far-reaching social and economic consequences. Many organisations are demanding greater flexibility and introducing new technologies and working practices in response to the pressures of competition. Innovation is needed to sustain and create new jobs. Training for job skills is now a crucial part of economic strategy. And the meanings and concepts of work and leisure are being reappraised.

For some organisations flexibility of working practices are being coupled with policies for a balanced work and non-work life, sometimes in response to new attitudes, values and aspirations of key workers, but also to enhance creativity, improve company loyalty, and reduce the corporate health bill. Yet many employees are experiencing long hours, increasing workloads, changing work practices, and job insecurity. Stress at work and home is viewed as a major problem. At the same time, major social differentiation exists with increasing numbers of women in the paid workforce facing particular challenges, with resources in Western societies being increasingly unequally distributed, and significant variations arising in health, well-being and quality of life. The leisure environment has also changed radically with increasing commercialisation of leisure services and experiences, the influence of the Internet and globalisation, and a widespread decline in community-based activities.

This book brings together specially commissioned chapters from a number of leading experts in a wide range of disciplines concerned with work, leisure and well-being. The book is envisaged as a high-level text for final year undergraduates and postgraduates in the social sciences, and an accessible source for policy-makers in private sector and government organisations. Each author takes stock of the current position in relation to a particular aspect of work and leisure, identifies core theoretical and practical issues, and discusses research and policy implications.

In 1975, work seemed assured and increasing leisure the promised reward for all. Three decades later, the world seems to be a less certain place. But equitable access to work, and leisure, and a satisfactory well-being, remain key objectives for individuals and communities around the world. Our aim is for this book to contribute to the debate concerning ways and means of meeting these objectives.

## Related books by the editors

Haworth, J. T. (1997) *Work, Leisure, and Well-Being*. London: Routledge.
Haworth, J. T. and Smith, M. A. (eds) (1975) *Work and Leisure: An Interdisciplinary Study in Theory, Education and Planning*. London: Lepus.
Veal, A. J. (1987) *Leisure and the Future*. London: Allen and Unwin.
Veal, A. J. (2002) *Leisure and Tourism Policy and Planning*. Wallingford, UK: CAB International.

# Introduction

*John T. Haworth and A. J. Veal*

In the mid-1970s, the volume *Work and Leisure* (Haworth and Smith 1975) established a number of parameters which shaped the study of work and leisure then and which remain salient three decades later. The first was the complexity of the field of study, due in part to the multifaceted nature of the concepts involved. Second, it was observed that the field of study necessarily involved a considerable range of disciplines. Third, the field reflected the ongoing 'agency–structure' debate in the social sciences: that is, the extent to which individuals act on and influence their life situations rather than being shaped primarily by wider social and economic forces and events. Fourth, as a result of its increasing social and economic significance, leisure had become a public policy and planning issue and was caught up in debates on public participation, the environment and the quality of life.

The question of definitions of work and leisure raised by the editors of the 1975 volume was not resolved – except to suggest that the definitions used should be broad rather than narrow, in order not to restrict the concepts used in research (Haworth and Smith 1975: 1). The question of defining leisure at the time had been influenced by a normative, 'classical' view of the phenomenon promulgated by writers such as Josef Pieper (1999 [1952]: 26) and Sebastian De Grazia (1962: 5), who saw leisure as a 'condition of the soul' or a 'state of being' which might or might not be achieved during 'free time'. Today, the so-called 'residual' definition of leisure, that is time which is not occupied by paid work, unpaid work or personal chores and obligations, is widely accepted for its proven utility in research (Roberts 1999: 5) and is inclusive and non-normative. However, Roberts (1999: 23) notes that the residual definition of leisure proves difficult to apply to unemployed and retired people, as well as among women, regardless of their employment status. He also recognises that technological, economic and social changes in society impact on leisure, making it 'necessary to ask repeatedly whether we need to revise our notions about what leisure is' (Roberts 1999: 5).

It is important to emphasise that the residual approach does *not* define leisure only, or even primarily, in relation to paid work. The normative dimension is omitted from the residual definition: leisure is not, of itself, seen as 'good' or 'bad'. Leisure time and activity can be used for good or ill and that itself will often be a contested, subjective judgement. Of course public policy related to leisure is inevitably normative – leisure policies seek to promote those activities which are deemed, through a political process which may or may not be contentious, to be socially beneficial and to restrict, or even prohibit, those activities deemed to be socially harmful. Acceptance of the 'residual', time-based definition of leisure does not imply a view of leisure as necessarily culturally residual and does not deny that leisure has many complex meanings and functions for the individual and society, which are open to research and investigation (Roberts 1999: 153).

Yet many researchers view leisure in terms of what it is, focusing on dimensions of positive experience, such as intrinsic motivation and autonomy, and enjoyment (Iso-Ahola 1980; Neulinger 1981; Mannell and Kleiber 1997; Stebbins 1998; Thompson et al. 2002). Interestingly, some of the dimensions of positive experience studied by leisure researchers have been found to be very relevant to the study of well-being, which is now an important area of research, and will be returned to later in this introduction. It is therefore important to recognise that both residual and experiential definitions of leisure are important. Both types of definition are used by the contributors to this book, with residual definitions usually being used when large-scale survey research and trends are discussed, and experiential definitions being used more often when leisure and well-being are discussed, though they are not mutually exclusive.

The definition of work has been less problematical than that of leisure. Usually, work is considered to be paid employment. But a significant change since the mid-1970s has been to emphasise that 'work' not only includes paid work, but also includes unpaid domestic and childcare work and some community voluntary activity. Work has often been equated with labour, in line with the Hebrew view that it was imposed on humankind to expiate the original sin committed by its forefathers, or the Protestant view that work was of service to God. Yet, as noted in Haworth and Smith (1975), if

> a restricted definition of work is used, such as 'to earn a living', this can equally restrict the constructs which are used to study work and thus have important theoretical significance. Practically, it may encourage the attitude in management, trade unions and employees, that work need not be a meaningful experience.
>
> (Haworth and Smith 1975: 1)

But work is important to human functioning. Kohn and Schooler (1983) indicate that where work has substantive complexity there is an improvement in mental flexibility and self-esteem. Csikszentmihalyi and LeFevre (1989), studying 'optimal experience' or 'flow' in a range of occupations, found that this came more from work than leisure. The historian of work, Applebaum (1992), considered that

> Work is like the spine which structures the way people live, how they make contact with material and social reality, and how they achieve status and self-esteem . . . Work is basic to the human condition, to the creation of the human environment, and to the context of human relationships.
>
> (Applebaum 1992: ix)

In modern society, paid work has been found to be important for well-being (Warr 1987).

The study of the work–leisure relationship brings together two separate multidisciplinary research traditions: the study of work and the study of leisure. Each field of study encompasses a wide range of issues in addition to those directly concerning the work–leisure relationship. Thus the study of work also involves work organisation, industrial relations and workplace behaviour and experience, while the study of leisure includes a concern with participation in different leisure activities and the leisure behaviour of those not in the paid workforce, including children and retired people. The perceived importance of the work–leisure relationship has therefore fluctuated over time within each of the research traditions. The relationship was important in the early 1970s because leisure was a relatively new field of study and a relatively newly discovered 'social problem', and the possibility that leisure might supplant work as the 'central life interest' of individuals in Western society was being actively discussed. It re-emerged as a central issue in the 1990s as the century-old trend in Western societies towards less work time and more leisure time seemed to go into reverse (Schor 1991) and many began to experience the phenomenon of 'time-squeeze' or 'time-bind' (Hochschild 1997) and associated stress and threats to health and well-being.

Despite the common relevance of the work–leisure relationship, there is, therefore, a difference in the two periods. In the 1970s the work–leisure nexus was pushed to the fore because of issues raised by the emerging abundance of leisure; in the 1990s and currently, a key issue is the emerging lack of leisure, at least for some. A further difference in the two periods is that the intervening years have witnessed a significant development of research on work and leisure, involving new theoretical insights and a substantial programme of empirical study. The range of theoretical perspectives and the amount of empirical evidence on which to draw is therefore substantially changed. Thus theoretical frameworks, such as neo-Marxism, feminism and postmodernism, and concepts such as well-being, 'flow' and serious leisure, have all had an influence on the field of study since the mid-1970s. These developments are reflected in the contents of the current book compared with those of the 1975 volume.

As indicated earlier, research into work and leisure has been important for research into well-being. Haworth (1997) reviewed the then current literature and presented findings of the latest research which showed the importance of both personal and situational factors for well-being. Enjoyment was found to be important for well-being, as was the support, structure and a range of other experiences provided by employment. The diversity of individual experience and requirements was recognised. This was seen to be something which is not merely a function of rational knowledge, but is built into the bodily fibre of experience and social networks of practice (Haworth 1997: ch. 7) reflecting both the social and temporal nature of human endeavour.

The picture of our human condition is continually being informed by research, analysis, and new perspectives. The UK Economic and Social Research Council (ESRC) launched the 'Future of Work' research programme in 1998 to help close the gap in our understanding of the changing world of work. A report from the programme (Taylor 2002) considers that class and occupational differences remain of fundamental importance to any understanding of the world of work. The research also found that the present-day world of work is much less satisfying to employees than the one they were experiencing in the mid-1990s, particularly in relation to pay, job prospects and training. The report considers that if employees are going to cooperate in a positive and active manner with the management of workplace change, they are going to need a greater sense of well-being, status and control over the work they perform. In addition the report argues that a determined effort is required to assess the purpose of paid work in all our lives, and the need to negotiate a genuine trade-off between the needs of job efficiency and leisure.

In 2001–2, the UK Economic and Social Research Council also funded a trans-disciplinary series of four invitational seminars on 'Wellbeing: situational and personal determinants' (see www.wellbeing-esrc.com). The aim was to address positive outcomes, and how best to realise them, the objective being to complement the emphasis of research on stress and ill-health. The seminars concluded that social position significantly influences access to resources, well-being and health in the United Kingdom. Wellness was seen to be achieved by the simultaneous and balanced satisfaction of personal, interpersonal and collective needs, and by a therapeutic relationship with natural, built and social environments. It was recognised that there are cultural and social group differences in perceptions of well-being, and factors influencing well-being, and that there are global level prerequisites for societal and individual well-being, including a reduction of poverty and inequality across the world.

In the United States, a new focus on 'Positive Psychology' is concerned with factors leading to well-being, positive individuals and flourishing corporations and communities (Kahneman et al. 1999; special edition of the *American Psychologist*, January 2000; Snyder and Lopez 2000; see also website www.positivepsychology.org). Positive Psychology at the subjective level is about positive experience: well-being, optimism, hope, happiness and flow. At the individual level it is about the character strengths: the capacity for love and vocation, courage, interpersonal skill, aesthetic sensibility, perseverance, forgiveness, originality, future-mindedness and genius. At the group level it is about the civic virtues and the institutions that move individuals toward better citizenship: leadership, responsibility, parenting, altruism, civility, moderation, tolerance, and a work ethic. The US Positive Psychology programme is very praiseworthy, and will stimulate much-needed research in other countries as well as in the United States. The programme could be enhanced by the study of the influence of social institutions on behaviour and well-being, as instigated by Jahoda (1982).

This book is divided into two parts. The first, 'The changing face of work and leisure', is partly historical, both in terms of the history of work and leisure and in terms of the recent history of developments in the fields of study, and partly forward-looking, considering the adequacy of traditional theory to address new economic and social conditions and trends. The second part, 'Quality of life and work and leisure', focuses particularly on quality of life and well-being issues. The contributions in each section will now be briefly summarised.

## Part I The changing face of work and leisure

This part of the book contains six chapters, each of which provides a review of the state-of-the-art of research in the field of study of work and leisure from a particular viewpoint: historical, critical, postmodern, feminist, economic and sociological.

In 1975, when the original *Work and Leisure* volume was published, the challenge of leisure was immediate: the contributed chapters were generally concerned with the 'here and now' and the immediate future – history was all but ignored. Since that time, numerous historical studies have addressed the issue of the historical development of leisure and work. Taken as a whole, these contributions have, however, been fragmentary, with some authors harking back to classical Greece and Rome, some focusing on the Middle Ages, and most concentrating on the period of the industrial revolution and nineteenth-century Europe and North America. Chapter 1 seeks to provide a brief overview of the history of work, based on available literature – in fact it begins with prehistory, examining the question of whether the way of life of members of hunter-gatherer societies could be said to include 'work' and 'leisure'. The clear common message is that, throughout history, although religious as well as economic forces have been influential, the development of leisure has consistently been 'the other side of the coin' of developments in work and the economic organisation of society. This is reinforced by the general thrust of the other chapters in this section, that leisure is very much subject to the effects of the changing national and international economy and their resultant effects on work. In the words of Bill Clinton's US presidential campaign: 'It's the economy, stupid'.

The development of the field of leisure studies since the mid-1970s has been characterised by what Chris Rojek (1985: 5) termed 'paradigmatic rivalry'. Nowhere was this more clearly demonstrated than in John Clarke and Chas Critcher's seminal work of the mid-1980s, *The Devil Makes Work: Leisure in Capitalist Britain*, in which they outlined the shortcomings, as they saw them, of earlier perspectives on leisure, such as those expounded by Stanley Parker, Ken Roberts, Rhona and Robert Rapoport and Michael Young and Peter Willmott, and presented their own critical analysis of the phenomenon of leisure. They sought to discover 'what leisure can tell us about the development, structure and organisation of the whole society' (Clarke and Critcher 1985: xiii). In Chapter 2 of this volume Chas Critcher and Peter Bramham review the changes which have taken place in work and the economy, in the family and social structure and in leisure and culture in Britain, and in social theory, since the late 1970s. They conclude that the analysis in *The Devil Makes Work* stands the test of time. Changes in the labour market have been such that increasing productivity and wealth have failed to produce the anticipated across-the-board increase in prosperity and leisure time, but have resulted in a growing division between those with highly skilled and paid and pressurised jobs and the casualised and marginalised. Changes in family and household structures and patterns of child-bearing and rearing have not, Critcher and Bramham argue, dislodged the family or household unit as the major site for leisure. As for leisure itself, despite increasing commodification and globalisation of providers and products, and the associated increased focus on consumption, the traditional critical concerns with *production* and biological and cultural *reproduction* still provide the essential basis for understanding leisure. It is nevertheless suggested that there is a need for 'some engagement with new kinds of theories which purport to encapsulate the nature of recent societal change'.

In Chapter 3 Chris Rojek picks up from this point. He considers many of the same issues concerning recent economic and social change, in particular the polarisation between the overworked section of the community identified in Juliet Schor's (1991) *The Overworked American* and the increasingly marginalised and insecure mass identified by Ulrich Beck (2000) in the 'Brazilianization thesis'. Rojek addresses the question of solutions to the 'post-work' world, including the idea of a guaranteed income and the possibility of harnessing unpaid *civil labour* to undertake work of community benefit. But he notes the likely problems of adopting such measures given the currently entrenched values of Western society.

One of the major criticisms of the study of work–leisure relationships prior to the 1980s was that it was 'gender-blind'. This was certainly reflected in the 1975 *Work and Leisure* book. While data were available at the time on the differences in men's and women's patterns of leisure participation and non-participation, there was little by way of explanation of these differences, and when work–leisure relationships were discussed, the assumed model of *work* was the full-time paid job. During the intervening three decades, one of the major social and economic changes in Western societies is that substantially more women have full-time and part-time paid jobs; however, they also continue to shoulder the bulk of the burden of unpaid work in childcare and homecare. In Chapter 4 Judy White describes the developing feminist consciousness and epistemology which arose during the 1970s to challenge the 'malestream' view and which led to the emergence of substantial research on women's experience of leisure and work, paid and unpaid. But, as in other areas of social life, while there has been noticeable change in women's patterns of work and leisure, many of the fundamentals remain unchanged. White notes a parallel impasse in feminist leisure research concerning desirable future theoretical, empirical and political directions, and concludes that the emancipatory battles which emerged in the 1970s are not over.

Economic forces have been the driver of change which has produced such significant social and cultural change since the mid-1970s, with monetarism emerging to challenge unbridled Keynesianism in the world of economic policy and the rise of the political 'New Right' based on 'economic rationalism'. In Chapter 5, Chris Gratton and Peter Taylor provide an economic perspective on the changing relationship between work and leisure over recent years. The economic theory of 'income/leisure trade-off' posits that work and leisure time operate in connected markets, mediated in particular by the wage rate: workers choose more or less work depending on their own desires and needs and on the going wage rate – that is, what employers will pay the worker to give up an hour of leisure time. The changes seen in work patterns in Britain over recent years do not, however, conform to the predictions of the trade-off model. Gratton and Taylor conclude that the model, as normally promulgated, is too simplistic and ignores the power of employers in the market situation and the social realities of the labour market.

In Chapter 6 A. J. (Tony) Veal reviews three research traditions which have addressed the issue of the relationship between work and leisure since the mid-1970s or so, namely, first, the early work of Wilensky and Parker in devising typologies of work–leisure relationships, second, research on the relationships between leisure participation and occupation-based socio-economic groups, and third, the phenomenon of occupational communities. Although these research traditions were largely eclipsed during the 1980s and 1990s, by theoretical approaches and concerns which were seen to be more intimately related to broader social theory, the chapter suggests that they were, in fact, more theoretically informed than they are often given credit for and, further, that all three traditions provide a legitimate basis for current concerns in the study of leisure.

If it was ever the case that the study of leisure was insufficiently connected with wider social, cultural and economic issues and processes, the chapters in Part I suggest that this is no longer the case. In fact, it can be said that, while it has been more extensively studied and become more fully understood, the phenomenon of leisure has been healthily 'decentred' (Rojek 1995).

## Part II   Quality of life and work and leisure

The chapters in the second part of the book bridge traditional and new approaches to the study of well-being and quality of life. They address the relationship between work and leisure patterns and time-pressure and stress; stress among working parents; work and leisure and the concept of well-being; the reciprocal relationship between leisure and health; and serious leisure, volunteerism and the quality of life.

In Chapter 7, on 'Work, leisure, time-pressure and stress', Jiri Zuzanek notes that the questions of whether people living in modern societies are working longer or shorter hours, or have gained or lost free time, and the implications of any such trends, have been at the centre of sociological, political and economic discussion since the 1930s. The analyses of Canadian time-use trends suggest that, for the employed part of the population, the total combined paid and unpaid workload has been increasing since the early 1980s. However, in the competition for time triggered by higher workloads, employed Canadians have sacrificed time spent on personal needs and possibly education rather than their leisure pursuits. Rather than involving *discretionary* time, feelings of time-pressure seem to be primarily rooted in competition among various forms of *contracted* and *committed* time, that is paid work, family obligations and, possibly, voluntary work. Time-use data point to society becoming increasingly polarised along time-pressure lines, with some groups exposed to considerably higher levels of time pressure than others. The length of paid and unpaid working hours is an important, but not the sole, determinant of subjectively felt time-pressure. Lack of choice, interest, and control over working and non-working time, and a rapid change-over of activities contribute significantly to elevated levels of 'time crunch' in modern societies. Zuzanek notes the growing awareness that individual coping strategies and lifestyle modifications alone are not sufficient to offset the negative impacts of time-pressure and psychological stress on health. Many pressures faced by people in modern societies are social or *structural*. They are embedded in the competitive demands of globalised economies, changing workplace environments, value orientations emphasising rapid material gains and conformity with standardised and fast forms of expression prevalent in popular culture. Yet, Zuzanek argues, technological and economic progress should and *need not* clash with the goals of social solidarity, cohesion and human development.

In Chapter 8 Barbara Schneider, Alisa Ainbinder and Mihaly Csikszent-mihalyi examine stress among working parents using the Experience

Sampling Method, questionnaire surveys and qualitative interviews. By way of background, it is noted that, in the past few decades, the number of dual-earner families in the United States has increased substantially. Balancing the demands of work and family, maintaining a healthy marriage and providing adequate care for one's children are just a few of the demands that create stress for dual-career couples. Parents in the study were drawn from middle-class and upper-middle-class communities. Stress was found to be negatively correlated with the positive emotional states of happiness, enjoyment and feeling good and strong, and with self-esteem. The study found a lack of variation in stress by gender, income or level of education, though this may be related to the range of people included in the sample. The study found that the relationship between stress and excitement is relatively low in comparison to other emotions. The authors consider that some stress may be a reasonable response when attempting tasks that involve some uncertainty. However, high levels of stress, sustained over time, are associated with a lack of control over one's activities and a sense of frustration – conclusions similar to those presented in Chapter 7.

In Chapter 9 John T. Haworth presents a model of well-being focusing on the characteristics of persons and situations and the pivotal role played by enjoyment. The model is based on nine 'situational' factors or Principal Environmental Influences identified by Warr (1987) as being important for well-being, namely: opportunity for control; environmental clarity; opportunity for skill use; externally generated goals; variety; opportunity for interpersonal contact; valued social position; availability of money; and physical security. These features of the environment are considered to interact with characteristics of the person to facilitate or constrain psychological well-being or mental health. An important development of the model is the inclusion of the role of enjoyment in well-being. Research using the Experience Sampling Method suggests that enjoyment and situational factors are conjoined, and that enjoyment can give rise directly to well-being. Also, that enjoyment and feelings of control might enhance a person's locus of control disposition, which in turn may lead to enhanced well-being either directly or through greater access to Principal Environmental Influences. Research into locus of control suggests that positive successful life experiences increase internal locus of control beliefs through optimistic attributions. These may increase confidence, initiative and positive motivation, and thus lead to more successful experiences. Positive subjective states may influence personal factors, such as locus of control, through both reflective and non-reflective interactions: through actively thinking about situations and just being in enjoyable situations. The chapter concludes that social science research into well-being, work and leisure can be valuable, but that implementation is embedded in socio-political processes and requires negotiation and compromise.

Seppo E. Iso-Ahola and Roger C. Mannell, in Chapter 10, examine the reciprocal relationship between leisure and health. They recognise that many people feel stressed because of financial difficulties and the dominance of work and that in such situations leisure is used primarily for recuperation from work. The result is a passive leisure lifestyle and a reactive approach to personal health. They argue, on the basis of considerable research, that active leisure is important for health and well-being. Participation in both physical and non-physical leisure activities has been shown to reduce depression and anxiety, produce positive moods and enhance self-esteem and self-concept, facilitate social interaction, increase general psychological well-being and life satisfaction, and improve cognitive functioning. However, many people fail to discover active leisure. Trying new things and mastering challenges are discouraged and undermined by the social system and environment. And maintaining motivation for active leisure is possible only if it is marked by enjoyment. Of course, active leisure is not a panacea. If it is used as avoidance behaviour in order not to face up to problems which require attention, it can increase stress; and for people who are experiencing heavy demands from work and family, trying to undertake too much active leisure may exacerbate rather than ameliorate stress.

In the 1975 volume, the question was raised as to whether Western society as a whole was becoming 'leisure centred'. Such a possibility is rarely considered in the current era, but it is clear that leisure can take on varying levels of significance in individual lives. In Chapter 11 Robert A. Stebbins considers this phenomenon through his examination of 'serious leisure', volunteerism and quality of life, and argues that an optimal leisure lifestyle includes both serious and 'casual' leisure. Serious leisure is seen as the systematic pursuit of an amateur, hobbyist or volunteer activity that participants find so substantial and interesting that, in the typical case, they launch themselves on a 'career' centred on acquiring and expressing its special skills, knowledge and experience. Stebbins distinguishes between 'serious leisure' and 'casual' or 'unserious' leisure, which is characterised as comprising immediately intrinsically rewarding, relatively short-lived pleasurable activity requiring little or no special training. In the course of pursuing their activities, many participants in serious leisure try to find an optimal leisure lifestyle, conceived of here as the pursuit during free time of one or more substantial, absorbing forms of serious leisure carefully balanced with sessions of casual leisure as needed for a change of pace. Quality of leisure life is influenced by many factors, among them the very people with whom leisure participants pursue their leisure, and the number and intensity of rewarding experiences found in this part of life. The particular case of how career volunteering can lead to an optimal leisure lifestyle and quality of life is discussed.

The final chapter of the book identifies and addresses five themes or issues, which emerge from the preceding chapters. These are: the desirability of locating our current concerns in an historical context; the distribution of work and leisure; processes of change; well-being; and the question of policy.

# References

*American Psychologist* (2000) Special issue: Positive Psychology. 5(1).

Applebaum, P. D. (1992) *The Concept of Work: Ancient, Medieval, and Modern.* Albany, NY: State University of New York Press.

Beck, U. (2000) *The Brave New World of Work.* Cambridge: Polity.

Clarke, J. and Critcher, C. (1985) *The Devil Makes Work: Leisure in Capitalist Britain.* London: Macmillan.

Csikszentmihalyi, M. and LeFevre, J. (1989) Optimal experience in work and leisure. *Journal of Personality and Social Psychology* 56: 815–22.

De Grazia, S. (1962) *Of Time, Work and Leisure.* Garden City, NY: Anchor.

Haworth, J. T. (1997) *Work, Leisure and Well-being.* London: Routledge.

Haworth, J. T. and Smith, M. A. (eds) (1975) *Work and Leisure: An Interdisciplinary Study in Theory, Education and Planning.* London: Lepus.

Hochschild, A. R. (1997) *The Time Bind.* New York: Metropolitan.

Iso-Ahola, S. (1980) *The Social Psychology of Leisure and Recreation.* Dubuque, IA: Wm C. Brown.

Jahoda, M. (1982) *Employment and Unemployment: A Social Psychological Analysis.* Cambridge: Cambridge University Press.

Kahneman, D., Diener, E. and Schwarz, N. (1999) *Well-Being: The Foundations of Hedonic Psychology.* New York: Russell Sage Foundation.

Kohn, M. and Schooler, M. (1983) *Work and Personality: An Enquiry into the Impact of Social Stratification.* Norwood, NJ: Ablex.

Mannell, R. and Kleiber, D. (1997) *A Social Psychology of Leisure.* State College, PA: Venture.

Neulinger, J. (1981) *To Leisure: An Introduction.* London: Allyn and Bacon.

Pieper, J. (1999 [1952]) *Leisure, the Basis of Culture.* Indianapolis, IN: Liberty Fund.

Roberts, K. (1999) *Leisure in Contemporary Society.* Wallingford, UK: CAB International.

Rojek, C. (1985) *Capitalism and Leisure Theory.* London: Tavistock.

Rojek, C. (1995) *Decentring Leisure: Rethinking Leisure Theory.* London: Sage.

Schor, J. (1991) *The Overworked American: The Unexpected Decline of Leisure.* New York: Basic Books.

Snyder, C. R. and Lopez, S. J. (2000) *Handbook of Positive Psychology.* Oxford: Oxford University Press.

Stebbins, R. (1998) *After Work: The Search for an Optimal Leisure Lifestyle.* Calgary: Temeron.

Taylor, R. (2002) Britain's World of Work-Myths and Realities: ESRC Future of Work Programme. Available from the ESRC (tel: 01793 413001).

Thompson, S. M., Grant, B. C., and Dharmalingam, A. (2002) Leisure time in midlife. *Leisure Studies* 21(2): 125–43.

Warr, P. (1987) *Work, Unemployment and Mental Health.* Oxford: Clarendon Press.

# Part I

# The changing face of work and leisure

# Chapter I

# A brief history of work and its relationship to leisure

*A. J. Veal*

## Historical perspectives

In the 1975 volume *Work and Leisure* (Haworth and Smith 1975), history was virtually ignored; the early 1970s was a period of economic and demographic growth and leisure researchers in Britain were more concerned with planning for the future rather than mulling over the past. History was neglected despite the existence of a considerable body of literature on the historical aspects of the work–leisure relationship, including Thorsten Veblen's *Theory of the Leisure Class* (1899) and Johann Huizinga's *Homo Ludens* (1950) which discuss the emergence of leisure and play in prehistory, Sebastian De Grazia's *Of Time, Work and Leisure* (1964) which begins with classical Greek ideas about leisure, and Stella Margetson's (1968) *Leisure and Pleasure in the Nineteenth Century*. In the late 1970s and into the 1980s, however, a veritable cornucopia of historical research on work and leisure was published, including, for example, that by Helen Meller (1976), Peter Bailey (1978), James Walvin (1978), Gary Cross (1990), Hugh Cunningham (1980) and Roy Rosenzweig (1983). Essentially these histories concentrated on the nineteenth century and the overall theme was the struggle between the masses and burgeoning capital over the control of work and leisure time during the process of industrialisation and urbanisation. Thus students of leisure came to see contemporary forms of leisure and work as a product of industrialisation, with only a hazy impression being gained of work and leisure in non-industrial societies.

More recently, research on women and leisure has drawn attention to the fact that not everyone in contemporary Western society has experienced the formal compartmentalisation of work and leisure, the emergence of which had been chronicled by the historians. Even in industrial society much work continues to be unpaid and is not regulated, recognised or rewarded as part of the industrial economy (see Judy White's Chapter 4 in this volume). The current phase of globalisation draws attention to the fact that non-industrial work and leisure is still the norm for most of the planet's population and for millions the experience of industrialisation is the present or the future, not the past, while for further millions the experience of industrialisation may be bypassed altogether, with a rapid translation from non-industrial to post-industrial lifestyles. Leisure, and work, predate the Western industrial revolution and are at the heart of the development not just of industrial society but of human culture (Rojek 2000: 115). Many current Western leisure forms, practices and values carry the traces of pre-industrial, religious and secular traditions (Shivers and deLisle 1997; deLisle 2003).

The aim of this chapter is therefore not to engage directly with current debates on relationships between work and leisure, but to provide a broad-ranging overview of the history of work as a backdrop to the later chapters in the book, with their emphasis on contemporary debates concerning work and leisure. In the main it follows a chronological pattern, beginning with an examination of pre-industrial societies, namely hunter-gatherers, classical Greece and Rome and the early Christian era. This is followed by consideration of the first 300 or so years of the so-called 'modern' era, and then the contemporary era, or the first two-thirds of the twentieth century. Finally, since much contemporary debate is centred on the recent growth in working hours in some Western countries, there is a brief examination of trends in working hours since the middle of the nineteenth century.

## In the beginning

In the Book of Genesis the work of creation takes six days and the Creator rests on the seventh day. Later in Genesis, when Adam and Eve are expelled from the Garden of Eden, in addition to acquiring the knowledge of good and evil, Adam is condemned to *work*. He is 'sent forth from the Garden of Eden to till the land from whence he was taken' (Genesis 3: 23) and is told: 'In the sweat of thy face shalt though eat bread' (3: 19). Thus the biblical historians' view was that humankind engaged in work, in the form of tilling the land, from the very earliest times and that such work was to be viewed negatively compared with the idyllic life in the Garden of Eden. At the time of the writing of the Book of Genesis, work in Jewish society clearly possessed a moral and cultural significance. Work was seen as a burden and a punishment for Adam; indeed, the Hebrew view was that work was imposed on humankind 'to expiate the original sin committed by its forefathers in the earthly Paradise' (Tilgher 1977: 11).

Whether the biblical story is seen as history or as ancient religious metaphor, or both, it illustrates two themes of this chapter: first, that attitudes to work and leisure have been central themes in human cultural development since the earliest times (Veblen, 1899). Second, since two world religions continue to hold the Old Testament to be essentially true, ideas about work and leisure clearly transcend historical eras (deLisle 2003).

## Hunter-gatherer societies

Historical accounts confirm that the negative biblical *attitude* towards work has indeed been the norm for most people for most of the time, but anthropology raises questions about the biblical portrayal of the earliest *type* of work being agricultural. Hunter-gatherer society preceded agrarian society, so agricultural work was not part of earliest human experience, but emerged quite late in the process of human development – perhaps as recently as 10,000 to 15,000 years ago.

There is debate among anthropologists and leisure theorists as to whether the concepts of *work* and *leisure* are applicable in hunter-gatherer societies because of the lack of any clear dividing line in such societies between time spent engaging in actual hunting and gathering tasks and time spent in other activities. Direct evidence on the nature of the hunter-gatherer way-of-life has been assembled within the past century or so from the declining numbers of tribal groups leading traditional ways of life in areas as diverse as Australia, Papua New Guinea, South America and the Arctic, and efforts have been made to construct 'time-budgets' for individuals living in such circumstances. If work is activity deemed 'necessary for survival' then the acts of hunting and gathering should be considered to be work. Conversely, some of the time left over from such activities might plausibly be considered leisure time. Sahlins (1974: 15–20) notes that the number of hours spent in obtaining food in hunter-gatherer societies was probably little more than between three and five hours a day for most communities for most of the time and that, even in daylight hours, a great deal of time was spent in 'resting'. The Australian anthropologist, W. E. H. Stanner (1979), speaking of traditional Aboriginal societies contacted in the nineteenth and early twentieth centuries, notes that limited material needs were often met with limited expenditure of time, which

> left free time, energy and enthusiasm to be expended – as they were, without stint – on all the things for which life could be lived when basic needs had been met: the joys of leisure, rest, song, dance, fellowship, trade, stylized fighting and the performance of religious rituals . . . The true leisure time activities – social entertaining, great ceremonial gatherings, even much of the ritual and artistic life – impressed observers from the beginning.
>
> (Stanner 1979: 162, 38)

As Rojek (2000: 115) puts it: 'Human culture did not begin with the need to work, it began with language, dancing, laughing, acting, mimicking, ritual and a variety of play forms'. In a functionalist sense, the evolution of such activities can be seen as an early solution to the 'problem of leisure'.

In contemporary Western society the balance between work and leisure is, and has been at least since the Enlightenment, considered an earnest matter because work is seen as the means to human *progress* – at both the individual and societal level and in a material and spiritual/intellectual sense. From such a viewpoint, Sahlins (1974: 15–20) notes, anthropologists have inferred that the lack of material possessions of hunter-gatherer communities suggests an existence involving scarcity and a ceaseless round of relatively unsuccessful effort to overcome the environmental odds. But he disagrees with this view, referring to hunter-gatherers as 'the original affluent society'. Lack of material possessions, Sahlins argues, was far from being an indicator of poverty and a wretched existence, but can be seen as evidence of a society in which a satisfactory balance had been achieved between material needs, work and leisure. Achieving such a balance has been a major task for human culture throughout history and is at the heart of much debate about work and leisure today.

While the creation of artifacts, such as tools, pots, bags and clothing, resulted in the development of work activity among hunter-gatherer groups, it is the development of agriculture, and the permanent human settlements that came with it, that created a form of work which is particularly recognisable to the modern eye. Land, crops and domesticated animals created obligations and a daily and seasonal rhythm to labour. The creation and maintenance of physical, communal human settlements and the social organisation which went with them gave a further boost to development of the phenomenon of work. With the growth of the size of settlements specialist occupations, such as workers in stone, leather, wood and metal, also arose. As Veblen (1898) pointed out, it was this phenomenon which created the possibility for social structures to evolve which included chiefs, warriors and priests, and their immediate family members, the 'leisure class', who did not engage in manual work, but extracted a surplus from the rest, whether voluntarily or otherwise – a phenomenon which continued into the industrial era. Membership of the elite was associated with exemption from work, thus creating the status divide between work and leisure echoed in the Genesis story.

## Work and culture in ancient Greece and Rome

It is often reported in the leisure studies literature that ancient Greek philosophers celebrated the life of leisure and looked down on manual work as an activity fit only for non-citizens and slaves. The implication is that this, at least in part, has provided the basis for modern attitudes towards work and leisure and potentially provides a normative basis for an elevated status for a 'pure' form of leisure. But the negative attitude of ancient Greeks towards work was more subtle. While work in general was despised, *farming* was held in high esteem. In the Homeric period (before the eighth century BC), the Greeks

> looked upon farming as submitting to the laws and rules of nature as much as applying technique to the soil. Agriculture was a form of

morality, involving daily struggles with nature, which must be performed
at the appointed time and in the right way ... The Greek view that the
earth was a goddess wedded the subject of agricultural work with nature.
Work on the land was a noble way of life, which bred robust bodies and
men of high repute ... In the Homeric poems, work on the land was
not viewed as acting upon nature in order to transform it, but rather
participation in a divine order that is superior to man.

(Applebaum 1992: 17)

In the Archaic and Classical periods, with the emergence of the Greek city-
state (eighth to fourth centuries BC), the respect for farming continues,
as shown in Aristotle's writings. The type of work which individuals did
was believed to shape their character and 'worthiness'. Thus Aristotle, in
distinguishing between the various occupations of the general population,
in regard to their potential for inclusion as citizens of the state, with
corresponding rights and duties, states:

> The first and best kind of populace is one of farmers ... The other kinds
> of populace ... are almost without exception of a much poorer stamp.
> They lead a poor sort of life; and none of the occupations followed by a
> populace which consists of mechanics, shopkeepers, and day labourers,
> leave any room for excellence.
>
> (quoted in Barker 1948: 262, 265)

In general the negative attitudes towards work continued in Roman times.
Cicero listed a wide range of occupations which were considered to be
'unbecoming to a gentleman ... and vulgar', including tax-gatherers and
usurers, all hired manual labourers, mechanics, shopkeepers and small traders
and 'all those trades which cater for sensual pleasures: fishmongers, butchers,
cooks and poulterers and fishermen'; but of all the gainful occupations, he
asserted, 'none is better than agriculture, none more profitable, none more
delightful, none more becoming the freeman' (quoted in Applebaum 1992:
95).

## Work and leisure in the Christian era

The teaching of Christ would appear to convey a 'withering scorn of prudent
work, and wealth' (Tilgher 1977: 22), as exemplified by the following:

> Ye cannot serve God and mammon. Therefore I say unto you, take no
> thought for your life, what ye shall eat, or what ye shall drink; nor yet for
> your body, what ye shall put on. Is not the life more than meat, and the
> body than raiment? Behold the fowls of the air: for they sow not, neither
> do they reap nor gather into barns; yet your heavenly Father feedeth

them. Are ye not much better than they? . . . And why take ye thought for raiment? Consider the lilies of the field, how they grow; they toil not, neither do they spin. And yet I say unto you, that even Solomon in all his glory was not arrayed like one of these. Therefore, take no thought, saying, What shall we eat? or, What shall we drink? or, Wherewithal shall we be clothed? for your heavenly Father knoweth that ye have need of all these things. But seek ye first the kingdom of God, and his righteousness: and all these things shall be added unto you.

(Matthew 6: 24–33)

While such teaching appears to advise against a concern for work, it is arguably more a sermon against materialism. Christ's followers were not to be concerned with earthly wealth, but were to focus on rewards in heaven. God and heaven were brought into the material goods, work and leisure equation. In fact, far from scorning work, Christians came to see it as virtuous when it served God or helped others, although the Jewish idea of work as expiation for sin also remained. The *spiritual* life was revered: to spend one's life in prayer and contemplation, particularly as priest, monk or nun, was the ultimate 'calling'. These values were enshrined in many of the rules of existence of monastic orders, in which life for the monk or nun consisted of a rigidly prescribed round of prayer and work, including manual work. Spending non-work time in the contemplation and worship of God, which all Christians were exhorted to do, can be seen as a harnessing of many non-work activities (music, art, storytelling, drama, ritual) to a single religious purpose.

The cloistered approach to virtuous work and worship changed with the rise of Protestantism in sixteenth-century Europe. Martin Luther rejected monasticism as being unworldly and saw every occupation, not just the religious one, as a 'calling'.

Luther swept away the idea of the superiority of one type of work over another. As long as work is done in a spirit of obedience to God, every variety of work has equal spiritual dignity and each is the service to God on earth. All work contributes to the common life of mankind. Hence no one is more necessary than another to piety and blessedness ... He believed that, if all activity of all types is divine, then there is no basis for making distinctions between the work of clerics in 'God's work' and the work of everyday tradesmen, craftsmen, and peasants.

(Applebaum 1992: 322)

Nevertheless, certain forms of work were considered undesirable: Luther saw the world of trade, banking, credit and capitalist industry as part of the 'kingdom of darkness'. Calvin, however, while preaching that wealth was not to lead to material self-indulgence and that any surplus should be used for the public good and philanthropy, 'saw the profits of trade and finance as being on the same level as the earnings of workmen, with the merchant's profits coming from diligence, industry, and hard work' (Applebaum 1992: 325–6). Thus can be seen the link which Max Weber described in *The Protestant Ethic and the Spirit of Capitalism* (1930).[1] It is the Puritan attitude towards work which, Weber argues, provided the basis for the emergence in the West of modern capitalism. Based on a review of early writing, Weber summarises the principles of Puritanism, thus:

> on earth man must, to be certain of his state of grace, 'do the works of him who sent him, as long as it is yet day'. Not leisure and enjoyment, but only activity serves to increase the glory of God . . . Waste of time is thus the first and deadliest of sins . . . Loss of time through sociability, idle talk, luxury, even more sleep than is necessary . . . is worthy of absolute moral condemnation . . . every hour lost is lost to labour for the glory of God.
>
> (Weber 1976 [1930]: 157–8)

The extent to which these ideas directly influenced the behaviour of the mass of the people in Christendom is debatable. Cross (1990: 28) notes that the Protestant work ethic was particularly embraced by the English middle classes, notably in southern England, but not by either the aristocracy or the 'improvident' poor. Most of the aristocracy lived a life of unvirtuous idleness, while most of the poor, being dependent on an agricultural economy, experienced seasonal and weather-related variations in work intensity with bursts of intense work interspersed with lighter duties and even periods of idleness. Dedication to or celebration of work for its own sake was not fostered by this variable agricultural round, or the folk traditions of rural life or the Catholic church, which remained strong in much of Europe. The year was punctuated by many regular and irregular interruptions to work, including numerous saints' day holidays and annual fairs and carnivals which traditionally involved days off work, although it should be noted that saints' day holidays required attendance at church as well as involvement in festivities. In European cities, prior to the capitalist industrial revolution of the late eighteenth and nineteenth century, there was considerable development of industry – sometimes referred to as 'proto-industrialisation' (Watkins 1987: 3) – but it was a culture in which attitudes towards work, time and sobriety were far from the Protestant model. Thus the institution of 'St Monday' was common among urban workers, involving the taking of an unofficial holiday to recover from the, often alcoholic, excesses of the Sunday of rest (Cross 1990: 20–1).

## Work in the modern world

The 'modern' world can be said to have started with the Renaissance, in sixteenth-century Italy, bringing new ways of thinking about technology and social and economic *progress* – and work. Industrialisation and urbanisation, which began to gather pace in the eighteenth century, brought with them a change in *time sense* which became an essential prerequisite for the growth of industrial capitalism. Along with these changes came long-term *increases in material rewards* for the masses. Change, however, did not come about automatically: there was some *resistance* and persistence of existing habits – what would today be called 'industrial inefficiency'. These concepts – progress, time sense, increasing material rewards and resistance – will now be discussed in turn.

### The idea of progress

The Renaissance was marked by new ideas about human possibilities. Christianity had provided a fixed, unchanging, view of the world and humankind's place in it, in which the purpose of human existence, it was believed, was to follow God's will; 'improvement' or 'progress' was not a social task but a moral journey for the individual. In medieval European society, 'The aim of work was not economic progress' (Le Goff 1988: 222). Renaissance thinking, by contrast, saw progress as being possible for the wider human society here on earth. Philosophy, art, architecture and engineering flourished; labour aimed at improvement of human conditions on earth was celebrated. Tilgher summarises the thoughts of the sixteenth-century philosopher Giordano Bruno:

> Bruno exalts the human age of toil in which man, driven by hunger, creates day after day still more wonderful arts and inventions, draws ever further away from the animal, nearer to the divine – makes for himself a second and higher nature of which he is the true god.
>
> (Tilgher 1977: 75)

But while Renaissance humanist thinking and Protestantism may have laid the moral foundations of capitalism, it is clear that they did not succeed in immediately transforming the work culture of the masses which, as discussed, was based on the rhythms of agricultural and pre-capitalist urban life. Much of the history of industrialisation, in eighteenth- and nineteenth-century Europe and North America, is the history of efforts to develop workers with a non-industrial work culture into a disciplined industrial workforce capable of realising the modern secular dream.

### Time sense

Historical changes in *time sense* were analysed by E. P. Thompson in his well-known 1967 essay. He noted that, some time before the industrial revolution, the appearance of clocks began to change people's sense of time from the *task-orientation* typical of traditional and agricultural societies to an increasing awareness of *clock-time*. Lewis Mumford, in chronicling the role of the machine in the development of civilisation, noted that it was the medieval monasteries and their strict daily regime of prayer and work, which gave rise to the need for clocks:

> one is not straining the facts when one suggests that the monasteries – at one time there were 40,000 under Benedictine rule – helped to give human enterprise the regular collective beat and rhythm of the machine; for the clock is not merely a means of keeping track of the hours, but of synchronizing the actions of man . . . by the thirteenth century there are definite records of mechanical clocks, and by 1370 a well-designed 'modern' clock had been built by Heinrich von Wyck at Paris . . . The instrument presently spread outside the monastery; and the regular striking of the bells brought a new regularity into the life of the workman and merchant. The bells of the clock tower almost defined urban existence. Time-keeping passed into time-serving and time-accounting and time-rationing. As this took place, Eternity ceased gradually to serve as the measure and focus of human activities . . . The clock, not the steam-engine, is the key-machine of the modern industrial age.
>
> (Mumford 1934: 13–14)

He goes on to note that 'A generalised time-consciousness accompanied the wider use of clocks . . . dissociating time from organic sequences' (Mumford 1934: 17). Thus a changing sense of time was underway in Europe, at least in urban areas, from the fourteenth century. However, as Thompson and other historians record, at the time of the beginning of the industrial revolution at the end of the eighteenth century, the transformation from a *task-orientated* sense of time to a *clock-time* orientation was far from complete among urban workers and was still quite alien to the thousands, and eventually millions, who flocked from the countryside to the towns as industrialisation and urbanisation unfolded. Steam-driven factory machinery tended by large labour forces raised the demand for clock-based discipline to a new level: all hands needed to be in place when the machines started and they could not stop until the machines did so; and every minute the machines were idle meant lost output and lower profits. Despite the fact that, as Bailey (1978: 13) points out, factories were also subject to irregularities, caused by breakdowns or fluctuations in business conditions, the unrelenting demands of machines in factories and their owners' determination to maximise profits, called for an increasingly 'disciplined' labour force.

O'Malley (1992), however, cautions against an oversimplistic acceptance of this thesis. He argues that a life without clocks was not necessarily a leisurely or disordered life. In particular, in medieval Europe, in 'everyday affairs and for all practical purposes time's authority . . . came from the Church'

(O'Malley 1992: 347) – and religious observances could involve substantial calls on an individual's time. Further, among Puritans (as discussed) a devotion to hard work and prohibition of idleness predated widespread use of clocks and the factory system.

But changes in work culture did not happen overnight. The continuing process of urbanisation, industrialisation and migration meant that the clash of traditional and new industrial cultures persisted for some time. Thus Herbert Gutman (1977), in analysing the process of industrialisation in the United States, based on local and immigrant labour from rural backgrounds, noted that:

> Common work habits rooted in diverse pre-modern cultures (different in many ways but nevertheless all ill fitted to the regular routines demanded by machine-centered factory processes) existed among distinctive first-generation factory workers all through American history ... workers new to factory production brought strange and seemingly useless work habits to the factory gate. The irregular and undisciplined work patterns of factory hands before 1843 frustrated cost-conscious manufacturers and caused frequent complaint among them.
>
> (Gutman 1977: 19)

### Increasing material rewards

Economic factors played a direct part in changing the lifestyles of the masses. While industrialisation brought with it widespread poverty and exploitation, this was not true for all, and urban poverty was often seen as preferable to the rural alternative. Wages for skilled workers in particular were historically high. One feature of the non-industrial work culture which industrialists found frustrating was the tendency for employees to work until they had earned a certain amount of money, sufficient for their needs, and then to stop, perhaps disappearing from the workplace for extended periods – a phenomenon seen today in situations where modern industry is superimposed on non-industrial society, such as South African gold mines. However, higher wages also meant that at least some working people could, through hard work and long hours, improve their material conditions. Further, the very products of industry resulted in more and more goods being produced that were within reach of working people. Capitalism began to offer a form of prosperity for the masses. The idea of wealth from hard work, particularly in the New World, transformed the hopes and aspirations of many ordinary people. It was no longer necessary to persuade the masses that work was a moral duty or for the glory of God, with its rewards in the hereafter; work now had its own, increasing, rewards here on earth.

### Resistance

Changes in work patterns under industrialisation did not happen smoothly and without resistance. Thompson (1967), in referring to the many ways in which factory owners sought to impose the new discipline on their labour forces, notes:

> In all these ways – by the division of labour; the supervision of labour; fines; bells and clocks; money incentives; preachings and schoolings; the suppression of fairs and sports – new labour habits were formed, and a new time-discipline was imposed. It sometimes took generations . . . and we may doubt how far it was ever fully accomplished [but] this is a place of the most far-reaching conflict . . . the historical record is not a simple one of neutral and inevitable technological change, but is also one of exploitation and of resistance to exploitation.
>
> (Thompson 1967: 90, 93–4)

The nineteenth century saw the development of organised labour and associated political movements designed to stem the worst excesses of employer exploitation, notably in relation to the employment of children and women, and to improve the worker's lot by campaigns for better working conditions, increased pay and reduced working hours. Political analysis was brought to bear on the phenomenon of labour in industrial capitalism. At the heart of Karl Marx's analysis was the observed increasing level of exploitation of labour by the capitalist, which was seen as unsustainable and destined to lead eventually to revolutionary overthrow of the capitalist system (Marx and Engels 1952 [1848]: 60).

The persistence of pre-industrial leisure patterns can also be seen as a form of resistance. When the tasks of the industrial worker were done there was time left over, however little. The Puritan ethic, the nineteenth-century 'Samuel Smiles' type ethic of self-improvement (Anthony 1977: 77–9) and the modern materialist ethic would require the individual to find other wholesome and 'self-improving' activity to fill this residual time. In fact, it would appear that, apart from the minimal demands of church attendance, which not all heeded in increasingly secular urban centres, free time was generally filled with diversionary pastimes such as drinking and entertainment, and quasi-leisure activities such as attendance at fairs and markets. Such was the attraction of these activities, that they often impinged on supposed working hours – the best known example being the institution of 'St Monday', referred to earlier. Thus work was 'kept in its place' and had to compete with leisure for a share of the worker's time.

Leisure historians note that the nature of many of the leisure activities engaged in by the urban industrial working class, such as violent and cruel sports, gambling and extensive consumption of alcohol, prompted moral reformers to join with industrialists in attempts to rein in the perceived excesses of urban working-class leisure (Bailey 1978; Cunningham 1980; Cross 1990). These alliances of reformers and industrialists achieved some success through the 'stick' of legislative controls and the 'carrot' of providing for 'rational recreation', such as, in Britain, the Mechanics Institutes.

Thus it can be seen that the idea of progress, changing time sense and increasing material rewards radically disrupted the nexus between work, leisure and material needs which had for centuries been determined by an agrarian, feudal society overlain with Christian moral sanction. Capitalist expansion was forging a new balance in which work and material rewards formed the central elements, with leisure and, arguably, religion forced to take a back seat.

## The contemporary era

By the end of the nineteenth century industrialisation had brought about the transformation of work for a large proportion of the labour forces of Europe and North America. The epitome of this transformation was seen in the research of Frederick W. Taylor, whose *scientific management* involved minute analysis of industrial work processes, designed to simplify and routinise them to maximise efficiency and profits. The most celebrated example of such ideas in practice was the automobile factories of Henry Ford, developed in the early part of the twentieth century and based on the moving production line, where each worker undertook a small, fixed, routinised part of the production process. This approach to routinisation of work and division of labour came to be called 'Taylorism' or 'Fordism' and dominated industrial thinking for much of the rest of the century, resulting in massive increases in productivity and output (Giddens 1993: 494).

Whereas the eighteenth and nineteenth centuries had seen the massive struggles and transformations resulting in a new industrial culture with the 'gospel of work' at its core, in the twentieth century the possibility that industry and technology, by solving the problem of material scarcity, might actually deliver more leisure, even a 'leisure society', began to be discussed. In the 1920s, the philosopher Bertrand Russell wrote:

> If every man and woman worked for four hours a day at necessary work, we could all have enough . . . it should be the remaining hours that would be regarded as important – hours which could be devoted to enjoyment of art or study, to affection and woodland and sunshine in green fields . . . Man's true life does not consist in the business of filling his belly and clothing his body, but in art and thought and love, in the creation and contemplation of beauty and in the scientific understanding of the world.
>
> (Russell and Russell 1923: 50)

In the 1930s, the economist John Maynard Keynes, in an essay entitled 'Economic possibilities for our grandchildren', foresaw a reduction in working hours brought about by technology and wrote:

> It will be those people, who can keep alive, and cultivate into a fuller perfection, the art of life itself and do not sell themselves for the means of life, who will be able to enjoy the abundance when it comes . . . We shall once more value ends above means and prefer the good to the useful. We shall honour those who can teach us how to pluck the hour and the day virtuously and well, the delightful people who are capable of taking direct enjoyment in things, the lilies of the field who toil not, neither do they spin.
>
> (Keynes 1972 [1931]: 331)

The Second World War brought such speculation to an end: the war effort reasserted the primacy of work. In the post-war period, however, in the fully industrialised West, with a skilled and disciplined workforce and highly productive, consumer-orientated industries, the question arose as to how committed workers were to the work ethic. Dubin (1958: 215) observed that, while 'work has long been considered a central life interest for adults in most societies, and certainly in the Western world', among the American industrial workers he studied, only 24 per cent 'could be labeled job-orientated in their life interests' (Dubin 1958: 219). There were other studies during the 1960s, 1970s and 1980s which suggested that workers in a number of Western countries were beginning to see more leisure as a preferred option to more work and more consumption (Veal 1987: 70–1).

By the 1960s, rapidly rising affluence and receding memory of war saw a fall in working hours and increased holiday entitlements, leading to renewed talk of a 'leisure society' (Dumazedier 1967), later spurred by ideas of a 'post-industrial' era (Veal 1987: 46–62). One 'Delphi' forecasting exercise in the 1970s foresaw an average working week of 32 hours by 1985 (Shafer et al. 1975). In some Western countries, notably Western Europe, some attempt to reassert the status of leisure in the work, leisure, material needs equation had been achieved. But in the United States the decline in working hours came to a halt in about 1950. Owens (1979: 10–13) shows average weekly working hours of non-agricultural workers in the United States falling from 58 in 1900 to 42 in 1948, but then remaining static until 1977. Hunnicutt (1988) notes that the attainment of the 40-hour week in the post-Second World War era brought to an end a century of campaigning for shorter working hours.

In the 1970s the West became unsettled by the apparently more intense work ethic of the Japanese, and later the newly industrialised countries of South-East Asia, which resulted in massive inroads being made by those countries into the markets of the West. Globalisation trends and further dispersal of investment to low-cost developing countries, or 'flexible accumulation' as discussed elsewhere in this book, caused further economic disruption. Thus by the 1990s, as will be discussed, working hours in some Western countries stopped falling, and even began to rise again, and talk of a 'leisure society' all but disappeared.

Since it is this 'crisis' in the work, leisure, material rewards balance, characterised by pressure on working hours and its consequences for leisure and well-being, which forms the basis of much of the rest of the book, this chapter concludes with an historical overview of trends in working hours.

## Trends in working hours

Juliet Schor, in *The Overworked American* (1991), drew on numerous sources to analyse trends in working hours, initially in England and later in the United States and United Kingdom, over a 750-year period. This analysis suggests that typical working hours for peasants and casual labourers in thirteenth-century, pre-industrial England may have been as low as 1500 hours per annum, rising to 2000 in the fifteenth century. Schor notes that records indicate that peasants worked their land for only 150 days a year and other groups of hired workers were employed for only 175–80 days a year. Further, she notes:

> All told, holiday leisure time in medieval England took up probably about one-third of the year. And the English were apparently working harder than their neighbors. The *ancien régime* in France is reported to have guaranteed fifty-two Sundays, ninety rest days, and thirty-eight holidays. In Spain, travellers noted that holidays totalled five months a year.
>
> (Schor 1991: 47)

However, 'working their land' is an ambivalent term, in that it may exclude the time worked on the feudal lord's land. In medieval Europe half of all peasants were serfs, required to work their lord's land as well as their own (Sylvester 2000: 5–6). Marx saw this as a forerunner of the capitalist system of extracting 'surplus value' and indicates how the amount of work required by the lord was, in the hands of unscrupulous, almost without limit (Marx 1930 [1867]: 238–9).

With the coming of industrialisation, however, working hours increased, reaching over 3000 a year in the mid-nineteenth century (Schor 1991:45). However, estimates of working hours for manual worker provided by Young and Willmott (1973), as shown in Figure 1.1, indicate that the range of these estimates prior to the twentieth century is wide.

Having reached a peak in the mid-nineteenth century, working hours began to fall substantially, as a result, initially, of restrictions on working hours for women and children, followed by the campaign for the eight-hour

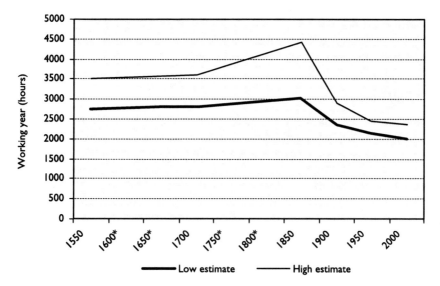

*Figure 1.1* Estimates of length of working year: male manual workers in Britain, 1550–1950

Source: based on Young and Willmott 1973: 132
Note: *author's interpolations

working day for all, the move to the five-and-a-half-day and then the five-day working week and the advent of paid annual holiday entitlements. As a result, the typical working year for full-time employed workers fell to less than 2000 hours in the post-Second World War era.

These historical trends, indicating that working hours of most workers in pre-industrial England were considerably shorter than those of industrial workers at the height of the industrial revolution, are widely acknowledged. The case for a pre-industrial leisured society, made by Schor (1991) and others is, however, arguably somewhat exaggerated, since it seems to ignore a number of issues, including women's work; the disciplines of animal husbandry; the demands of feudal society and the Church; and the difference between agricultural, industrial and other sectors. These are now discussed in turn.

### Women working

Schor (1991: 44) herself notes that little is known about women's working patterns, but suggests that their work commitments were probably more continuous than those of men. In addition to their contribution to the agricultural labour of the peasant household, women had childcare and other domestic duties which in earlier times would have involved such activities as weaving and the making and mending of clothes. All this suggests long and continuous working hours and suggests that data on fluctuations in men's working hours are unlikely to be representative of women's working hours.

### Animal husbandry

Accounts of agricultural work often refer to the bursts of activity at seed-time and harvest, with periods of idleness in between, but both women and men were also responsible for animal care in peasant households – a 365-day-a-year responsibility. Cows have to be herded to and from the fields and milked twice a day. Most animals require at least some form of attention on a daily basis – including Sundays and saints' days. In fact, such were the demands on them that peasants often resented rather than welcomed the many saints' day holidays because the various religious observances required of them took them away from their work.

### The feudal system

As already discussed, the feudal system required that, in addition to working their own land, at least half of the peasants of Europe were required to work on the land of the lord of the manor or other landlord in lieu of rent. Under unscrupulous lords, such requirements could be very onerous. Thus reference to the amount of work time peasants spent attending to their own land may significantly under-represent total hours worked.

### Industrial sectors

It is also notable that the available records tend to refer to peasant and hired labourers, but do not refer to those in domestic service, who would, no doubt, have been on call seven days a week. Later, data on working hours in the nineteenth century often refer only to those in industrial jobs, a category which never rose above 40 per cent of the labour force (Veal 1987: 10).

All this suggests that work outside the industrial sector may have been more onerous than available statistics indicate. It is notable that, in the data presented by Zeisel (1958: 146), working hours in agriculture in the United States in 1850 were higher, at 72 hours a week, than those in industrial occupations, at 66 hours a week. Thus, the view of Schor and neo-Marxist historians such as Bailey (1978), that long hours were imposed by industrialists on an unwilling workforce, might be countered by the view that industry attracted labour by offering a more attractive combination of working hours and wages than agriculture.

While industrialisation undoubtedly resulted in increased working hours for industrial workers, in the second half of the nineteenth century and thereafter, while industrialisation was still proceeding apace in Europe and North America, the trend was to reduce working hours. Workers' organisations campaigned for shorter hours not only because of the desire for more leisure, but also because it was felt that this would create more jobs and, through restrictions on the supply of labour, lead to increased wages. But the move was also supported by politicians and social reformers, and even by some industrialists, because 'they believed it would improve work performance and increase production', and have beneficial effects on 'health, citizenship, morality, family and religious duties' (Hunnicutt 1988: 15).

There is no doubt that working hours in Western countries fell dramatically between the height of the industrial revolution in the mid-nineteenth century and the middle of the twentieth century. However, as Figure 1.1 and Schor and others (e.g. Juster, in Zuzanek 1996: 67) indicate, in recent years the trend may have gone into reverse. Such trends are the focus of a number of other chapters in the book.

## Conclusion

An attempt has been made here to convey some of the broad characteristics of the history of work and its relationship to leisure from prehistoric times to the present. The topic is a substantial one which is addressed in a number of ways in a large and growing literature. The balance between work, leisure and material needs has varied markedly over time, in quantitative and qualitative terms, influenced by culture, religion, technology and social and economic structures and the relative power of different groups within those structures. In that sense, little has changed and history is a fair predictor of the future.

## Note

1   *The Protestant Ethic and the Spirit of Capitalism* was originally published as a two-part article in 1904–5 and in book form in 1920–1, appearing in English translation in 1930 (see p. 1 of Anthony Giddens' 'Introduction' to Weber (1976)).

## References

Anthony, P. D. (1977) *The Ideology of Work*. London: Tavistock.
Applebaum, H. (1992) *The Concept of Work: Ancient, Medieval, and Modern*. Albany, NY: State University of New York Press.
Bailey, P. (1978) *Leisure and Class in Victorian England*. London: Routledge and Kegan Paul.
Barker, E. (1948) *The Politics of Aristotle*. Oxford: Clarendon Press.
Cross, G. (1990) *A Social History of Leisure since 1600*. State College, PA: Venture.

Cunningham, H. (1980) *Leisure in the Industrial Revolution*. London: Croom Helm.

De Grazia, S. (1964) *Of Time, Work, and Leisure*. Garden City, NY: Anchor.

deLisle, L. J. (2003) Keys to the kingdom or devil's playground? The impact of insti-
tutionalised religion on the perception and use of leisure. *Annals of Leisure
Research* 6(2): 83–102.

Dubin, R. (1958) Industrial workers' worlds. In E. Larrabee and R. Meyersohn (eds)
*Mass Leisure*. Glencoe, IL: Free Press.

Dumazedier, J. (1967) *Toward a Society of Leisure*. New York: Free Press.

Giddens, A. (1993) *Sociology*, 2nd edn. Cambridge: Polity.

Gutman, H. G. (1977) *Work, Culture, and Society in Industrializing America*. Oxford:
Basil Blackwell.

Haworth, J. T. and Smith, M. A. (eds) (1975) *Work and Leisure*. London: Lepus.

Huizinga, J. (1950) *Homo Ludens: A Study of the Play Element in Culture* 1955 edn.
Boston, MA: Beacon Press.

Hunnicutt, B. K. (1988) *Work without End: Abandoning Shorter Hours for the Right to
Work*. Philadelphia, PA: Temple University Press.

Keynes, J. M. (1972 [1931]) Economic possibilities for our grandchildren. In *The
Collected Writings of John Maynard Keynes, Volume 9: Essays in Persuasion*.
London: Macmillan.

Le Goff, J. (1988) *Medieval Civilization: 400–1500*, trans. J. Burrow. Oxford: Basil
Blackwell.

Margetson, S. (1968) *Leisure and Pleasure in the Nineteenth Century*. London:
Cassell.

Marx, K. (1930 [1867]) *Capital, Volume 1*. London: Dent.

Marx, K. and Engels, F. (1952 [1848]) *Manifesto of the Communist Party*. Moscow:
Progress Publishers.

Meller, H. E. (1976) *Leisure and the Changing City, 1870–1914*. London: Routledge
and Kegan Paul.

Mumford, L. (1934) *Technics and Civilization*. New York: Harcourt, Brace.

O'Malley, M. (1992) Time, work and task orientation: a critique of American histori-
ography. *Time and Society* 1(3): 341–58.

Owens, J. D. (1979) *Working Hours: An Economic Analysis*. Lexington, MA: Lexington
Books.

Rojek, C. (2000) *Leisure and Culture*. London: Macmillan.

Rosenzweig, R. (1983) *Eight Hours for What We Will: Workers and Leisure in an
Industrial City, 1870–1920*. Cambridge: Cambridge University Press.

Russell, B. and Russell, D. (1923) *The Prospects of Industrial Civilization*. London:
Allen and Unwin.

Sahlins, M. (1974) *Stone Age Economics*. London: Tavistock.

Schor, J. (1991) *The Overworked American: The Unexpected Decline of Leisure*.
New York: Basic Books.

Shafer, E. L., Moeller, G. H. and Russell, E. G. (1975) Future leisure environments.
*Ekistics* 40(236): 68–72.

Shivers, J. S. and deLisle, L. J. (1997) *The Story of Leisure: Context, Concepts, and
Current Controversy*. Champaign, IL: Human Kinetics.

Stanner, W. E. H. (1979) *White Man Got No Dreaming: Essays: 1938–1973*. Canberra:
Australian National University Press.

Sylvester, T. L. (2000) *Slavery throughout History*. Detroit, MI: UXL.

Thompson, E. P. (1967) Time, work-discipline, and industrial capitalism. *Past and Present* 38(1): 56–97.

Tilgher, A. (1977 [1930]) *Work: What it has Meant to Men through the Ages*, trans. D. C. Fisher. New York: Arno Press.

Veal, A. J. (1987) *Leisure and the Future*. London: Allen and Unwin.

Veblen, T. (1970 [1899]) *The Theory of the Leisure Class*. London: Allen and Unwin.

Walvin, J. (1978) *Leisure and Society, 1830–1950*. London: Longman.

Watkins, P. (1987) *An Analysis of the History of Work*. Canberra: Curriculum Development Centre.

Weber, M. (1976 [1930]) *The Protestant Ethic and the Spirit of Capitalism*, 2nd edn. London: Allen and Unwin.

Young, M. and Willmott, P. (1973) *The Symmetrical Family*. London: Routledge and Kegan Paul.

Zeisel, J. S. (1958) The workweek in American industry 1850–1956. In E. Larrabee and R. Meyersohn (eds) *Mass Leisure*. Glencoe, IL: Free Press.

Zuzanek, J. (1996) Canada. In G. Cusnman, A. J. Veal and J. Zuzanek (eds) *World Leisure Participation: Free Time in the Global Village*. Wallingford, UK: CAB International.

## Chapter 2

# The devil still makes work

*Chas Critcher and Peter Bramham*

## Introduction

During the 1960s, American academics heralded the emergence of post-industrial societies, blessed with rapid technological innovations, high rates of productivity and economic growth. Time devoted to work would decline, career patterns would change and society could look forward to a 'leisure revolution'. Future shock became 'leisure shock'. All societies – capitalist and communist, Western and Eastern – would eventually converge around similar meritocratic occupational structures, identical technological infrastructures and common lifestyles. A future of leisure seemed inescapable.

In Britain, futurology was regarded with more scepticism. Nevertheless, leisure studies emerged in Britain during the 1970s out of a pragmatic alliance between policy-makers, leisure managers and academics, all interested in the increasing economic, social and psychological importance of leisure. The sociological strand explored the relationship between leisure, paid work and family life. Though subsequently challenged by alternative emphases on the social divisions of gender, class and ethnicity, the original triumvirate remained constant. Since the mid-1970s, this research agenda has been increasingly challenged for at least two reasons. First, British society, along with many other capitalist democracies, has undergone significant changes in each of the key areas of work, family life and leisure. Second, and as a consequence, new kinds of theorising about society have emerged, with apparently greater claim to explain these new formations than traditional models.

This chapter concentrates on the precise nature of changes in work, family and leisure in Britain since the mid-1970s and how to interpret them. The patterns are often complex. In work there have been severe economic recessions and mass unemployment, as well as periods of near full employment. The family remains an entrenched ideal but has become so varied that the term itself no longer seems adequate to encompass the variety of household formations. In leisure, commercial influences have increased, yet a previously impoverished public and voluntary sector has been given fresh stimulus by funding from the National Lottery, itself an innovative kind of state-licensed gambling. The unevenness of these patterns makes it difficult to identify the thrust and nature of change, to differentiate between the form and the substance of social experience or between permanent structural change and ephemeral cultural fashion. Basic questions emerge: has the period since the mid-1970s seen the emergence of a new kind of society, radically different from the one preceding it? How do we conceptualise such changes? What implications do they have for our understanding of leisure? In the rest of the chapter we address these questions by looking in turn at paid work, family and leisure. For each we review the major quantitative changes, comment on their qualitative implications and examine one account of their significance. We also note in each case how much or little governments have responded to social change.

Our argument is that work, family and leisure remain recognisable divisions of social experience. They demarcate boundaries of time and space which are permeable only to a limited extent. Most people know when and where they are at work or working, even though such activities may be punctuated by others which, in another time and place, might be construed as leisure. Similarly, what is located and timed as leisure might have within it activity which otherwise might be called work. The family is precisely characterised by the interplay of activity which is quite clearly work, notably domestic labour, and that which is as unequivocally leisure, such as holidays. The boundaries between work, leisure and family derive from our own experience; they are taken-for-granted and help us make sense of the world. It is only when there are episodic fractures – unemployment, divorce or depression – that we think about their roles and boundaries. That does not mean that social science should automatically inherit commonsense notions of work, family and leisure. Under intellectual scrutiny, they may not stand up. They may prove misleading, even illusory. Yet nor can they be jettisoned as self-evidently unsatisfactory. Many accounts of the new society do not seem to take sufficient account of the ways in which daily life is structured by the experience of work, family and leisure. Accounts of consumption subordinate production; accounts of identity marginalise primary relationships. The assumption that leisure has achieved a primacy over other areas of experience is based on a skewed perception of everyday life. We therefore make no apology for beginning with what most people experience at some time in their lives as a necessity: paid work.

## Work

There is general agreement about the overall trends in employment in the British economy since the mid-1970s, though there are differences in the significance attributed to fine detail, with even more divergence about what the changes in total signify. The main agreed features are the continued decline of the manufacturing sector, the expansion of the service sector, in which the quaternary or information-based sector is especially important, and the rapid expansion of the number of women in paid employment. The extent and pace of these changes have been disruptive for many local economies, exacerbating regional inequalities in the distribution and quality of jobs.

Since manufacturing tends to be regionally concentrated, men in older industrial areas are the main victims of contraction. Unemployment is the clearest, though inconsistently defined, measure. All estimates admit that one in six of households with potential earners are workless. Unemployment is higher for men than for women and concentrated among the younger age groups. Long-term unemployment is more common for men in their thirties and forties. Older long-term unemployed men frequently opt for a form of early retirement, claiming invalidity benefit until they can 'officially' retire. Only half of men aged 60–64 are in paid employment. All this is regionally imbalanced. In some of the older industrial areas, estimates of real male unemployment run as high as 30 per cent. Contrary to those who gleefully announce the end of 'jobs for life', employment tenure has not altered for those in work. What has happened is that those without work experience life on the fringes of the labour market, moving from one insecure job to another.

Three-quarters of women aged 25–44 are now in paid employment. Some 80 per cent of part-time workers are women. Their occupations are gender-specific. While some inroads have been made into professional and managerial jobs, the main clusters of female employment remain in secretarial and clerical, sales and public administration sectors, while men still rely heavily on skilled and unskilled jobs in manufacturing. The sexual divisions of labour and the labour market have been resilient. Women still carry the burden of combining domestic with paid work. As largely part-time employees, they are excluded from many benefits available to core male workers.

The changes are clear and decisive: paid employment in male-dominated primary and assembly-line mass production has diversified into flexible, feminised, batch-production for increasingly differentiated niche markets. Technological changes – computerisation, robotics, new information technologies and mass communications – have produced new occupational hierarchies, underscored by new patterns of unemployment, deskilling, reskilling and professionalisation. The quality of new jobs is a matter of dispute. While some are clearly highly skilled and well rewarded, involving elaborate use of new technologies, others are more mundane. The lowest paid sectors are in catering and retail trades, the highest in finance and utilities. The 'call centre' – with highly regimented and standardised working practices, fragmented working hours and comparatively low pay – has become the touchstone of the new economy.

Hence the experience of paid work is one of unevenness. The security, rewards and working conditions of employment vary considerably. There is no doubt that what the new economy wants and needs is a 'flexible' labour force. In practice, this means workers who will work the hours employers want, under conditions they cannot collectively negotiate and in a state of permanent insecurity. Employers clearly predominate in the balance of power with employees. Work and class inequalities still remain centre stage in the struggle over time. Selling labour power is still at the heart of people's everyday experience of capitalism. Postmodernists may write about how cultural intermediaries skilfully celebrate the aestheticisation of everyday life, as they experience dedifferentiation and the blurring of the boundaries between work and leisure, as workplaces become more leisurely and people 'work out' in their leisure time. But for the majority of workers, dedifferentiation means work time invading the rest of life, eroding the boundaries with family and leisure. The material reality of the 'online society', Sunday and late-night shopping or the 24-hour call centre, means that someone else is working antisocial hours, with contractual conditions lightly regulated by the state and outside trade union influence. Some people can embrace new flexible patterns and construct new lifestyles which run counter to the biological rhythms and task-based routines of traditional work. But it is always the employer's prerogative to choose flexibilisation, to introduce new technologies to monitor performance and measure output and to introduce new patterns of work. Self-employment often means high risks and long hours. Indeed, the middle class as a whole has experienced changes in conditions of work which are qualitatively significant.

In Beck's (1992) thesis of the *risk society*, power relations and power differentials in employment are transformed. Growing insecurity of tenure and intensification of bureaucratic control and surveillance applies to all sectors of paid employment. The traditional confidence and trust reserved for middle-class professions is dissipated. With demands for quality control procedures and transparency of performance, the majority of professions, particularly within the public sector, have had their traditional work practices subject to increased surveillance (Sennett 2000).

The common experience of those selling labour power has been the actual intensification of work. The leisure revolution has been betrayed on two counts – people in paid work are not only working longer but also working harder. Ironically the very architects of post-Fordist regimes of de-industrialisation and work flexibilisation find that they themselves are subject to the same logic of work discipline as their subordinates, such as downsizing, stress, casualisation, increased workloads and long-term insecurity. Career patterns and trajectories change; the harried middle class experiences an excess of work (Seabrook 1988; Schor 1996).

Of the many ways in which employment status impacts upon leisure, its effect on individual and household income remains central. Where access to leisure increasingly rests on the capacity to purchase goods and services in the market, the distribution of income becomes an important determinant of leisure life chances. The overall trends are clear, if only occasionally recognised. With the exception of brief periods in the early and very late 1990s, the distribution of income has become more and more unequal since the early 1980s. The taxation and benefit systems which might redress imbalances have been redesigned to exacerbate inequality. The shift from direct to indirect taxes, for example, is universally acknowledged to have a disproportionate effect on the purchasing power of the poor.

The statistical evidence is overwhelming (Office for National Statistics 2001). In 1971 the average income of the richest tenth of the population was three times that of the poorest tenth; by 1999 it was four times. Real incomes have risen across the society but the rich have got richer much faster than the poor have got less poor. There remain substantial differences of income between men and women, becoming smaller for single people but remaining constant among married couples. Households experiencing unemployment or headed by a lone parent, pensioners, disabled and low-paid people are all denied access to the increasing disposable incomes of society as a whole. The distribution of wealth is even more extreme, the most wealthy 5 per cent holding half of the nation's wealth. On the whole society has been getting more prosperous, often measured by the decreasing amount of time necessary to work in order to purchase any nominated good. But this increase, like the increase in employment, is distributed in ways which are systematically unequal.

These overall changes in paid employment have been described graphically as the emergence of the '40–30–30 society' (Hutton 1995). The economic class division between rich and poor in the labour market has been complicated by the emergence of an insecure middle class. Changes in patterns of employment have resulted in new patterns of work and time inequalities. New Right economic strategies of privatisation, casualisation and deregulation have, according to Hutton, reshaped class cleavages and the nature of inequalities. The top 40 per cent are relatively privileged, since their market power has increased since the early 1980s. They include the minority of full-time employees whose jobs are secure or unionised, as well as the long-term self-employed. The middle 30 per cent are marginalised and insecure. Their jobs are precarious, often with few substantial benefits. They include part-time and casual workers, low paid people and those whose self employment is short term. Finally, the bottom 30 per cent are those who are disadvantaged, largely excluded from the employment market. Here we find unemployed people and their dependants, people on government schemes and those in the benefits trap (Hutton 1995: 105–10). Hutton is quite clear about the implications of this new employment structure for social divisions.

> For the majority of the population this is an irrational state of affairs. They do not have the wherewithal to cover all the eventualities that might hit them, from divorce to unemployment, nor can they build up a

cushion of savings against hard times. The extension of the market principle into wider and wider areas, all in the name of individual choice and
personal responsibility, has begun to destabilise society.

(Hutton 1995: 194)

Hutton's thesis, though powerful, has its limitations. As a new model of class
divisions, it collapses distinctions between managers and managed. It may
also now seem anachronistic, as unemployment has fallen. But it does remind
us of the profound insecurity of employment, its effects on financial status
and the domination of the free market in the distribution of employment. It
is certainly a more viable account than that adopted by the Office for
National Statistics, whose response to the changing occupational structure is
to abandon the old socio-economic categorisation in favour of one based on
a 'grouping of occupations' which is 'not hierarchical in nature' (Office for
National Statistics 2001: 21). Thus are the inequalities of paid work wished
away.

What all this means for leisure is far from clear. Changes in the structure
of the economy should not be assumed to alter perceptions of paid
employment. The commonly expressed idea that work has lost out to leisure
as a source of identity is simply speculative. What is clear is that the dur-
ation and intensity of work has increased. The average Briton in employment works longer hours than in any other country in the European Union.
Whatever else it has done, economic change has clearly decreased the
amount of time which is free from paid employment. Others can find no, or
only a marginal, place in the new economy. They eke out a life as best they
can, mixing benefits with the black economy or opting for premature
retirement.

For all categories of those excluded from employment, the UK government has a clear message: get back to work. Lone mothers, disabled people,
young people, short- and long-term unemployed, are all targeted by the
'New Deal'. They are regarded as lacking the motivation, aptitudes and
skills to find employment in the new economy. Indeed, contrary to those
who identify the decline of the work ethic, it has never been stronger in
political life. An essentially puritanical New Labour regime proclaims the
virtues of work: it will solve the problems of poverty, alienation and devi-
ance, all categorised in the handy concept of social exclusion. Given trends
in longevity, the present government is also considering legislation to
encourage men and women to work beyond retirement age. Far from realising a life where paid employment can use up less time and energy and
become less important to our sense of who we are, contemporary economic
trends and political ideologies insist that we should work harder and longer
under conditions dictated by employers. In that sense, ours has become a
more work-centred society.

## Family, life cycle and generation

Consideration of the second of the leisure studies triumvirate, the family, must begin with demographic trends, without which changes in household structure make little sense. The United Kingdom has an ageing population. Of all adults, half are aged 45 or over, one-fifth over 65. It is too easy to mistake the activities of the young for those of the population at large and attribute to choice changes in household composition which are more likely to be the outcome of ageing. Longevity has had a dramatic impact on households and family networks. In 2000 the average life expectancy was 75 for men and 80 for women, increases of seven years since the early 1960s. Class inequalities in health are still evident among elderly people, one-third of whom live in poverty. Two-thirds of women over 75 who live alone are crucially dependent on family members to provide care and support but one in three have no near relatives.

These factors bear on household composition. Compared with the early 1960s, the proportion of single person households has almost tripled, while households containing couples with or without children have decreased by 50 per cent. The biggest group of people living on their own are not surprisingly pensioners, especially women. The second largest group of people living alone turns out to be men under 65, whose numbers are increasing at an even faster rate than pensioners. Since young men are comparatively slow to set up home independently, it would appear that this group are men of middle age.

If we consider persons rather than households, the 'family' has not decreased to such an extent. In the early 1960s eight in ten people lived in such units; now it is seven in ten. Four in five children still live in recognisable families, if not necessarily with both biological parents. It is not, then, that the family is being rejected as a residential grouping but that it is no longer a constant unit. It is also subject to ethnic variation. White society mobilises polarised views of family structures among African Caribbeans as too loose and Asians as too close.

Families for life have been disappearing much faster than jobs for life. Still, the process of family formation remains the most common pattern. It, and what follows, is undertaken later. Young women leave home earlier than men. Most will eventually live with a man whom they will then marry. Since the mid-1970s the age of marriage has increased by five years (to 27) and the age of first childbirth for women by three years (to 29). The numbers declining to do one or the other have increased. One-quarter of women born in the mid-1970s will have no child by their mid-forties. One in six couples who live together are not married. Rising numbers of unmarried, separated and divorced mothers have resulted in one in five families being headed by a lone parent. Fewer than 10 per cent of births occurred outside marriage in 1961; by 2000 it was 40 per cent and rising – though mostly to cohabiting couples. At the turn of the millennium, 40 per cent of first marriages end in divorce, though most involved will remarry, men rather more than women.

Changed attitudes towards cohabitation, marriage, parenting and child-care have transformed generational experience and household composition. The traditional nuclear family, though remaining an aspiration, has proved difficult to sustain. Yet many of the cultural patterns inside the intact family change but little. A key example is domestic labour. Though men have become marginally more involved in the maintenance of the home, the division of labour is still highly gendered. Women spend half as much time again as men on household tasks. They have primary responsibility for cleaning and tidying, cooking and childcare, washing and ironing. Men's contribution to these tasks is consistently less, the only areas where they outperform the women being do-it-yourself (DIY) and gardening. Like the single good-time girl, the 'new man' is largely a myth. Based on their own restricted experience, media commentators and dramatists, and some sociologists, take the experience of a tiny minority as an index of change, when much behaviour inside families is relentlessly conventional.

As in the case of work, political ideologies have taken an ultra-conservative position. Divorce and lone parenting are lamented, with constant threats to make either or both more difficult. Tax and benefit systems do little to support parents living apart. The traditional family is assumed to be the optimum condition for social integration. Labour and Conservative parties vied with each other to be identified as the 'party of the family' in the run-up to the 2001 election. The family has been placed ideologically at the heart of community-care policies by various New Right and then New Labour initiatives of privatising welfare. This is at the precise time when families are too culturally fragmented, geographically dislocated and financially stretched to respond to increased responsibilities for caring. The burden of dependency between generations has consequently changed. As the state withdraws public funding from collective consumption, parents have to fund their children through education; adults become 'liable relatives' for the care of their elderly parents. On the other hand, current rates of longevity ensure the present working population has to pay for a growing pensions bill, which was generously crafted, index linked and enhanced in the welfare-state era. The state's response is to devalue the state pension, encourage private schemes and defer retirement.

These chains or patterns of dependency become even more financially and legally complicated if considered in the context of growing numbers of single parents, common-law marriages, and high rates of both divorce and remarriage. Heritage and inheritance are not only national but also local problems. For many people, even kinship ties are negotiable and problematic rather than the taken-for-granted bedrock of solid family and local community identities. The ideology of the 'traditional family Christmas' (Finnegan 1981) becomes less convincing and less binding on all family members whose duties, allegiances and contradictory wishes are stretched across generations and diverse family networks.

Beck (1992) has interpreted such changes to indicate the family as a site of contradictions. A basic one is that the logic of the market, driving inexorably towards modernisation and individuation, undermines what it is posited on: the existence of a 'normal' nuclear family and its inherent gender divisions. The equality of the market is incompatible with the inequalities of family life. The normative constraints of gender dissolve in the face of increasing individuation so that the definition of roles in a heterosexual partnership become more fluid and problematic. The very proliferation of apparent lifestyle choices of residence, work and household structures reveals the constraints on choice, opening up greater possibilities of conflict within the family. It becomes 'the setting but not the cause' (Beck 1992: 103) of the disjunction where 'production and family work are subjected to contrary organisational principles' (Beck 1992: 107). The freeing of women from their traditional roles is attributed to five changes: increasing life expectancy, the restructuring of housework, contraceptive and family planning, the fragility of marriage and educational opportunity. As women gain greater control over their biographies, so their enforced dependence on men becomes irksome. The family is where these contradictions are acted out, with the result that 'the traditional unity of the family breaks apart in the face of decisions demanded of it' (Beck 1992: 117). Since the clock cannot be turned back and equality is not achievable within the confines of the family, the only solution is to reform employment and family structures so they can be made more compatible with each other.

Beck's portrait may seem overblown. Perhaps more couples do, if not at the first attempt, find ways of living through these tensions. Yet it may remind us that the creation of a family is psychologically wearing and its dissolution no less devastating for being commonplace. The solutions found by individuals – nuclear families, lone parenting, divorce with or without remarriage, living alone or cohabiting – may appear to be choices but cumulatively they indicate that the changes in work and family are interconnected, both for individuals and for the society as a whole.

For Giddens (1999), one dimension of globalisation is this decline of tradition, changing gender relations and a growing 'democracy of the emotions'. Long-term structural processes express themselves and are mediated by changes in family structures and personal relationships, especially between generations. Traditional nuclear families, sustained by patriarchal divisions of labour, put localised community identities at the heart of post-war Fordist social policies. Men were occupational breadwinners, contributed to national insurance schemes and determined public policy; in contrast women and children were confined to the private domain, expected to participate in local neighbourhood networks but dependent on husbands/fathers for state benefits and services. As Clarke and Critcher (1985) have argued, it is crucial to differentiate between the ideology, structure and experience of families in advanced industrial capitalism.

In post-war Britain, family structures and household relationships are apparent sites for fragmentation, destabilisation and individualisation, though overall 'the structures of both the household and the family are becoming diverse, but remain important to society and retain an integral role in people's lives' (Office for National Statistics 2001: 55). In the 1970s and 1980s, Young and Willmott (1973) and Kelly (1983) might have detected the consolidation and centrality of the 'symmetrical family' in leisure but this portrait seems increasingly anachronistic. However, in so far as leisure studies has traditionally identified the family as a site, participating group and central motivation for leisure, none of these trends seem likely to have dislodged the family or, more accurately, household unit from its strategic position. Its internal dynamics and precise composition may have changed but its role in society and its leisure patterns can be expected to have remained relatively constant.

## Leisure and lifestyles

We must again insist on the primacy of economic factors. Households now have, on average, greater disposable income than ever before. This is so, despite the proportion of income spent on mortgages having increased from one-tenth in 1971 to one-quarter in 2004. Otherwise, the proportion spent on essential items has decreased while that on non-essential items, including leisure, has increased. The purchase of financial services, tourism and telecommunications has shown some of the sharpest increases. New kinds of consumers emerge, most indicatively children. But again there are disparities. Unemployed people do not share in this expansion of disposable income, which is also regionally variable. The 'average' household spends one-sixth of its income on leisure goods and services but the figure is higher in London and the South East, lower in the North East, Northern Ireland and Scotland.

Of all leisure activities, the group which still consumes most time, though often in conjunction with other activities, comprises the mass media and related communication technologies. An average of 26 hours a week is spent watching television, with those of pensionable age spending twice as long as children. Some 19 hours is spent listening to the radio. Four in ten households have a home computer, even more where there are children. Listening to music is also a common home-based leisure pursuit. Indeed contact with relatives and friends is the only leisure activity which occurs with anything like the frequency of use of communications media. Overall, the trend towards home-based leisure has increased and become more and more dependent on the purchase of leisure technology. But DIY and gardening continue to be popular, heavily correlated with social class.

Outside the home, we meet some old friends. Cinema admissions, concentrated among the young, have doubled since the early 1980s. Library use has declined but museum entrances have increased, except where charges have been introduced. Trips out are still for mundane purposes such as eating or drinking, visiting friends, going shopping or for a walk and pursuing hobbies and sports. Young men dominate sport, though one-third of them and one-half of their female counterparts take no regular exercise. The young drink more alcohol than the old and a substantial minority take illegal drugs.

More organised excursions follow a familiar pattern. Visits to historic houses, zoos and theme parks have reached stable levels, with traditional venues to the fore. One-quarter of the population now take two or more holidays a year and one-third at least one, but four-tenths have no holiday at all, a proportion unchanged since the mid-1970s. In short, though new activities have been added, the overall patterns are remarkably predictable. More leisure is purchased in the market, especially at home. Almost all activities show considerable variation by class, gender and age. Much of leisure, it can be safely assumed, is still spent in and motivated by the company of others: family, relatives and friends.

More recent processes of globalisation should sensitise us to the profound changes taking place, particularly in the markets for sports goods, leisure wear, media and catering services. Global firms offer and produce global consumer culture, as national and regional markets are developed for the ubiquitous icons of Nike, Gap, Disney, Coca Cola and not least McDonald's. Bauman's (1992) early work on postmodern change suggests that we no longer live in the age of the single 'legislator' of taste and cultural consumption but rather rely on a variety of expert 'interpreters' to make sense of diversity and difference. The historical project of national elites to act as legislators of taste becomes less confident and more diffused with the globalisation and commodification of leisure experiences. Prescriptions for rational recreation and central government subsidies for legitimate leisure activities – whether in the sport, arts or serious leisure – appear not so much old-fashioned as irrelevant.

Leisure studies has not been blind to this growing commodification and privatisation of leisure experiences. For example, Rojek (1985) highlighted these processes, alongside pacification and individualisation, as the key to understanding modern leisure. Indeed, during the Thatcher years, New Right policies sought to restructure and dilute the welfare state, specifically to bypass or to redirect the energies of local government. In the 1980s the Audit Commission and Compulsory Competitive Tendering legislation for sport and leisure introduced an entrepreneurial edge to local authority provision. There was increased emphasis on income generation, customer care and quality assurance, as well as an ideological shift towards an economic rationale for local government policies. The social rationale of leisure access and community development was superseded by investments in tourism, heritage, museums and mega-events in sports and the arts, with ambitious plans especially favoured by de-industrialising cities seeking urban renaissance. Leisure researchers, too, started to question the role and boundaries of public sector provision in sport and leisure. Fred Coalter's research base into sports participation and deprivation and his polemic against public sector professionals has grown over the years (Coalter 1997, 1998). There has been a growing overlap between the public, voluntary and commercial sectors as all have adopted a business discourse that makes sense to investors, planners, quangos, sponsors, stakeholders and customers alike.

Roberts (1995, 1999) has tried to make sense of this kaleidoscope of continuity and change. In the earlier work he identified four trends in contemporary leisure. The first and most obvious is home-centredness. Many of the main items and services of the leisure industry are consumed at home or in household groupings. Alcohol consumption, for example, has increased but more of it is being drunk at home. In the second trend, out of home recreation, people still go out but for discrete activities, with the decline of communal life reinforcing the primacy of the home as a leisure site and the household as a leisure grouping. Only two areas of leisure outside the home, sports participation and tourism, have increased, both concentrated among more affluent sections of the population. Third, and again restricted to the more affluent, is the expansion of connoisseur or serious leisure. Committed enthusiasts join networks of the like-minded. The development of such committed leisure interests is one solution to the problems posed by premature retirement. Fourth is the alienation of youth from the commercial and public leisure provision. Exacerbated by youth unemployment, the leisure of youth is regarded as a growing problem, from teenage pregnancies to excessive drinking. Overall, the main paradox is the uneven distribution of the two preconditions for leisure: free time and spending power. 'Time released from employment has been given to the poorest sections of the population, while spending power has increased mainly for those with the least leisure time' (Roberts 1995: 18).

The face of leisure certainly seems to have changed. But often what happens is that long-standing pursuits take place in new kinds of environmental ambience: wine bars instead of pubs; shopping malls instead of city centres; multiplexes instead of flea pits; night clubs instead of discos. The Big Five of leisure – gambling, sex, alcohol, television and annual holidays – have all held their own. Each has experienced changes in dominant forms, such as the National Lottery, contraceptive techniques, wine consumption, multi-channel subscription television and the weekend break. And again it must be insisted that much leisure for most people most of the time is informal and mundane. In an ageing society, sedentary leisure is an even more common pattern. Some accounts of leisure seem to imply that the significant groups are under 30 and living in city centres; they are, statistically speaking, as likely to be middle-aged and living in the suburbs.

As pluralists and postmodernists rightly stress, some individuals in these new times are confronted with lifestyle choices. They are required to choose partners, diet, sexuality, exercise regimes, terrestrial and satellite television, foreign holiday destinations, gardens and houses. Indeed, there is a babble of experts out there advocating alternatives; with postmodern figural media, one can safely and vicariously spectate as people change rooms, change gardens, change places, change jobs, change continents or change channels. But this postmodern literary strategy of deconstructing and decentring leisure practices as cultural texts becomes less convincing when applied to people's everyday experience. People can and do make choices, do experience 'flow' and 'serious leisure' as well as pleasure and excess but leisure should not be decontextualised from the economic, political, social and cultural formations of modernity. With global flows of people, goods and services and a more flexible role for the nation-state, access to leisure experiences and leisure time becomes increasingly commodified and unequal. Divisions of class, race and gender still mediate patterns of inequality in material and cultural competencies.

The shifting patterns of paid work and their differential impact on the lives of family members still provide the decisive context for understanding leisure and individualised leisure practices. The previously localised networks of jobs, neighbouring and childcare have now been displaced. For those in secure paid employment, high levels of productivity have permitted high levels of investment in and consumption of commodified free-time experience – though many remain excluded (Taylor et al. 1996). 'Just-in-time' production techniques are mirrored by 'just-in-time' leisure patterns, with expensive mobile phones a ubiquitous prerequisite for managing busy work, friendship and leisure schedules. This is the cultural trend which Ritzer (2000) has argued dominates contemporary culture and its habitual modes of production and consumption.

## The McDonaldisation thesis

There is now a bewildering array of theories and concepts which endeavour to explain the broad contours of societal transformation of which changes in work, family and leisure form an integral part. The 'new' society has been characterised by postmodernity, risk, consumerism, to name but a few (Crook 1991; Featherstone 1991; Zukin 1991; Bauman 1992; Beck 1992; Smart 1993; Lyon 1999). Paradoxically, some of these hardly mention leisure at all while others place prototypical leisure at the heart of the new social order. Relatively few try to link changes in production and consumption at the level of lived experience. An exception is the thesis of the 'McDonaldisation' of society. Ritzer (2000) develops a Weberian perspective on the systematic rationalisation of industrial capitalism. He posits the McDonald's company as the exemplar of global capitalist organisation transforming the production, distribution and consumption of food and – more importantly – everyday life. McDonald's unique contribution is to apply Fordist or Taylorist assembly-line production techniques wholeheartedly to the fast-food industry. The application of standardised dehumanising technologies lowers costs and increases profits. Ritzer discerns four shibboleths of the McDonald's strategy – efficiency, calculability, predictability and control. Franchising enables a global firm to shape and retain ownership of the cultural capital, advertising and marketing the brand label, but permit others to busy themselves with its material production. Such strategies maximise the profits of giant corporations, while distancing them from exploitative work practices and environmental despoliation.

The insight driving Ritzer's polemical analysis is how such rationalisation of production and consumption styles has permeated other areas of social life – education, health care, politics, and travel and work in general (Rojek and Urry 1977; Smart 1999). However, McDonald's rationality also produces irrationalities, unintended negative consequences such as environmental impacts and dehumanised labour. It all means disenchantment, false friendliness and, importantly, junk food at high cost. The consumer provides the necessary labour power to realise consumption. Traditional service staff, such as waiters and waitresses, are no longer required. By offering flexible family-eating times and fun styles and promotions, these new forms of individualised self-service can rely upon the consumer to wait, queue and work in his/her free time. Examples elsewhere include microwaves, vending machines, and drink dispensers; EPOS (electronic point of sale) and EPOT bar-coding; scanners, copiers and self-service ticket machines.

Ritzer (2000) somewhat romantically counterposes the relaxed and interactive traditional family meal with the harassed and self-absorbed consumption of eating at McDonald's. Yet fast-food can be seen as complementing changing eating patterns and family lifestyles, especially the enormous marketing effort directed at children as consumers. For adults, too, American styles of eating such as 'snacking', 'grazing' or 'refuelling' are increasingly popular, also reflecting the erosion of shared tea and lunch breaks. People simply do not have the time to shop, to prepare ingredients, to cook food, often even time to sit down together and then clear up afterwards. The feminisation of paid employment and changing expectations in the sexual division of labour have resulted in 'eating out' becoming the major item of leisure spending in the United Kingdom.

But it is not just the money-rich, time-poor niche markets that constitute McDonald's customers. Rather than being locked in the iron cage of McDonaldisation, Bauman's (1992) contention is that the majority of the population in postmodern times are seduced into consumer culture; the excluded minority yearn to consume too. The nation-state is no longer interested in seeking legitimation, in binding producers into work, in socialising citizens into homogenous national culture. Politicians have relinquished the task of social integration to the market and the media. People are engaged in society as consumers not producers: spending therefore becomes a duty and political partisanship an irrelevance. The current hegemonic project is to produce willing consumers rather than obedient citizens immersed in national culture. Market inequalities may produce flawed consumers – poor, homeless and unemployed people – but they can be controlled and supervised. The whole culture is now impossible to escape and we may not even want to.

## Conclusion

We have tried, here, to confine our argument within clear boundaries, those of understanding the key changes in work, family and leisure in Britain since the mid-1970s. We considered the McDonaldisation thesis, less because we are necessarily persuaded by it but because it offered one coherent (not to say accessible and amusing) rendering of the connections across work, family and leisure. Accounts of this kind seem to us to be one way forward for considering the future of work and leisure. However, it is not easy to restrict the scope of the discussion. For one of the problems we posed at the beginning – how we conceptualise these changes – ultimately demands some engagement with new kinds of theories which purport to encapsulate the nature of recent societal change.

This is not the place to evaluate these perspectives but we must note that some of them would not only dispute the particulars of our analysis but its initial assumption: that work, family and leisure provide the basic framework for understanding everyday life. In this view, our social activity in all these spheres cannot be divorced from 'how contemporary consciousness is structured by the global economy of signs' (Rojek 1995:147). It is no longer the case, as sociology traditionally assumed, that society produces culture; rather, culture parades a 'hyperreality' of signs from which we construct our apprehension of daily experience. The symbolic activities of the mass media and communication technologies suffuse all areas of life – work, family, leisure, politics, consumption – which are now essentially postmodern in nature.

The implication is that what we call 'leisure' is where the new social consciousness finds its most powerful expression. Its modes of consumption and symbolic plenitude become the defining characteristics of the culture as a whole. While it is quite true, and something our own account may have under-stressed, that the leisure and media industries do occupy an ever more central role in the economic structures and cultural sign systems of contemporary society, they have yet to dislodge the fundamental sociological proposition that all societies must have – and it is an imperative – systems or structures of production, reproduction and consumption. If some traditional accounts have over-privileged production, it would seem equally erroneous to place excessive emphasis on consumption. Neither may take reproduction, biological and cultural, seriously enough. We hold to the project that the purpose of understanding any particular element of the social order is to *connect* – to understand the ways in which one particular element is shaped by other structures and ways in which that one area affects and contributes to the development of the rest.

(Clarke and Critcher 1985: xiii, original emphasis)

It remains our view, despite all the genuine difficulties it entails, that British society is still basically a capitalist one. Since capitalism is a dynamic system it has changed but not in its fundamentals.

Changes, when set against the basic rules of capitalist accumulation, appear more as shifts in the surface appearance rather than the emergence of some new kind of entirely new postcapitalist or even postindustrial society.

(Harvey 1989: vii)

This does not mean that changes in family life, leisure or even work can simply be 'read off' as inevitably and invariably capitalist. The challenge is to demonstrate, not that a theory can immediately and thoroughly explain everything but that it can account in broad terms for the major features of the phenomenon under discussion, in this case the sweep of social change recently undergone by British society. Despite all the real changes, especially in the cultural and leisure industries, the basic contours of daily life – of work, family and leisure – have remained remarkably recognisable. The effort to understand the connections between them continues.

## References

Bauman, Z. (1992) *Intimations of Post-Modernity*. London: Routledge.

Bauman, Z. (1998) *Globalization*. Cambridge: Polity.

Beck, U. (1992) *Risk Society: Towards a New Modernity*, trans. M. Ritter. London: Sage.

Clarke, J. and Critcher, C. (1985) *The Devil Makes Work: Leisure in Capitalist Britain*. London: Macmillan.

Coalter, F. (1997) Leisure sciences and leisure studies: different concept, same crisis? *Leisure Sciences* 19: 255–68.

Coalter, F. (1998) Leisure studies, leisure policy and social citizenship: the failure of welfare or the limits of welfare? *Leisure Studies* 17: 21–36.

Crook, I. (1991) *Postmodernisation*. London: Routledge.

Featherstone, M. (1991) *Consumer Culture and Postmodernism*. London: Sage.

Finnegan, R. (1981) Celebrating Christmas, Unit 2, *Popular Culture, Themes and Issues*. Milton Keynes: Open University Press.

Giddens, A. (1999) *Runaway World: Reith Lectures*. London: BBC.

Harvey, D. (1989) *The Condition of Postmodernity*. Oxford: Blackwell.

Hutton, W. (1995) *The State We're In*. London: Jonathan Cape.

Kelly, J. R. (1983) *Leisure Identities and Interactions*. London: Allen and Unwin.

Lyon, D. (1999) *Postmodernity*. Buckingham: Open University Press.

Office for National Statistics (2001) *Social Trends*. London: Stationery Office.

Ritzer, G. (2000) *The McDonaldization of Society*. Thousand Oaks, CA: Pine Forge Press.

Roberts, K. (1978) *Contemporary Society and the Growth of Leisure*. London: Longman.

Roberts, K. (1995) Great Britain: Socio economic polarisation and the implications for leisure. In C. Critcher, P. Bramham and A. Tomlinson (eds) *Sociology of Leisure: A Reader*. London: E and FN Spon.

Roberts, K. (1999) *Leisure in Contemporary Society* Wallingford, UK: CAB International.

Rojek, C. (1985) *Capitalism and Leisure Theory*. London: Tavistock.

Rojek, C. (1989) Leisure and recreation theory. In E. Jackson and T. Burton (eds) *Understanding Leisure and Recreation*. State College, PA: Venture.

Rojek, C. and Urry, J. (1977) *Touring Cultures*. London: Routledge.

Rojek, C. (1995) *Decentring Leisure: Rethinking Leisure Theory*. London: Routledge.

Schor, J. (1996) *The Overworked American*. New York: Basic Books.

Seabrook, J. (1988) *The Leisure Society*. Oxford: Blackwell.

Sennett, R. (2000) *The Corrosion of Character: The Personal Consequences of Work in the New Capitalism*. New York: W.W. Norton.

Smart, B. (1993) *Postmodernity*. London: Routledge.

Smart, B. (ed.) (1999) *Resisting McDonaldization*. London: Sage.

Taylor, I., Evans, K. and Fraser, P. (1996) *A Tale of Two Cities: Global Change, Local Feeling and Everyday Life in the North of England*. London: Routledge.

Young, M. and Willmott, P. (1973) *The Symmetrical Family*. Harmondsworth, UK: Penguin.

Zukin, S. (1991) *Landscapes of Power: From Detroit to Disney World*. Berkeley, CA: University of California Press.

# Chapter 3

# Postmodern work and leisure

*Chris Rojek*

## Introduction

The classical political economy of Ricardo, Bentham and J. S. Mill presented paid employment as the primary means through which the individual develops the self, morally and economically, and contributes to the wealth and well-being of the commons. Leisure was acknowledged to be the necessary complement to work since, in the voluntary chosen activities of non-work time, individuals replenish themselves and freely develop their faculties and interests. Nonetheless, classical political economy seldom departed from the postulate that the *a priori* of leisure is paid employment.

Interestingly, emancipatory politics in the nineteenth and for most of the twentieth centuries typically confirmed this position. Karl Marx has some claim to be regarded as the foremost critic of the work ethic in the nineteenth century. His analysis emphasised the forced nature of work, the usurpation of value by the capitalist, the alienation and self-estrangement of the work process, and the need to rethink the relationship between work and society from top to bottom. Nevertheless, he was always blistering about his utopian disciples who mistook communism for the end of work. In Marx's view, capitalism condemned workers to exploitation and brutalisation. He held that the solution to this state of affairs was the determination of the lengths and ends of the work by the 'socialized, associated producers, through the transcendence of capitalism' (Marx 1977: 820). He famously distinguished between the realm of necessity and the realm of freedom. He argued that under communism the individual participates in multi-activity, which is voluntarily chosen and socially enriching. Underpinning this activity, however, is the requirement to produce socially and economically necessary work. The relevant passage in *Capital* submits:

> The realm of freedom actually begins only where labour which is determined by necessity and mundane considerations ceases; thus in the very nature of things it lies beyond the sphere of actual material production. Just as the savage must wrestle with Nature to satisfy his wants, to

maintain and reproduce life, so must civilized man, and he must do so in all social formations and under all possible modes of production. With his development this realm of physical necessity expands as a result of his wants; but at the same time, the forces of production which satisfy these wants also increase. Freedom in this field can only consist in socialized man, the associated producers, rationally regulating their interchange with Nature, bringing it under common control, instead of being ruled by it as by the blind forces of Nature; and achieving this with the least expenditure of energy and under conditions most favourable to, and worthy of, their human nature. But it nonetheless still remains a realm of necessity. Beyond it begins that development of human energy which is an end in itself, the true realm of freedom, which however can blossom forth only with this realm of necessity as its basis.

(Marx 1977: 820)

However, communism would not result in the end of work. Rather, it would create the basis for enhancing the individual's faculties through voluntarily chosen activity and the reaffirmation of the indissoluble bond between the individual and the commons through socially necessary labour. By the term 'socially necessary labour' Marx meant the indispensable work required to reproduce life and achieve the surplus wealth that guarantees the benefit of all. Marx therefore regarded work to be ineradicable in the development of character and society.

In this proposition, the movement of organised labour has been a sturdy accomplice. As indicated in Chapter 1 of this volume, Hunnicutt (1988) notes that the campaign for shorter working hours had climaxed by the time of the Second World War. During the Great Depression average working hours declined, but this was due principally to the lack of demand for workers rather than the campaigning zeal of trade unions or the wishes of workers. Since the 1930s, organised labour has adopted the right to work as a traditional principle of collective bargaining (Sayers 1987). While workers have, naturally, not rejected vacation time or flexible working arrangements, their collective bargaining processes have generally verified the standpoint of classical political economy, that paid employment is the *a priori* of leisure.

## The work–leisure relationship in leisure studies

For the most part, leisure studies has followed suit. The key debates have focused on two issues: the relationship between work and leisure and principles of redistributive justice regarding access to work and leisure. To begin with the relationship between work and leisure, Wilensky (1960) famously posited 'compensatory' and 'spillover' patterns between work and leisure, in which leisure forms were explained as, respectively, the reaction to the requirements of work, or the continuation of behavioural regimes established in the workplace. Parker (1983), whose approach was clearly influenced by Wilensky, devised a threefold typology of work and leisure:

- *extension:* work and leisure are not clearly demarcated, and the behavioural regime of voluntarily chosen activity resembles the regime of the workplace
- *opposition:* work and leisure are sharply divided, and the behavioural regime of voluntarily chosen activity is diametrically opposed to work experience
- *neutrality:* no causal relations between work and leisure are identified.

For many feminists, the debate about the relationship between paid work and leisure is beside the point. Instead they focus upon the second issue, the question of redistributive justice. Two further issues have emerged from this. First, feminists have demonstrated that women have been systematically excluded from paid employment, with the resultant negative implications for occupational and state contributory benefits. Second, they have explored how women's access to leisure time and leisure space is constrained. However, while important points about redistributive justice and the sexual division of power in work and leisure have emerged from this debate, the exploration of what a 'post-work' society might look like is substantially underdeveloped (Deem 1986; Shaw 1994).

On the whole, with one or two exceptions, notably Dumazedier (1967) and Veal (1987), students of leisure studies have not participated in conceptualising societal-wide alternatives to existing work–leisure patterns. Although debate and research in the field often reinforce the presupposition that the coming of the 'leisure society' is inevitable, the institutional form, fiscal arrangements, citizenship rights and obligations that will obtain in such a new social form remain substantially under-theorised. Indeed, the main impetus for clarification in this area has come, not from leisure studies, but from students of trends in the capitalist labour market.

## The 'overwork' thesis: Juliet Schor

Juliet Schor's (1991) important contribution to the debate on work and leisure certainly supports traditional feminist concerns. Her study demonstrates the perpetuation of obstacles to the full employment of women in the labour market and demands redistributive justice in the existing division of work and leisure between the sexes. However, it is written from the presumption that the character of the labour market has changed in crucial ways, making traditional feminist demands for sexual equality in work and leisure too limited. According to Schor the real problem confronting Western society is not realising full employment for both sexes, but coping with the problems of overwork.

Her 'overwork' thesis argues that workers are forced into multiple jobs, often on a casualised, non-renewable basis. Her study concentrates on American experience, but the thesis applies throughout the West. Casualisation and the threat to secure incomes posed by automation and globalisation, have produced the general condition of the overworked worker. Overwork is associated with generalised time-famine and what Harriman (1982), in an earlier study, refers to as 'harried' work and leisure experience. Schor identifies a variety of social and medical problems with the condition of overwork, including stress, hypertension, gastric illness, heart disease, cancer, depression, broken homes, marital violence, and under-socialised and antisocial children.

Overwork has been related to the pre-eminence of the work ethic in capitalist society. Max Weber (1976) ingeniously proposed a causal link between the axial attachment to work and the salvationist psychology of Protestantism. On balance, most commentators, including Schor, tend to believe that his analysis was faulty. Historians of work have made three points in this respect (Moorhouse 1989; Applebaum 1992). First, the historical evidence does not unequivocally support the proposition that a universal connection exists between the rise of Protestantism and the domination of the work ethic. Second, Weber underestimated the significance of the continuation of play forms in the Puritan revolution. In particular, he neglected to convey the vitality of the antinomian tradition in theatre, dance, sport and literature which challenged Puritan hegemony. Third, he did not grasp the reflexive relationship that workers develop in respect of the workplace. Certain play forms proved to be highly compatible with the workplace. The origins of soccer, rambling and picnic groups, the health and keep-fit movements and workers' fiction and poetry, can be partly be traced back to the work setting.

Schor's (1991) explanation for overwork focuses principally on globalisation, the deregulation of the labour market and the ascendancy of consumer culture in everyday life. She argues that the motive to develop 'portfolio-work' derives from anxieties about the effect of globalisation and automation on secure incomes and the desire to participate fully in consumer culture. In so far as capitalism requires consumer desire to be alienable, since the principle of economic accumulation requires wants to be transferable in relation to commodity and brand innovation, the consumer is permanently split between having and wanting. Schor's study therefore suggests a double bind of alienation in consumer culture. First, consumers experience the dissatisfaction of a time-famine in leisure because they are driven by an insatiable desire to earn more in order to partake of all that consumer culture offers. Second, workers are fundamentally alienated from consumer culture because it perpetuates the division between having and wanting.

## Postmodern work and leisure

Schor's study is part of a growing wave of arguments which insist that globalisation and deregulation have fundamentally transformed the nature of the capitalist labour market (see in particular: Lash and Urry 1987; Harvey 1989; Castells 1996, 1997, 1998; Gorz 1999; Beck 2000).

These arguments are sometimes grouped together under the category of postmodernism. Incidentally, it should be noted that the term postmodernism is probably losing its *cachet*. If Western society has entered a new epoch, it has done so unevenly. Some economic sectors and social strata have unquestionably adopted the mobile, flexible, global lifestyles posited by postmodern authors as the new norm in the West. Others have not. Fully blown postmodernists are rightly criticised for exaggeration and hyperbole and for not testing their propositions empirically. Nonetheless, the debate around postmodernism has raised many pertinent issues and themes about identity, power and lifestyle that traditional pluralists and radicals either ignored or treated insensitively.

Regarding the relationship between work and leisure, the main contextual changes in the market identified by postmodernism are fourfold.

### The end of Fordism

As discussed in Chapter 1 of this volume, Fordism is the method of industrial production introduced by Henry Ford to produce a standardised product that would achieve mass consumption. The system extended the principles of scientific management devised in the late nineteenth century by F. W. Taylor. It was capital-intensive, involved large-scale plant organised around an inflexible production process with rigid, centralised, hierarchical chains of command. Semi-skilled labour was employed in repetitive, routine tasks. Products were aimed at protected national markets and the labour process was highly regulated through collective bargaining. The climax of Fordism was between the late 1940s and early 1970s, when the system was extended to reconstruct the post-war economies of Europe and Japan, but it has gone into relative decline in the West as a result of decentralisation and the rise of flexible accumulation and globalisation.

### The rise of flexible accumulation

Flexible accumulation refers to the capacity of capital to switch investment according to market initiatives. Its increasing economic significance is related to the globalisation of production and consumption. Globalisation has transferred some of the capital intensive production that was once situated in the capitalist core nations, into the peripheral nations of the world system. In the periphery, the labour market is relatively unregulated and the cost of the main factors of production – labour, raw materials, plant, transport – is more competitive than in the West.

The rise of flexible accumulation was accelerated by the growth of the knowledge-based sector. Biotechnology, computers and service industries require a different skills-base than Fordism. Flexible accumulation is based in innovation, adaptability and mobility. Fordism is based in predictability, standardisation and routine. Flexible accumulation requires flexible workers, with a knowledge and skill-base that enables them to switch operations according to market challenges. Flexible workers are concomitant with the individualisation of the work contract, since the essence of innovation, adaptation and mobility is versatility.

### The reconstruction of the concept of 'work career'

The globalisation and deregulation of the labour market brings with it the individualisation of work, which in turn redefines the traditional post-war concept of the work career. The notions of a job for life, or of following an unbroken career pattern between leaving school or university and retirement, are no longer tenable for the mass of workers. Flexible workers must be prepared to follow work opportunities and retrain. Portfolio and fixed contract employment becomes more pronounced in the labour market. This has implications for old-age provision, since the globalisation and individualisation of employment is not compatible with traditional national insurance and occupational pension arrangements. Flexible workers have a high propensity to develop their own private pension schemes, and also to default on contributions if they fail to renew employment contracts.

### The increasing significance of the trans-national corporation

Globalisation and flexible accumulation imply global brand recognition. Companies intent on maximising margins, and therefore minimising the risk of takeovers, aim to achieve monopolistic or quasi-monopolistic market shares. Trans-nationalism is the inevitable consequence of the globalisation of production and consumption. Both capital and the consumer become increasingly de-territorialised and disembedded. Mass communications intensify this by eliciting 'real-world' time, in which data are instantly exchanged and consciousness of interdependence and simultaneity are heightened.

## Sociological consequences

The sociological consequences of these changes in the market for the work–leisure relationship are varied. The decline of Fordism and the rise of flexible accumulation in the West, have increased the size of the knowledge and service sectors, and globalisation and deregulation bring with them the individualisation of the work contract. Aronowitz and Cutler (1998) contend that we have already moved into 'post-work' society, in which technological innovation and the deregulation of the market have combined to drastically reduce the requirement for human labour. With this, the salience of the work ethic diminishes. Their study of the United States parallels Gorz's (1999) arguments that all workers in Europe are now 'makeshift' workers, and that the individualisation of the work contract produces the casualisation of work experience.

In terms of stratification, most commentators argue that the salariat in Western society now consists of four strata.

### Professional and executive class

Professional and executive class workers are the beneficiaries of globalisation, deregulation and privatisation. Many have experienced an exponential increase in salary, which is frequently augmented with bonus schemes and share-ownership. Their power base and opportunity for accumulation have expanded as corporations have switched from national to trans-national organisation. The increasingly flexible conditions in the market, and the continued competition for monopolistic or quasi-monopolistic market share, have increased job insecurity and status anxiety and the professional and executive class is not immune from redundancy and unemployment. Further, as studies by Pahl (1995) and Hochschild (1997) demonstrate, members of this stratum often suffer acutely from time-famine, which impacts upon their family life and the quality of their leisure time. Nonetheless, in financial and status terms, they are the winners among the post-Fordist salariat.

### Skilled middle managers, professionals, technical and service staff

Skilled middle managers, professionals, technical and service staff are salaried workers who are often well paid, and enjoy access to bonus schemes, and sometimes share-ownership schemes. They are situated at the cutting edge of innovation and charged with the task of operationalising flexible accumulation. Gorz's (1999: 51) estimate that these 'elite knowledge workers' represent no more than 1 per cent of the workforce is perhaps tendentious, since his argument is dedicated to the proposition that post-Fordism benefits only a privileged cadre of the salariat. However, that they form a small proportion of the workforce is not in doubt. Yet, although privileged, the knowledge elite has not escaped the experience of job insecurity. A significant trend in this class is the shift towards temporary, fixed-term contracts as the typical employment contract. Attendant with this is the trend towards 'portfolio working', anxiety about unemployment and the increased workload involved in the self-management of personal fiscal arrangements. This stratum also suffers from time famine, with vacations often postponed on the grounds that they cut into work time and the building up of a reliable market network. The move towards the individualisation of employment contracts means that occupational health and pension schemes are replaced with private alternatives.

### Low-skilled and unskilled workers

Globalisation and deregulation have weakened the bargaining power of the low-skilled and unskilled group. They suffer a 'double squeeze' as automation threatens to replace them, and the over-supply of labour in other countries encourages the professional and executive class to transfer demand. These are the classic 'overworked' workers described in Schor's (1991) study. They are often forced to take multiple jobs to make ends meet. An important trend in the work experience of this class is the move towards casualisation and fixed-term contracts, with the consequent diminution of benefits, notably in respect of health and pension rights. This intensifies the motivation for multi-work, with the result that time-famine is often acute in this class with the resultant negative consequences for health and family life described by Schor (1991).

### The new residuum

The term *residuum* is used by historians of nineteenth-century labour conditions to describe the class of unskilled workers who constitute either the localised poor, or the migrant jobbing seasonal labour force (Steadman-Jones 1971). The residuum consists of the classic 'emiserated' worker, identified by Marx, who suffers from poverty, ill-health and low life-expectancy. This is the class that the post-war welfare state sought to eliminate through the provision of universal public education, health care and housing. However, with the retrenchment of the market during the Thatcher-Reagan era and the associated rolling back of the welfare state, the size and prominence of this class has increased. For this stratum, the casualisation of work and the experience of regular unemployment combine to intensify poverty. The welfare safety net is not the last resort for this class, but the staple form of support. According to World Bank estimates, global unemployment stands between 600 million and 800 million, and to fully employ the economically active population which will come on to the labour market between now and 2025, some 1200 million new jobs must be created (Gorz 1999: 25).

## The 'Brazilianization thesis': Ulrich Beck

Prima facie, deregulation has created conditions in the labour market which are reminiscent of work experience at the height of the Victorian era. Acute poverty, unemployment, migratory work patterns, social dislocation and isolation are prominent features of the social and economic landscape at the present time, as they were for much of the nineteenth century. Yet, if pushed too far, the analogy wears thin. Victorian deregulation applied to national markets and was combated by national collective bargaining and the establishment of the welfare state. Deregulation now applies to the global labour market, with unions often pitched in fierce competition with one another to save or gain jobs, to flexible accumulation at the global and national level, and to a weak or declining welfare state.

Instead of regarding the current condition of the labour market as a reprise of nineteenth century trends, Beck (2000) has introduced the 'Brazilianization of the West' thesis. In semi-industrialised Brazil, Beck argues, the economically active population employed in full-time paid employment constitute only a minority of the working population. The majority are migratory workers involved in low wage, multi-activity employment. Until now this form of employment has been a feature of mainly female patterns of work in the West, but deregulation and globalisation are now coalescing to make this pattern a significant feature of the overall labour market. Labour market flexibility is attractive to the state because it redistributes risks away from the public purse and transfers them to the individual. However, it comes with great social costs, notably insecurity, low pay, intermittent work experience and social dislocation.

Beck's thesis provides a nice counterpoint to the post-industrial society theorists of the 1960s and 1970s (e.g. Dumazedier 1967; Bell 1973; Kerr et al. 1973). These writers operated on societal-wide levels. They proposed that automation would increase productivity and reduce the demand for human labour. As a result, they concluded that Western society must rapidly move into the condition in which machinery produces a perennial, exponential surplus and therefore reduces the need to work. On the whole, an over-optimistic attitude was adopted in relation to the question of the social consequences of this change. It was assumed that workers would welcome being unchained from repetitive and psychologically and socially unrewarding work. Protests at job losses would be insignificant because graduated work arrangements and welfare support would alleviate distress and leisure would be recognised as a compelling social benefit. Kerr et al. (1973) predicted the emergence of 'pluralistic industrialism' in which post-work strata develop enriching cultural and aesthetic activities and the cultural and social stock of society appreciates in value. This line of argument enjoined that 'the leisure society' is a viable alternative to industrial capitalism. The 'leisure society' was seen as a social form in which work is rationally planned and restricted to produce surplus wealth for leisure experience. It assumes that leisure, understood as the free and full development of the individual in a harmonistic, mutual relationship with civil society, can be the central life-interest. The basis for this is a socially guaranteed income, provided from the enhanced fiscal revenues and surplus wealth, generated via automated productivity.

The post-industrial society underplayed the possibility of mass un-employment, civil unrest and schisms between the technocratic elite and the rest. This is because it tended to support a rational choice theory of change, in which the universal benefits of a shorter working life outweighed the cost to particular interest groups. However, critics regarded the thesis as funda-mentally flawed in failing to identify the new power struggles over wealth, time and status that would inevitably occur in the wake of mass automation. In particular, they attacked post-industrial society theorists for being woolly about the allocative mechanisms of distributive justice and the rights, responsibilities and obligations of citizenship under the leisure society (Touraine 1974).

Beck's 'Brazilianization' thesis can be read as further exposing the limita-tions of post-industrial society theory. It argues that society is moving into an indefensible polarisation between an economically active minority, with full-time employment, carrying good pay and occupational benefits, and an economically active majority driven to the poverty line by the absence of full-time remunerative work. Three consequences make this polarisation indefensible.

First, the economically active minority are beset by an acute time-famine which prevents them from gaining satisfaction from the fruits of their labour. Studies by Pahl (1995) and Hochschild (1997) show that economically suc-cessful workers frequently complain that they are slaves to work and do not know how to enjoy time off. The balance between work and leisure which has traditionally been presented as the foundation for good health, is fractured.

Second, the economically active majority are already economically and politically marginalised and their life chances are deteriorating. Gorz (1999) argues that effective citizenship rights are tied to full-time or regular employment; the casualisation of work and the trend towards intermittent employment contracts create unbearable social and economic strains which destabilise political and cultural stability.

Third, the ethical foundations of redistributive justice are undermined by the polarisation of work experience. The fiscal burden upon the economically active to sustain welfare delivery to the majority poses a threat to innovation and initiative. High progressive taxation may be necessary to fund minimal welfare services, but they disincentivise workers. Conversely, the economically active majority gain fiscal dividends by participating in the informal econ-omy. Polarisation creates a crisis in state funding which poses the threat of a disinvestment and economic slump.

In terms of leisure practice and experience three major consequences follow from the Brazilianization of work.

### Modularisation of leisure

For the economically active in full-time or regular work, leisure becomes modularised. The Greek *polis* advocated a balanced existence between philosophy, public activity, politics and leisure as the proper end of civilisation. Work was held to belong to the realm of obligation and, hence, had nothing to do with freedom. In Ancient Greek society leisure was conceived of as harmonious, coherent and holisitic. The rise of industrial civil society involves the individualisation of work and the development of an instrumental attitude to leisure. Typically, leisure is not conceived of, or practised, as an essential part of a harmonious whole. Rather, it is adjustable and flexible. Leisure values are not universalistic, but fit the circumstances of the time-famine set by work or the time-surplus which derives from the lack of work. Throughout the life cycle, modules are added and subtracted. It may be, for many people, that the full fruits of labour are only enjoyed *after* retirement when the various multi-modular modes of leisure activity in working life can be reassembled or rationalised into what Stebbins (1992) has called 'serious leisure' activities. Increasing numbers of the economically active minority with full-time or regular employment plan for early retirement by contracting into private pension schemes to supplement occupational and state schemes during their peak earning years.

### Social dislocation and an increased propensity for invasive leisure patterns to develop

Globalisation requires professional, technical and managerial staff to be mobile. Flexible work regimes impose significant burdens on family life. Pahl's (1995) study of successful workers documented the high incidence of stress in conjugal role relationships and parenting responsibilities which derive from the physical absence of husbands and/or wives from the home.

The new residuum face a different set of problems. Brazilianization elicits peaks and troughs in the pattern of their work experience, with intensified bursts of working in full employment, often in multiple contracts, followed by periods of unemployment or semi-employment. Globalisation and deregulation propagate migratory, nomadic work–leisure experiences. The consequence of this is the disruption of interaction in family and kinship groups and intermittent work–leisure regimes, punctuated by unemployment–leisure regimes.

Workers on either side of the full employment divide are vulnerable to the development of invasive leisure symptoms. In invasive leisure, free time is not experienced as a source of validation or self-worth, but as a cause of self-engulfment and isolation. Under invasive leisure patterns, the individual's public face may outwardly represent sociability and harmony. Inwardly however, the veridical self is beset by waves of inauthenticity and worthlessness. Alcohol and drugs may deaden these oppressive feelings. However, in the long run, they contribute to a general retreat from engagement with others into a private world of leisure. In extreme cases, the sense of invalidity and inauthenticity in the veridical self may result in a desire to negate feelings of worthlessness and oppression by burying the self from the sight of others either through psychological breakdown or suicide (see Rojek 2000: 178–80).

### Alienation and the development of mephitic leisure symptoms

Time-famine brings with it a permanent sense of being besieged and overworked. Unemployment produces feelings of rejection, mourning at the loss of status, and anger. In both cases, feelings of invalidation may be transferred from the veridical self to others who are perceived as either the causes of time-famine and unemployment, or stereotyped as incapable of empathising with the existential problems of time famine and unemployment.

Mephitic leisure refers to the transformation of attachments from solidarity to antagonism or revenge. Individuals are estranged from the community and society: they feel that their pain and anxiety is abstracted from the commons, so that the commons themselves become a source of invalidation. Mephitic leisure patterns tend to be dominated by two sets of morbid symptoms. First, the veridical self is identified as being more real, and therefore more significant, than other members of society. As such, abusive or violent behaviour towards others in leisure is legitimated by an appeal to the individual's superior or finer feelings in relation to other members of society. Second, the veridical self transfers its own feelings of invalidation upon the abstracted mass. In practice the two sets of symptoms are often related. In both cases individuals are deprived of genuine feelings and become objectified as resources for self-gratification through the off-loading of frustration and aggression (Rojek 2000: 180–6). Mephitic leisure is associated with violent and antisocial conduct and in extreme cases, may be a causal factor in homicide (Leyton 1986).

### Post-work and civil labour

Aronowitz and Cutler (1998) hold that postmodern conditions produce a post-work society. It might be objected that this is an extravagant proposition, since paid employment under postmodern conditions is clearly still widely sought and highly valued. In addition, there are some grounds for speculating that time-harassment is a new source of status, as workers 'without a minute to spare' and 'with no free time to enjoy themselves' patently demonstrate that they are in high demand. Conversely, the concept of the 'post-work society' powerfully represents the disequilibrium between increasing productivity and full employment in the cybernated economy. Automation sheds labour and, while the short-term economic benefit of this is lower wage costs, as more and more workers compete for fewer and fewer jobs, the long-term social consequences of Brazilianization are social unrest and political tension.

Aronowitz and Cutler (1998) follow Gorz (1999) and Beck (2000) in concluding that the cybernation of work requires the rethinking of the work ethic. Modern industrialism equated rights and status with paid employment. But the fecundity of technological and organisational forms created by modern industrialism reduces the requirement for full employment and therefore contradicts the equation of rights and status with paid employment. If the labour market has moved into a structural position in which the individualisation of the employment contract produces the casualisation of work and intermittent experience of paid employment, the continued equation between paid employment, rights and status is counter-productive.

Although these writers work in very different traditions, they reveal a remarkable degree of consensus on the relationship between policy, leisure and work. They propose that the socially guaranteed income, rather than paid employment, should now be introduced as the *a priori* of leisure. Workers must commit to *civil labour* – that is, the necessary social and economic labour which guarantees the growth of economic and social capital. However, the status of this labour is distinct from paid employment since it is expended to increase the general economic and social value of the community and society, rather than the conventional ends of possessive individualism. The introduction of the socially guaranteed wage and civil labour does not preclude individuals from seeking paid employment. However, it does neutralise the compulsion to engage in abstract labour as the necessary means of subsistence and acquired status. By the term 'abstract labour' is meant a form of labour that is measurable, quantifiable and alienable from the person who provides it. It is the 'time-centred' work that the historian E. P. Thompson (1967) argued replaced 'task-centred' work regimes during the rise of industrial capitalism. Gorz (1999: 55–6), in particular, is scathing about the social bonds produced under industrial capitalism, damning abstract labour for the superficial and weak levels of social cohesion that it accomplished.

The socially guaranteed income and civil labour overturn established thinking on the work–leisure relationship. If paid employment ceases to be the *a priori* of leisure, the sphere of leisure is divested of its connotations with paid employment. Leisure will cease to be thought of as the reward for work or the portion of the week given over to the renewal of energies depleted by the work process. Instead it will fully assume its potential as the sphere, par excellence, of self-development. In picturing communist society, Marx (1977:

820) held that 'the realm of freedom' begins only when the labour that is determined by necessity ceases. The various notions of civil labour now being debated make the same assumption. Human and social reproduction requires socially and economically necessary labour. Under civil labour, necessary labour is voluntarily given to increase the stock of social and economic capital held by the commons. It no longer carries the connotation of imposition or burden which accompanies paid employment in market society. This is because the individual is a full and integrated part of the commons and therefore directly profits from the increase in social and economic capital. Beyond the boundaries of civil labour lies the area of free self-development: the true sphere of leisure in post-work society.

## Critical commentary

Casualisation and globalisation bestow considerable moral force upon the argument that society must take steps to switch from a time and income system based upon abstract labour, to one organised around civil labour. Nonetheless, there is good reason to be sceptical about the realpolitik of this transformation. Those who make the case for the replacement of paid employment with generalised civil labour have not got beyond proposing national solutions to global problems. Capitalism is a global system based on the principle of competition between economic units. Without binding global checks and balances, the decision of one economic unit to introduce civil labour would simply confer competitive advantage on other units which set their face against civil labour. The guarantee for providing effective global checks and balances is world government. While this is implicit in the case for civil labour, it is substantially under-theorised. At the empirical level, economic and political regulation in global relations is still primarily dependent upon bilateral and multilateral agreements. While these agreements have some effect in introducing a 'level playing field' around the globe, in the nature of things, they are not ubiquitous and their perpetuation may be rescinded according to circumstance. Without a viable form of world government, many observers will conclude that the case for civil labour is, perforce, utopian.

This criticism is reinforced if one considers the case of the 'third world'. The case for civil labour is strongest in the most economically advanced countries where the consequences of post-work are most apparent. In the third world, the problem is not post-work, but a disequilibrium between the economically active population and the capacity of the economy to generate sufficient wealth to sustain life and acceptable living standards. Castells (1998) maintains that this disequilibrium is produced by the dynamics of the global economy which tend to concentrate resources in the economically advanced countries. According to Castells, it is no longer accurate to refer merely to a third world. A 'fourth world' has emerged in which over-exploitation of workers, social exclusion and 'perverse integration' are endemic. The term 'perverse integration' refers to the labour process of the criminal economy. Sub-Saharan Africa and large areas of the former Soviet Union experienced a decline in most of the vital indicators of living standards in the 1990s. Most of Latin America regressed in the 1980s (Castells 1998: 70–1). As the formal economy shrinks, acute poverty intensifies and criminal activity becomes rife. Weapons trafficking, smuggling illegal immigration, trafficking in women and children, trafficking in body parts and money laundering have all become significant elements in the fourth world economy. Addressing the chasm between the economically advanced nations and the third and fourth worlds, must be part of a tenable programme of civil labour. Currently, it is a neglected part of the case for the socially guaranteed income and the reconstitution of paid employment.

Finally, the discussion of civil labour and post-work society tends to be glib about the question of transgression. It assumes that releasing labour from the chains of alienated paid employment will result in the fully socialised citizen who voluntarily places individual energies at the disposal of society. But this is to misconceive the egoism of individualised society as an epiphenomenon of capitalism which will vanish once the antagonism between capital and labour that is inherent in the employment contract is dismantled. But egoism, and the desire to go beyond socially accepted boundaries are, perhaps, not so easily eliminated. The anthropologist, Victor Turner (1969, 1982), has postulated that the formal legal and moral systems of society inevitably create 'anti-structures' in which behaviour that transgresses official boundaries is sanctioned and incentivised. Leisure activity is not just about reproducing existing ethical frameworks and habitual practices; it is also about challenging and transcending them. If free and full development mean anything they mean perpetuating some forms of behaviour which others find reprehensible or offensive. The discussion of civil labour as a moral category is seriously underdeveloped. The competing moral values that define the limits of constraint and permissiveness in work society are unlikely to vanish in post-work society. However, it is reasonable to propose that the removal of the antagonistic element inherent in the employment contract under capitalism, would alter the dynamics and content of the moral struggle over free time. The nature of this moral struggle in post-work society is the black hole in the various discussions over civil labour. Before we can situate the concept of civil labour at the centre of leisure policy, as is perhaps desirable given the transparent effects of deregulation and globalisation, there is still much work to do.

## References

Applebaum, H. (1992) *The Concept of Work*. Albany, NY: State University of New York Press.

Aronowitz, S. and Cutler, J. (eds) (1998) *Post-Work*. New York: Routledge.

Aronowitz, S. and Di Fazio, W. (1994) *The Jobless Future*. Minneapolis, MN: University of Minneapolis Press.

Beck, U. (2000) *The Brave New World of Work*. Cambridge: Polity.

Bell, D. (1973) *The Coming of Post-Industrial Society*. Harmondsworth, UK: Penguin.

Castells, M. (1996) *The Rise of Network Society*. Oxford: Blackwell.

Castells, M. (1997) *The Power of Identity*. Oxford: Blackwell.

Castells, M. (1998) *The End of the Millennium*. Oxford: Blackwell.

Deem, R. (1986) *All Work and No Play? The Sociology of Women's Leisure*. Milton Keynes: Open University Press.

Dumazedier, J. (1967) *Toward a Society of Leisure*. London: Collier-Macmillan.

Gorz, A. (1999) *Reclaiming Work*. Cambridge: Polity.

Harriman, A. (1982) *The Work/Leisure Trade-Off*. New York: Praeger.

Harvey, D. (1989) *The Condition of Postmodernity*. Oxford: Blackwell.

Hochschild, A. (1997) *The Time Bind*. New York: Metropolitan.

Hunnicutt, B. (1988) *Work without End*. Philadelphia, PA: Temple University Press.

Kerr, C., Dunlop, J., Harbison, F. and Meyers, C. (1973) *Industrialism and Industrial Man*, 2nd edn. Harmondsworth, UK: Penguin.

Lash, S. and Urry, J. (1987) *The End of Organised Capitalism*. Cambridge: Polity.

Leyton, E. (1986) *Hunting Humans*. Toronto: McLelland and Stewart.

Marx, K. (1977) *Capital, Volume 3*. London: Lawrence and Wishart.

Moorhouse, H. F. (1989) Models of work, models of leisure. In C. Rojek (ed.) *Leisure for Leisure*: 15–35. London: Macmillan.

Pahl, R. (1995) *After Success*. Cambridge: Polity.

Parker, S. (1983) *Leisure and Work*. London: Allen and Unwin.

Rojek, C. (2000) *Leisure and Culture*. London: Macmillan.

Sayers, S. (1987) The need to work. *Radical Philosophy* 46(1): 17–26.

Schor, J. (1991) *The Over-Worked American*. New York: Basic Books.

Shaw, S. (1994) Gender, leisure and constraint: towards a framework for the analysis of women's leisure. *Journal of Leisure Research* 26(1): 8–22.

Steadman-Jones, G. (1971) *Outcast London*. Harmondsworth, UK: Penguin.

Stebbins, R. (1992) *Amateurs, Professionals and Serious Leisure*. Montreal: McGill University Press.

Thompson, E. P. (1967) Time, work-discipline and industrial capitalism. *Past and Present* 38(1): 56–97.

Touraine, A. (1974) *The Post-Industrial Society*. London: Wildwood House.

Turner, V. (1969) *The Ritual Process*. Chicago: University of Chicago Press.

Turner, V. (1982) *From Ritual to Theatre*. New York: Cornell.

Veal, A. J. (1987) *Leisure and the Future*. London: Allen and Unwin.

Weber, M. (1976) *The Protestant Ethic and the Spirit of Capitalism*. London: Routledge.

Wilensky, H. (1960) Work, careers and social integration. *International Social Science Journal* 4(4): 543–60.

# Chapter 4

# Gender, work and leisure

*Judy White*

## Introduction

In 1970, Germaine Greer wrote:

> The first exercise of the free woman is to design her own mode of revolt; a mode which will reflect her own independence and originality. The more clearly the forms of oppression emerge in her understanding, the more clearly she can see the shape of future action. In the search for political awareness there is no substitute for confrontation. It would be too easy to present women with yet another form of self-abnegation, more opportunities for appetence and forlorn hope, but women have had enough bullying. They have been led by the nose and every other way until they have to acknowledge that, like everyone else, they are lost. A feminist elite might seek to lead uncomprehending women in an arbitrary direction, training them as a task force in a battle that might, that ought never to eventuate . . . Freedom is fragile and must be protected. To sacrifice it, even as a temporary measure, is to betray it. It is not a question of telling women what to do next, or even what to want to do next. The hope in which this book was written is that women will discover they have a will; once that happens they will be able to tell us how and what they want . . . Unless the concepts of work, play, and reward for work change absolutely, women must continue to provide cheap labour, and even more, free labour exacted of right by an employer possessed of a contract for life, made out in his favour.
>
> (Greer 1970: 23–4, 25)

It is hard to explain the overwhelming feelings of recognition and amazement that women felt on first reading *The Female Eunuch*: here was an articulate, funny, serious, subversive writer expanding and setting out arguments for the foundations of a second-wave feminism. There had been nothing else like it in our lifetimes. The book offered women the right to be seen as independent individuals in their own right. It resonated personally with many women, most of whom had tales of discrimination to tell.

Greer's forensic analysis, always individual and idiosyncratic, gave women heart and energy to feel that, not only were we not alone, but also there were possibilities for change and things could get better. Applying her arguments to women at work in 1968, Greer noted that women formed almost 40 per cent of the workforce in England, so half of the women aged 16–64 were in paid employment (Greer 1970: 132), but the wages of women were on average half that of men in the same industries. But, she asserted:

> equal pay for equal work will not make as great a difference in these figures as women might hope. The pattern of female employment follows the course of the role that she plays outside industry: she is almost always ancillary, a handmaid in the more important work of men.
>
> (Greer 1970: 132)

Greer saw her book as a part of the second feminist wave:

> The old suffragettes . . . have seen their spirit revive in younger women with a new and vital cast. The new emphasis is different, and the difference is radical, for the faith that the suffragettes had in the existing political systems and their deep desire to participate in them have perished.
>
> (Greer 1970: 13–14)

The final chapter, entitled 'Revolution', speculates about what might be and how it might happen. She states:

> Revolution is the festival of the oppressed. It does not understand the phrase 'equality of opportunity'. For it seems that the opportunities will have to be utterly changed and women's souls changed so that they desire opportunity instead of shrinking from it.
>
> (Greer 1970: 370)

To secure this revolution, Greer argued that women needed to reclaim their bodies, their souls, their love and their hate. It was tough and exciting stuff, and women would need to be resolute to follow it through. And the amount of work that was required was, it transpired, much more than anyone could have anticipated: the strength and resilience of the existing edifices of power and control, of objectivity, of 'acceptable' ways of knowing, of denying difference, and of the overall lack of willingness to listen and take seriously other ways of thinking and theorising, were palpable.

Nearly 30 years later, in 1999, Greer wrote, as a 'recantation', a sequel to *The Female Eunuch*, in *The Whole Woman* – 'the book I said I would never write':

I believed that each generation should produce its own statement of problems and priorities, and that I had no special authority or vocation to speak on behalf of women of any but my own age, class, background and education . . . it was not until feminists of my own generation began to assert with apparent seriousness that feminism had gone too far that the fire rose up in my belly. When lifestyle feminists chimed in that feminism had gone far enough in giving them the right to 'have it all', i.e. money, sex, and fashion, it would have been inexcusable to remain silent.

(Greer 1999: 2)

The 1999 book may be more measured in its anger, but it is as clear as in the 1970 book that women still have to struggle to be considered on their own terms and in their own right as people and individuals, with values and beliefs which are not conditional on their status in relationship to men. As early 'second-wave' feminists, we had to learn how to work with different groups of people and, painfully, to acknowledge that there were differences in what we felt we wanted and how we might achieve it. We might have agreed that we were oppressed and undervalued, and that this was a condition of the Western industrialised world, but there were disagreements about the extent to which this was a reflection of the lack of women in positions of power and influence in organisations outside the home (roughly the liberal view); the domination of capital systems (Marxist); women not receiving their rightful share of resources (socialist); or of women positioning themselves in relation to men rather than to each other and their own independent networks and power relations (radical).

If diagnoses were different, so were prognoses and possible ways in which change might be brought about, and to what ends. While these differences were inevitable (if there was acceptance of the belief that there is much diversity between women themselves), it also made it extremely difficult to manage the processes of changing attitudes towards women and the intellectual debates and theoretical developments to underpin these changes. Indeed, as Greer suggests, although academic feminists did all that their male colleagues did to gain power and prestige through attempts to make the study of gender respectable, few women won the glittering prizes.

This chapter unfolds from the personal to the political, and back again. In it I try to weave threads and join them together, using work which I consider provides essential signposts, to be outstanding epistemologically and to have methodological rigour and ethical robustness in the development of feminist approaches to leisure and gender research and theory. So the chapter starts with an exploration of the 'new' epistemologies of feminism which have emerged and been battled over since the 1960s, and then the impact of the new methods of inquiry which such epistemologies have engendered. The two sections following these discussions lay out the foundations of theoretical discussions from the 1970s and the consequences of undertaking research in

gender and work and leisure. The large-scale seminal research work undertaken in Sheffield in the 1970s, which teased out attitudes to leisure and work
among a variety of women, is analysed, alongside a small-scale project
undertaken two decades later, exploring perceptions of, and rights to, leisure
among women in full-time employment and with small children. The discussion points up the continuities of experience and expectations between these
two diverse populations. The chapter draws to a close using some recent
reflections by feminist theorists and thinkers on the state of feminist research
and the academy and the impact this is having on gender and leisure research.

## New epistemologies

One of the themes which has preoccupied feminists throughout the three
decades being surveyed is the debate about epistemology and the search for
developing epistemologies which could be embraced as feminist. Traditional
epistemology was based on the Enlightenment model, which attempted to
transform abstract versions of 'knowledge' into 'truth'; definitive knowledge
is possible only if 'necessary and sufficient' conditions are established.
Reason is seen as the objective foundation for all knowledge, and all human
behaviour is rule-governed, so that it can be investigated, measured, analysed
and assessed using positivist normative approaches. This approach denies
that knowledge is socially situated and constructed and that the underlying
values and attitudes of the 'knower' will impact on the research. Knowledge
producers, epistemologists in the traditional mode, could not admit to their
subjectivities or emotions and sought to retain their absolute objectivity.
These 'knowers', however, were predominantly a fairly homogeneous group
of white, middle-class males.

Feminists suggested that this Enlightenment model was a distinctly
'male' way of thinking, which reinforced male domination and power. By
assuming that knowing is universal, they assumed that gender, ethnicity
and sex are neutral, hence denying that 'differing social positions generate
variable constructions of reality and afford different perspectives on the
world' (Code 1993: 39). Work, such as that by Stanley and Wise (1993),
however, argued comprehensively that 'the personal is political' and
Enlightenment epistemology had marginalised or negated the experience of
women in the world and critically limited their political power. It is not
possible to have one single 'truth' which is applicable in all situations and
contexts: all truths inevitably are partial, contain distortions and are not
fully representative.

It has taken a long time for feminist epistemologies to gain some degree of
understanding and acceptance within parts of the academy and doubt
remains as to how far they have permeated other bastions of power. Harding
(1993: 56) identified three phases in the development of feminist epistemology: empiricism; standpoint; and postmodernist. These phases are not distinct

and they exist alongside each other (Stanley and Wise 1993: 191; Maynard and Purvis 1994: 19).

Feminist *empiricists* emerged from the 1960s 'liberal tendency' which hoped and believed that it would be possible to engage traditional epistemologists with changes by using reason and logic in ways similar to theirs, to show not only that there could be several worldviews but also that these could be measured, and so new types of knowledge could be acknowledged and given status. The belief that debate, the use of rigorous research methods, and common sense would sway the traditionalists was, in retrospect, naive. It also underestimated the power of rationality, the criteria used for the reception and acknowledgement of knowledge and, simply, the deep suspicion of any knowledge which was seemingly grounded in gender. The difficulties for liberal empiricists were compounded in the 1970s by the scarcity of women in the academy, and the multiple campaigns with which they were involved; there was too much to do and neither enough time or resources with which to do it. This was as true of leisure studies as any other field. It had been defined and dominated by men, who had invented and sustained the 'work–leisure' divide as it fitted their experience and seemingly kept them in a dominant position. It is notable that only one chapter out of thirteen in the 1975 volume *Work and Leisure*, which the current volume celebrates, was by a woman (Emmett 1975). Feminist academics recognised this world but knew it was not theirs.

*Standpoint* epistemologists have tried to explain the impact and effect of different value systems on knowledge; they have seen a need to work with and articulate the views of those groups of women who have been marginalised by the dominant groups of women who have tended to be more like the dominant groups of men in the liberal empiricist tradition: white, middle-class, heterosexual intellectuals. Standpoint epistemologies argued that for feminism to have any acceptability it had to recognise the diverse and differing standpoints of different women, accepting and celebrating these and incorporating them into knowledge and common, conflicting, or contrasting standpoints (Harding 1993: 56). Harding saw this as a 'strong objectivity', demonstrating the essential social 'situatedness' of beliefs and thoughts which could be used to develop analysis and policy in ways not dissimilar to those used by 'objective scientists.' Although Stanley and Wise (1993) applauded the concept, which allowed diversity to be acknowledged through embracing a variety of feminist viewpoints, they were worried about its potential ethnocentricity.

More recently, feminist *postmodern* theorists have adapted a Foucauldian approach, the argument being that, as power resides within individuals, each of us has the opportunity to create our own distinctive knowledges, which are uniquely our own and not rule-bound by tradition (Wearing 1998; Aitchison 2000). Attractive as this may be, and despite its potential to empower individuals in ways which are not otherwise available, there are concerns about its relativism which denies all generalisations. While it is of limited application for policy-based research, its contribution to feminism more generally is nevertheless important, as it enables better understandings and more opportunities for exploration of differences and diversity and their legitimacy and the role of power relations in shaping women's experience.

## Women's leisure: what leisure? Feminist research in the 1980s

Feminists in the 1970s and 1980s were taken up with establishing the inappropriateness of the traditional epistemological notions of the separation of work and leisure (Anderson 1975; Green, Hebron and Woodward 1987a) and the complexity of women's caring roles (Deem 1986; Wimbush 1986). A start was made to push open the door examining women's sexuality and ethnicity in relation to their involvement in 'leisure activities' (Scraton 1986).

The seminal research study of the 1980s, which illustrates the conundrums of feminist research at that time, became known as 'the Sheffield study'. It provided a theoretical analysis of the impact of gender on leisure experiences, based on empirical research. A random sample of 707 women in Sheffield, aged between 18 and 60, were interviewed at their homes for about an hour, in discussions designed to establish how much free time they felt they had available to them and to relate this to their life situations and personal circumstances. This was augmented with less structured and more qualitative interviews with five groups, each of about five women, who were selected from the first group surveyed, together with their resident men partners, if they had them. The groups were chosen 'to represent those likely to have varying types and levels of constraints and opportunities for leisure, because of their life cycle stage and domestic situation, and their household's level of affluence' (Green et al. 1987a: 2).

While the research was neither a preliminary nor a pilot project, it was certainly the first to attempt to explore the interaction of socio-economic, demographic and cultural factors which influence women's opportunities for free time and which shape how individual women perceive and use their leisure. The research team argued that it was vital that there should be quantitative work to establish a base of knowledge about women's access to leisure time and their use of it, and that this should be done using feminist values and approaches. From this work, it was possible to collect qualitative material from the interactive interview discussions which explored the processes of decision-making and negotiations which lay behind observed leisure behaviour.

The Sheffield study was the first UK study to set out to explain in detail what leisure experiences mean to those people experiencing them, and its significance in relation to other aspects of people's lives. The investigation of the impact of gender on leisure was a 'study of the influence of prevailing notions of male and female roles on access to free time, and of ways of spending it' (Green et al. 1987: 3). So, although both men's and women's leisure opportunities may be bounded by apparently similar constraints, such as paid employment and parenthood or poverty and loneliness, these factors impinge in different ways and to a greater or lesser extent on women and men. For example, some constraints, such as the fear of being out alone after dark, apply to most women but to few men. Others apply to both women and men in particular social groups, such as those in the same age group or socio-economic category, but here gender can be a significant source of difference. For example, elderly white men on low incomes who are lonely, still generally have available the choice of going out to a pub or club, even if one drink has to last them the evening, whereas this is less likely to be seen as a viable leisure activity for a similarly placed woman.

The study showed categorically that women had less time for leisure than men and less time which was 'unambiguously free', mainly because wives and mothers hold primary responsibility for domestic labour, which is not conditional on any paid work they may do. Outside the home, women undertake a smaller range of leisure activities less frequently than men. Any study must be situated in its broad social context: 'leisure cannot be adequately researched without taking into account the principal social divisions of gender, class, race, and age group, because it is clearly structured by them' (Green et al. 1987b: 9). It is clear that, in terms of gender, inequalities in access to the resources needed for leisure, such as free time, money and access to transport, are to some extent legitimised by prevailing definitions of masculine and feminine roles:

> This can be seen in common sense assumptions about differences between the sexes, not least the notion that somehow men 'need' leisure more than women, or are more entitled to it, because of their relation to paid work. The same belief explains the continuing male control of many public places where leisure activities take place.
>
> (Green et al. 1987b: 10)

This echoed the findings of Deem's (1986) research carried out in Milton Keynes during the same period.

The Sheffield study was also the first to signify and to provide evidence that, while all women are oppressed primarily by gender relations and patriarchy, they are nonetheless a heterogeneous group. The implications of this are that women have different inclinations and social situations and that their wants and needs are different: some issues do affect large groups of women, such as the cost of leisure, care facilities for children and older relatives and availability of activity sessions for women only, at times of the day when they feel comfortable. But the underlying need is to involve women themselves in determining what is to be provided on the basis of what they want, which may not be what policy-makers think they might want.

## Continuities and divergence: women's rights to leisure in the 1990s

There has been little empirical feminist research to develop and expand on the Sheffield study. No research funding agency has seen fit to support studies which might broaden and deepen the foundations erected by the Sheffield study. We are left with small-scale, individual or small team projects, funded by academic institutions, often as part of higher degrees or personal post-doctoral research. While meeting the feminist criteria for dealing with personal issues, and acknowledging that the researcher brings her own per-spective and partiality to research, they do not together constitute a large enough body of work in which to ground or grow effective theory. Neverthe-less, contributions have been made to the consolidation and the development of feminist leisure theory, including the work of Henderson et al. (1996), Wearing (1998) and Aitchison (2000). In particular, links have been made with recent debates and developments in feminist theory generally, such as the sociology of the body and poststructuralism and postcolonial theory.

An example of such small-scale, but valuable, research, self-described as 'exploratory', is that done by Tess Kay in 1997 with eleven women in high-status, full-time jobs and with one or more pre-school children. Many of these women identified the extent to which gendered inequality resurfaced with the coming of children, when women's unpaid labour increased disproportionately to those of their (male) partners. Kay found that:

> whilst this group of women stayed in full time employment, they had to adjust their work involvement, adopting informal strategies to reduce and contain paid work to accommodate the increased demands of motherhood. Male partners made little or no comparable changes. Therefore, within the household, although both parents continued to be categorised as full-time employed, women's practical and emotional commitment to paid work was perceived as lower than men's.
>
> (Kay 1998: 1)

She suggests that this divergence is pivotal in reintroducing traditional gender stereotypes to dual-earner households on the basis of the higher societal value accorded the paid work in which the male partner's role is rooted.

This research focused on a group of women which is becoming larger and more widespread: not just women with young children and working full-time, but who are doing so in employment areas which require considerable qualifi-cations, training and 'presence' in the workplace. Previously, women who worked long hours in paid employment tended to be in lower skill, lower status and lower paid occupations: but those in higher status occupations were equally disadvantaged in terms of perception and support for their family responsibilities, as well as in their needs for leisure. However, although their numbers may be growing, other research indicates that there is a continued problem of unequal pay. In a report from the Women's Unit of the UK Cabinet Office in 2000, it was estimated that the 'gender earnings gap' (the difference in men's and women's earnings which could *not* be attributed to motherhood) was worth just below a quarter of a million pounds for a mid-skilled woman over her lifetime. For women with two children, in mid-skilled occupations, the loss was an *additional* £140,000 (Cabinet Office 2000). The pay gap remains as wide as it did in the 1960s when Greer analysed the situation in *The Female Eunuch*. In 1999, men in full-time employment in the United Kingdom earned on average £23,000 a year, while women in full-time employment earned £16,000.

All of the eleven women interviewed by Tess Kay experienced inequality in their home, work and leisure: not only were they conscious of it, but also they were dissatisfied with it. Some of them had taken steps to redress the imbalances, such as the allocation of selected tasks to their partners. At other times, the women had used less deliberate action and the sheer practicalities of the activities of the household made it inevitable that there were some changes in responsibilities. However, the women felt that these changes were slight and the impact limited, and they were frustrated by prevailing gender ideologies in their attempts to negotiate more satisfactory agreements. The overall feelings of the group were that 'at the heart of the inequitable distribution of paid and unpaid work lies leisure' (Kay 1998: 13).

So by the end of the 1990s, not only had attitudes not shifted significantly compared with the reported outcomes from professional working wives and mothers interviewed in the Sheffield study, the clarity of their understanding of the differences between men and women in their perceptions of responsibilities for the family and of the individual rights to leisure had not dimmed. Progress seemed to be almost non-existent since the 1970s. As one woman in Kay's study said:

> I think attitudes towards leisure differ between men and women. The more I think about it the more I think we are different species from the same planet! I think men are much better at prioritising and saying I want this for me, so I'll walk out of this home and do this, than women are. I read a quote in a magazine which I found really true and interesting: women do all that they have to do, and then make time for themselves with what is left; men do what they want to do for themselves and then everything has to fit in around that. I think that is true, women do everything they have to do for other people and what is left, even if it is

only five minutes, that's for them, but fellas will say, well sorry, I've been to work, I'm going to the gym now.

(Kay 1998: 14)

Kay's conclusion is clear: as a consequence of the ways in which men invest in their personal leisure time and energy, together with their limited effectiveness in the home, it is inevitable that working mothers have a disproportionate burden, 'and it was women's ability to sustain this burden, however reluctantly, that allowed household activity patterns to remain so inequitable' (Kay 1998: 14). Overall, Kay concluded that the full-time employed mother remained highly committed to her work, but was frequently forced, commonly due to the intransigence of her partner to change his working patterns, to contain work within fewer hours and to reduce the range of activities contingent upon it, which appeared to give messages to employers about the depth of their commitment, whether the women liked it or not: 'Parenthood became a site of gender differentiation in work behaviour, despite women's commitment to employment' (Kay 1998: 14).

At home, women carried out more household tasks and more childcare tasks than their partners did and felt that they had overall responsibility for running the home. The unequal share of childcare tasks was especially important in bringing about a reduction in their work time. Women were very conscious that domestic demands were unequally shared with their partners, but had great difficulty in achieving more equitable divisions of labour within the home and showed awareness of the influence of broader social expectations affecting this. The differentiation in work and home roles was repeated in leisure: women recognised their own needs for leisure but this did not in itself give them a strong enough sense of entitlement to override other demands.

These findings suggest that even those women with relatively high employment status could not pose a substantial challenge to the traditional gendered distinctions in couples' lifestyles. The arrival of children seems to be the signal for the emergence, or re-emergence, of stereotypical divisions of responsibility, with women taking on 'parenting' roles much more positively than their partners, whose behaviour changes minimally, and only marginally in the direction of childcare.

The depressing and alarming feelings come from the association of these findings with the rate and directions of change. The term used by Hochschild (1990) is 'stalled revolution', in which women have entered the workplace at all levels and in all types of jobs, but neither men in the workplace nor the culture have adjusted to the new realities.

## Leisure and feminist theory and practice in 2000

In an essay in *Feminist Theory*, entitled, 'But the empress has no clothes! Some awkward questions about the missing revolution in feminist theory',

Stanley and Wise (2000) began by expressing their concern with the development of feminist meta-theory which was not subsumed within mainstream/malestream social theory. They highlighted three recent changes to the organisational context in which the conjunction of 'feminism/theory' takes place, as follows:

- The relationship between feminist theory and practice has changed markedly as a consequence of the institutionalising or mainstreaming of feminism in some areas of government, private enterprise, welfare bodies and education.
- 'Social theory' and its feminist theory parallel have become much more marked by claims to multidisciplinarity or post-disciplinarity: 'travelling theorists' characterise this tendency.
- Theorising in the formal sense has increasingly become the province of specialist groupings of academics rather than of feminists in general, with the effect that feminist practice is now considerably more on the periphery of feminist theory than it was previously.

A contrast pertinent for this chapter is their analysis of the differences in three distinct areas between when 'feminism entered the academy' and the current situation.

In the first area, originally, feminism recognised the legitimacy of the coexistence of different and contending points of view, as highlighted at the beginning of this chapter. There were different theoretical positions about the idea of women's oppression, each of which was seen as independent and legitimate but not as separate, self-reproductive or securely dominant. There was a considerable critique of 'Theory' of a mainstream kind because its generalising failed to see women's lives. Feminism theory on the other hand attempted to theorise the whole range of feminist practice. There had been a 'collective forgetting' of the earlier feminist critique of 'Theory'. Instead, there was the constitution of a homogenous notion of 'feminist Theory' out of the ashes of the 'theory wars' of the past. Contrary bodies of theory were characterised as wrong, misguided, outdated, or even essentialist, rather than as precisely 'contenders'. This amounted to passing judgement and exercising exclusion in ways that were common among positivist masculine theorists. The debate about women's leisure in a postmodernist framework is an example of this tendency.

In the second area, the range of contending theoretical positions that originally existed:

> were seen as the product of a collective endeavour symbiotically linked to feminist politics; theorists were seen as codifying and interpreting collective ideas rather than being the source, the fount, of feminist thought; and feminist theory was seen as the provenance of all feminists,

not the preserve of a specialist group ... [One of the differences that feminism made was to] insist on the common ownership and shared production of feminist ideas, seeing theorising as always grounded in a context, howsoever disembodied its male practitioners might pronounce it.

(Stanley and Wise 2000: 276)

Now, there is a situation in which the place of theory in feminism has become considerably more like its place in the traditional disciplines (middle-range theories of different kinds are developed, with a 'grand' theory – sociological, anthropological or literary – standing over them). But superordinate over all is 'social theory', which is presumed to 'travel' across disciplinary distinctions and to have general, even universal, applicability. In the 'leisure studies and gender debate' examined by Deem (1986, 1988) and explored earlier, there seems to be a desire for leisure to be incorporated within traditional disciplines for issues of inclusion, safety and generalisability. But the distinctive role of theory in feminism for women and leisure studies is not admitted and the development of grounded theory developed through researching the leisure practices of women remains marginalised by feminist theorists in the academy. Such 'Theorists' have become part of the mainstream in the academy and have become adept at defending their positions. Echoing Stanley and Wise, the question arises as to how leisure feminism theory, as earlier understood and practised and examined in this chapter, and seen as 'feminist theorising', has become 'feminist Theorising' – the specialist activity of a few. Does 'feminist Theory' belong to feminism in general or does it have primarily academic allegiance?

In the third area, originally, feminism rejected scientistic claims that knowing the category 'women' is best done from the outside; it situated the feminist knower as fully within and as a part of the analysis.

The feminist knower is a woman with a point of view located in a context of time, place and personal specificities ... The difference that feminism made was to insist that knowledge is always partial, local, and grounded. Now there is a situation in which 'feminist Theory' has taken on many of the characteristics of 'Theory', including its implicit claims to produce transferable general knowledge. The attempts to ground production of feminist theory in the location and situatedness of the knower are criticised as an essentialist claim about 'experience'.

(Stanley and Wise 2000: 277)

Again, there are trends in gender research in leisure which attempt to devalue the legitimacy of the knower, and to devalue or ignore the possibility of sustaining a multiple and varied group of 'contenders', each of whom has a contribution to make, but none of whom can represent the 'whole'. Feminist knowledge cannot be produced in ways that are separated from values, feelings and points of view.

## Is feminist leisure research stuck in a ghetto or in 'theory wars'?

In 1998 Rosemary Deem used her keynote speech to the Leisure Studies Association International Conference on 'Gender and the Ghetto' to revisit the state of research work on gender and leisure at the end of the twentieth century. Positively, she thought that:

> the small number of researchers studying gender and leisure in the western world have produced important new knowledge about women. They have also informed both academic and policy communities about the ways in which leisure and sport are socially and culturally constructed by different women in the same and different contexts, and hence thereby imbued with particular meanings in which gender identities, gender roles, and gender power relations are often significant. There are of course, theoretical and political disagreements between those working in the gender and leisure ghetto, but it is a sign of intellectual maturity that such disagreements can be and are aired and interrogated.
>
> (Deem 1998: 4)

However, she surmised that, for most leisure scholars, gender is still used as little more than a variable or a 'grudging acceptance' that gender is relevant, in some unspecified way, to many women, and sometimes to some men. She mused that this is a result of some researchers just not wanting to examine gender as an issue or, equally, being fearful, from their own observation, that gender and leisure research is a ghetto in which they may be trapped, 'for ghetto studies rarely attract much status or funding' (Deem 1998: 4). If the 'mainstream' did 'discover' gender it would not necessarily be on the same terms as feminists or proponents of masculinity theories and may have very different academic and political goals. If, she argued, leisure and gender researchers made more alliances with other researchers interested in feminisms and masculinity theories it could bring gender studies within wider perspectives and research problematics. But she also wondered whether

> we have to completely abandon studies of women's leisure: provided that we locate those studies within clear parameters and with a recognition of the many differences that there are between women, then in my view it is still worthwhile to continue to conduct such research. Nor does it only mean we can only do small scale research, valuable though this is. The development of analysis of complex quantitative data sets about various

aspects of women's lives remains important, even if it is a form of analysis held together by theorists of a post-modern persuasion.

(Deem 1998: 11)

Deem is clear that it is also important to see how we can accommodate those critiques of previous studies, which:

we regard as justified – in particular ensuring that we only prioritise gender over other forms of research when our research data and analysis seem to support that – and to adapt future research so that this becomes possible. We also need to ensure that leisure is researched in a proper manner so that we do not (if we ever did) assume that leisure is a wholly separable part of women's lives. We must also remember that methodologies need to remain sensitive to what we are studying, especially when or if we are looking at marginal or excluded groups.

(Deem 1998: 11)

Recent trends in social theory, she argues, have questioned concepts of social class and stratification as 'concepts more closely allied to ideas about modernist societies rather than post-modern societies: social structures have been replaced by signs and symbols, including new technologies and information structures' (Deem 1998: 12). But, however seriously we take differences within social groups such as women, there remain some elements of more commonly experienced social and cultural patterns (e.g. motherhood) which are not necessarily oppressive and, although they do not of course apply to all women, they display patterns which go beyond affecting single individuals. Critiques of conceptions of leisure, gender and social exclusion tend to focus on two aspects of previous studies, arguing about the extent to which there are common shared worlds of women and whether leisure is a source of enjoyment or a form of resistance to traditional gender stereotyping. The criticisms tend to both oversimplify and use selective research results to suggest that the differences between women need to be underscored and explored more, and that it is somehow wrong or inappropriate to suggest that women might actually be able to, and do, enjoy their 'relative leisure freedoms'!

Deem is concerned that these criticisms have affected the mind-sets of researchers and funding agencies, such that they perceive these areas of work to be, at best, of little policy importance and, at worst, irrelevant to theoretical development, that it is 'modernist nonsense.' But the attitude illustrated by Deem here is fundamentally dangerous, as it appears to equate 'worthwhile' research with that which can be funded; it suggests that a ghetto is inhabited by those who would rather be elsewhere and who do not feel that what they are doing is worthwhile. Not being taken seriously by funders has a different impact from not being taken seriously by the academy and feminist researchers. Would the location of 'women and leisure research' outside leisure studies but within sociology and consumption, provide any more than a shift into another ghetto, rather than, as Deem (1998) suggests, a 'way out of the ghetto'? Deem posits that if leisure research is gender-centred and remains so, in conception and analysis, then it is probably appropriate and possible to continue to encourage it. A move towards studies of women and leisure in which 'attention is paid to difference, increasingly focusing on commercial leisure, and situating gender analyses in wider research questions and problems' *can* be done within existing feminist frameworks. I do not believe 'relocating gender and leisure scholars outside their current ghetto' will do anything to encourage a serious debate about the research in feminist theory and practice. Building on the multidisciplinary and interdisciplinary modes of study, securing their foundations, and adhering to feminist principles, will provide a more robust future. This is the message of the latest essay and debate on feminist theory published by Stanley and Wise (2000), whose beacon of hope has kept many going in times of seeming despair.

## Conclusion

This chapter has provided a commentary on the changes observed over the past generation of research encompassing gender, work and leisure from feminist perspectives. It has highlighted some of the key debates and events in this erratic journey, which has been beset by continual doubts and uncertainties about the tasks to be accomplished and ways in which this might be done.

The key conclusions have to be, however, that the achievements of gender research in leisure are considerable. We now have evidence, from a variety of women, about how they experience leisure, and we have sufficient information and knowledge, grounded in women's values, feelings and points of view, to be able to develop theory 'from the bottom up'. In the words of Stanley and Wise:

> what counts as knowledge ... is marked by the politics of location and inevitably takes the form of situated knowledges ... and insists that all knowledge claims emanate from a point of view that makes a considerable difference to what is seen, how it is seen, how it is represented, and therefore what kinds of claims are made, on whose behalf.
>
> (Stanley and Wise 2000: 270)

The feminist scholarship reported here is grounded research and writing, which does not claim to be generalisable but is the result of shared ideas and epistemologies.

Stanley and Wise (2000) advocate the undertaking of a number of interesting meta-theory projects to 'greatly increase the stock of knowledge about how and why things are as they are, carried on by many people, in different parts of the world'. There is substantial scope for one of these projects to be involved with the continuing conundrum of 'women's leisure: what leisure?'

To finish as I began, with Germaine Greer:

> The personal is political still. The millennial feminist has to be aware that oppression exerts itself in and through her most intimate relationships, beginning with the most intimate, her relationship with her body ... She spends too much time waiting for things that will not happen, hoping for support and reinforcement that are withheld, apologising for matters beyond her control, longing for closeness to the ones she loves and being reconciled to distance ... The second wave of feminism, rather than having crashed on to the shore, is still far out to sea, slowly and inexorably gathering momentum. None of us who are alive today will witness more than the first rumbles of the coming social upheaval. Middle-class western women have the privilege of serving the longest revolution, not of directing. The ideological battles that feminist theorists are engaged in are necessary but they are preliminary to the emergence of female power, which will not flow decorously out from the universities or from the consumerist women's press.
>
> (Greer 1999: 330)

## References and further reading

Aitchison, C. (2000) Poststructural feminist theories of representing Others: a response to the 'crisis' in leisure studies' discourse. *Leisure Studies* 19(3): 127–45.

Anderson, R. (1975) *Leisure: An Inappropriate Concept for Women?* Canberra: Department of Tourism and Recreation.

Apter, T. (1985) *Why Women Don't Have Wives: Professional Success and Motherhood*. London: Macmillan.

Bell, D. and Valentine, G. (1995) *Mapping Desire: Geographies of Sexualities*. London: Routledge.

Bernard, M. and Meade, K. (eds) (1993) *Women Come of Age*. London: Edward Arnold.

Bordo, S. (1993) *Unbearable Weight: Feminism, Western Culture, and the Body*. Los Angeles: University of California.

Bowles, G. and Klein, R. (eds) (1983) *Theories of Women's Studies*. London: Routledge and Kegan Paul.

Butler, J. (1993) *Bodies that Matter: On the Discursive Limits of Sex*. London: Routledge.

Cabinet Office (2000) *Women's Incomes over the Lifetime: Report to the Women's Unit*. London: HMSO.

Chambers, D. (1986) The constraints of work and domestic schedules on women's leisure. *Leisure Studies* 5(3): 309–25.

Code, L. (1993) Taking subjectivity into account. In L. Alcoff and E. Potter (eds) *Feminist Epistemologies*. London: Routledge.

Deem, R. (1986) *All Work and No Play? The Sociology of Women and Leisure*. Milton Keynes: Open University Press.

Deem, R. (1988) Feminism and leisure studies: opening up new directions. In E. Wimbush and M. Talbot (eds) *Relative Freedoms: Women and Leisure*. Milton Keynes: Open University Press.

Deem, R. (1998) How do we get out of the ghetto? Strategies for research on gender and leisure for the twenty-first century. Paper presented to the *Leisure Studies Association International Conference*, Leeds, July.

Emmett, I. (1975) Masses and masters: a brief comparison of approaches to the study of work and leisure. In J. T. Haworth and M. A. Smith (eds) *Work and Leisure*. London: Lepus.

Fletcher, A. (1964) A feminist approach to leisure and social reality. Paper presented to the *Leisure Studies Association International Conference*, University of Sussex, July.

Glyptis, S., McInnes, H. and Patmore, A. (1987) *Leisure and the Home*. London: Sports Council and ESRC Joint Panel.

Green, E., Hebron S. and Woodward, D. (1987a) *Leisure and Gender: Final Report*. London: Sports Council and ESRC Joint Panel.

Green, E., Hebron, S. and Woodward, D. (1987b) Women's leisure in Sheffield: constraints and opportunities. In I. Henry (ed.) *Leisure Studies Association Newsletter Supplement: Women's Leisure: Constraints and Opportunities*, pp. 1–12.

Green, E., Hebron, S. and Woodward, D. (1990) *Women's Leisure, What Leisure?* London: Macmillan.

Greer, G. (1970) *The Female Eunuch*. London: MacGibbon and Kee.

Greer, G. (1999) *The Whole Woman*. London: Doubleday.

Gunew, S. (ed.) (1990) *Feminist Knowledge: Critique and Construction*. London: Routledge.

Harding, S. (1993) Rethinking standpoint epistemology: what is strong objectivity? In L. Alcoff and E. Potter (eds) *Feminist Epistemologies*. London: Routledge.

Henderson, K., Bialeschki, M. D., Shaw, S. M. and Freysinger, V. J. (1996) *Both Gains and Gaps: Feminist Perspectives on Women's Leisure*. State College, PA: Venture.

Hochschild, A. R. (1990) *The Second Shift*. New York: Avon Books.

Kay, T. (1998) New women, same old leisure: the upholding of gender stereotypes and leisure disadvantage in contemporary dual-earner households. Paper presented to the *Leisure Studies Association International Conference*, University of Loughborough, July.

Kelly, L. (1988) *Surviving Sexual Violence*. Cambridge: Polity.

Kemp, S. and Squires, J. (eds) (1997) *Feminisms*. Oxford: Oxford University Press.

Martin, J. and Roberts, C. (1984) *Women and Employment: A Lifetime Perspective*. London: HMSO.

Maynard, M. and Purvis, J. (eds) (1994) *Researching Women's Lives from a Feminist Perspective*. London: Taylor and Francis.

Maynard, M. and Purvis, J. (eds) (1995) *(Hetero)sexual Politics*. London: Taylor and Francis.

Scraton, S. (1986) Images of femininity and the teaching of girls' physical education. In J. Evans (ed.) *Physical Education, Sport and Schooling*. Lewes, UK: Falmer Press.

Scraton, S. (1994) The changing world of women and leisure. *Leisure Studies* 3(4): 249–61.

Skeggs, B. (ed.) (1995) *Feminist Cultural Theory: Process and Production*. Manchester: Manchester University Press.

Slater, D. (1997) Integrating consumption and leisure: hobbies and the structure of everyday life. Paper presented to the *British Sociological Association Conference*, University of York.

Stanley, L. (ed.) (1990) *Feminist Praxis: Research, Theory, and Epistemology in Feminist Sociology*. London: Routledge.

Stanley, L. and Wise, S. (1983) *Breaking Out*. London: Routledge and Kegan Paul.

Stanley, L. and Wise, S. (1993) *Breaking Out Again: Feminist Ontology and Epistemology*. London: Routledge.

Stanley, L. and Wise, S. (2000) But the empress has no clothes! Some awkward questions about the missing revolution in feminist theory. *Feminist Theory* 1(3): 270–80.

Talbot, M. (1979) *Women and Leisure: A State of the Art Review*. London: Social Science Research Council and Sports Council.

Wearing, B. (1998) *Leisure and Feminist Theory*. London: Sage.

Wimbush, E. (1986) *Women, Leisure, and Well-being*. Edinburgh: Centre for Leisure Research.

Wimbush, E. and Talbot, M. (eds) (1988) *Relative Freedoms: Women and Leisure*. Milton Keynes: Open University Press.

# Chapter 5

# The economics of work and leisure

*Chris Gratton and Peter Taylor*

## Introduction

In the early 1980s, economists joined with other analysts in forecasting the dawn of a leisure age in the United Kingdom (UK) (e.g. Vickerman 1980; Jenkins and Sherman 1981). There was a powerful economic logic to this forecast, both theoretical and empirical. On the theory side, so long as leisure is a normal good demand for it would rise as incomes rise and there would be pressure for leisure time to increase as long as real incomes continued to rise. On the empirical side, production processes were experiencing increased substitution of labour by technology, spending on leisure goods and services was increasing steadily, and long-term time trends demonstrated shrinking work hours, expanding holiday entitlements and increasing early retirements.

What happened since then has blown apart such a clear-cut forecast. The leisure age has not happened and in the UK at least there are signs of increasing work and reduced leisure, together with qualitative indications of increased pressures from work and domestic obligations. The core objectives of this chapter, therefore, are first to review the standard economic theory on work–leisure time choices by individuals, second to review major empirical indicators of work and leisure time in the UK, and third to put the UK in an international perspective. These stages will enable conclusions to be drawn about the efficacy of the standard economic theory, as well as likely developments in work and leisure time.

## The income/leisure trade-off

Neoclassical economic analysis assumes that the allocation of time between work and leisure is driven by individuals' decision-making. Rational utility-maximising consumers are faced with a continuous choice over how to allocate their time, principally between leisure, paid work, and 'obligated time' (for such activities as housework, hygiene and sleeping). Paid work is treated as disutility and consumers need compensation in terms of income to persuade them to give up their leisure time. If we make a simplifying assumption that obligated time is a constant (an assumption we will return to later), the key choice for individuals is between paid work and leisure – the income/leisure trade-off. Any time spent in leisure means losing potential earnings, so that the opportunity cost or *price of leisure* is the forgone earnings. If people behave rationally, they will enter the labour market and continue to work only as long as the benefits from income outweigh the benefits from leisure time.

If a decision is made to enter the labour market, it implies that the initial hours of paid work are worth more than the hours of leisure they replace. The next decision concerns how many hours to work. The more hours the consumer works the more valuable each hour of leisure time that is left becomes, as leisure time becomes increasingly scarce. Eventually there will come a point when the additional income earned from an additional hour of work (i.e. the hourly wage rate) is not sufficient to compensate for the loss of another hour of leisure time. The optimum trade-off between time spent at work and time spent at leisure will be at the point when the valuation of an hour of leisure time is equal to the wage rate. Working longer hours than this optimum would mean that the consumer was irrationally choosing to forsake leisure time that was worth more than the income from the extra work.

This choice mechanism has been used in economics to analyse individual decisions concerning whether or not to work, whether to take part-time or full-time employment, whether to work more hours in a week (overtime) or whether to take a second job (moonlighting).

A crucial part of the analysis is how people react to a change in the hourly rate of pay, the price of leisure time. Over time, rates of pay usually rise, even in real terms. How does this affect the income/leisure choice? In neoclassical economics theory there are two contrasting influences caused by a change in a price: the substitution effect and the income effect. First, because the price of leisure time is rising there is an inducement to take less leisure time and devote more time to work. This is the normal demand relationship: for any commodity, as the relative price rises, we demand less of it. This is the substitution effect.

Second, because rates of pay for all *existing* work hours are higher, total income will rise even if the amount of time spent at work does not change. Some of this extra income may be used to 'buy' more leisure time, by working fewer hours. If leisure time is a 'normal good', which in economics means that demand for it rises as incomes rise, then we would expect demand for leisure time to rise as rates of pay rise. This is the income effect.

Thus we have two effects pulling in opposite directions and the net effect on the demand for leisure time is uncertain. Whether leisure time increases or decreases as wage rates rise is an empirical question. In the next part we examine the evidence.

## UK evidence

The main statistical indicators of time allocation comprise:

- time spent in paid work, e.g. hours worked, overtime, labour force activity rates
- time allocated for leisure, e.g. holiday entitlement
- the identity of times worked, e.g. shiftwork, flexitime.

In addition to indicators of actual time allocations, there is also increasing evidence of what time allocations individuals would prefer and the extent to which these preferences differ from actual time allocations. This evidence suggests that actual time allocations may not be just the outcome of individual choices, in contrast to the neoclassical theory outlined earlier.

Two qualifying observations should be made about the indicators used to represent work and leisure time allocations. First, leisure time is rarely measured directly. Leisure time is more typically assumed to be the residual in any given time period after paid work time has been measured. Even holiday entitlement is a paid-work-related measure of time allowance, rather than an accurate measure of leisure time allocation. Second, the assumption that time not in paid work is leisure time ignores obligated time. There are also 'grey areas' in the use of time which are partly obligated and partly leisure, such as eating, shopping, travelling and DIY. At the simplest level of analysis these obligated or partly obligated time allocations may be assumed to be constant, but this may not be correct.

### Hours

In the long term, the basic working week (excluding overtime) in the UK has been falling. From an average of over 44 hours a week in 1950, it fell to around 40 in the late 1960s (Gratton and Taylor 1985). Thereafter it declined at a much slower rate. One estimate for 2000 is of a basic working week of 37 or 37½ hours for manual workers and 35–37 hours a week for non-manual workers (Incomes Data Services (IDS) 2000). A different picture emerges, however, when overtime is taken into account. The actual amount of hours worked per week for full-time employees, including paid overtime, declined to a low point of 41.7 hours a week for men in 1984 and 37.1 hours a week for women in 1982. Thereafter, hours of work have risen slightly, peaking at 42.3 hours a week for men in 1989 and 37.6 hours a week for women in 1988–9 and 1994–8.

Figure 5.1 shows the trends from 1976 to 2000 for four groups of full-time employees – male and female, manual and non-manual. Generally non-manual employees work lower paid hours than manual workers, although as we shall see later this does not take account of unpaid overtime. Male manual workers work about five hours a week more than the next group, female manual workers. The trends for the four groups show falling actual weekly

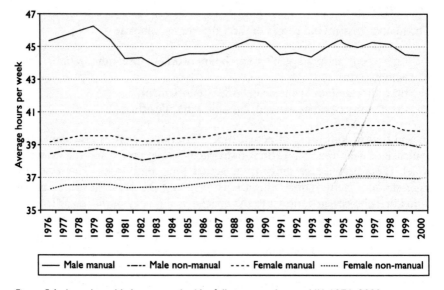

*Figure 5.1* Actual weekly hours worked by full-time employees, UK, 1976–2000

Source: New Earnings Survey, National Statistics website, www.statistics.gov.uk. Crown copyright
material is reproduced with the permission of the controller of HMSO.

hours of work until the early to mid-1980s, suggesting a dominant income
effect. Thereafter, a slight increase in actual working hours is indicative of a
dominant substitution effect.

### Overtime and long hours

One of the features of the UK labour market has been the predominance of
overtime working. In the early 1990s half of men in manual jobs worked an
average of ten hours a week paid overtime and 30 per cent of female manual
workers worked an average of six hours a week paid overtime. The scale and
length of paid overtime working for non-manual workers is typically lower.

The economic logic of overtime for employers is its flexibility and the fact
that there are far less fixed costs of employment associated with overtime
than taking on extra employees. The logic for employees is that the higher
overtime rate of pay will encourage only a substitution effect; i.e. demanding
less leisure time, because it is more expensive at the margin during overtime
hours.

Despite the long paid overtime hours of manual workers, it is not those at
the bottom end of the income distribution that are working the longest hours
in the UK, as might have been expected. Those who are contributing most to
a so-called 'long hours culture' in the UK are the better educated, the higher
paid, those in middle and senior management. Gershuny (1996), Britain's

most prominent economic researcher into time allocation, reports evidence from the British Household Panel Survey (BHPS) to indicate that those with the highest monthly income have clearly the longest working hours. He estimates that for men on average, excluding those who are unemployed, the highest paid 20 per cent of the workforce work ten hours longer per week than do the lowest paid. As he points out: 'Those with the highest earnings now have the least time to spend them' (Table 5.1).

Gershuny (1996) suggests the reasons for this pattern:

> More of the top jobs in the economy require high levels of specific technical knowledge, which, combined with increasing levels of education, intensifies competition for advantageous positions that were once less meritocratically allocated. The freeing of women from the imperatives of the reproductive cycle allows them also to compete for these top jobs. And one of the main mechanisms in this competition for top jobs seems to be to work long hours. Add to this increased competitive pressure from government deregulation of industries, and underfunding of services leading to overwork of senior staff, and the punishingly long hours of the top jobs are quite unsurprising.
>
> And of course, going along with the economic pressures, are powerful social influences. Just as, at the beginning of the twentieth century, the fact that the richest and most socially prominent were also the most leisured, gave social cachet to leisure itself, so that in turn all the classes strove to achieve leisure. By the end of the same century, in Britain and America at least, the richest and most powerful groups now have the least leisure – and busy-ness acquires its own cachet, long hours of work denote superior social status.
>
> (Gershuny 1996: 4–5)

The Institute for Employment Studies (Kodz et al. 1999) reported that one in four UK employees regularly worked more than 48 hours a week, exceeding

*Table 5.1* Weekly paid work hours by income, UK, 1994–5

|  | Work hours per week | |
| --- | --- | --- |
| Gross monthly income quintiles | Women | Men |
| Lowest | 18 | 22 |
| Second | 35 | 42 |
| Third | 40 | 46 |
| Fourth | 43 | 48 |
| Highest | 47 | 50 |
| Whole sample | 33 | 45 |

Source: British Household Panel Survey (Gershuny 1996)

the European Union's 'Working Time Directive'. One in five worked an extra 14 hours a week above their contracted hours, with managers, professionals and specialist occupations the most typical working such long hours. Nine out of ten people in this study blamed increased workloads as a major cause of long hours working.

An Institute of Management survey (Charlesworth 1996) also reinforced Gershuny's findings. Out of a random sample of 3000 managers, 1073 questionnaires were returned. Of these 12 per cent were chief executives/ managing director status and a further 36 per cent senior management, with 25 per cent junior management; 47 per cent of the sample were aged between 45 and 54. Thus the sample included a high proportion of people at the top end of the jobs hierarchy. Nearly six in ten respondents claimed that they always worked in excess of their official working week; 49 per cent of the sample regularly took work home, with 18 per cent always doing so, while 41 per cent of the sample regularly worked at weekends, with 14 per cent always doing so. More than eight in ten of respondents reported that their workload had increased over the past year, with 47 per cent stating that it had increased greatly.

Furthermore, it is apparent that for many managers and professionals working longer hours is not a simple substitution effect whereby leisure time is 'bought' by a premium pay rate. A study on work–life balance in the UK (Hogarth et al. 2000) reported that more than one in three employees who worked in excess of their standard or fixed hours of work received neither additional pay nor time off in lieu for any additional hours worked. The most common incidence of this was for senior managers – in two-thirds of workplaces they were neither paid nor had time off in lieu for additional hours.

> Manual workers were most likely to be employed on the basis of an hourly rate and a fixed number of hours each week with the result that overtime work strikes at the heart of the wage-effort bargain and, accordingly is paid. In contrast the nature of the wage-effort bargain for professional and managerial staff is much more nebulous, they are more likely to be employed to fulfil responsibilities without reference to working time. Hence, additional hours are probably not even referred to as 'overtime'.
>
> (Hogarth et al. 2000: 9)

This impression is reinforced by the Department for Education and Employment (DfEE 1999) which reported results from the Labour Force Survey in the winter of 1997–8. This indicated that while 23 per cent of male workers and 12 per cent of female workers worked paid overtime in the period covered, 18 per cent of men and 20 per cent of women worked unpaid overtime. Only 2 per cent worked both paid and unpaid overtime. While it was manual occupations which topped the list of those working paid overtime, it was managers and professionals who were most likely to be work-ing unpaid overtime.

Therefore a substantial part of the longer/overtime hours worked in the UK is not paid for directly, on an hourly basis. The income/leisure trade-off, if it exists, is much more indirect and longer term – with a perception that working longer helps to obtain and sustain senior positions with higher salaries.

### Labour force activity rates

The labour force activity rate is the percentage of working age people that are in the workforce. The long-term trend in labour force activity rates demon-strates a steady decrease in the percentage of working age men (16–65 years) working in paid employment, and a steady increase in the percentage of women of working age (16–60 years) in the paid workforce (see Table 5.2). In 1999 less than 72 per cent of men of working age were in paid employment, one of the main factors in the decline being that early retirement has reduced activity rates in the last years before 65. By 1999, over 54 per cent of women of working age were in paid employment and there is every expectation that this will continue to rise. These trends on the face of it demonstrate a domin-ant substitution effect for women and a dominant income effect for men. The picture for women, however, is more complex, as it may be that paid work is being substituted for unpaid (house) work, rather than leisure time.

Table 5.2 Labour force economic activity rates,[1] UK, 1984–99

| UK | Percentages of males age 16–65, females age 16–60 |
|---|---|
| Males | |
| 1984 | 75.9 |
| 1991 | 74.9 |
| 1994 | 72.6 |
| 1999 | 71.5 |
| Females | |
| 1984 | 49.2 |
| 1991 | 53.1 |
| 1994 | 53.0 |
| 1999 | 54.4 |

Source: DfEE Social Trends, National Statistics website, www.statistics.gov.uk. Crown copyright material is reproduced with the permission of the controller of HMSO.

[1] The percentage of the population that is in the labour force.

### Holiday entitlement

Apart from earlier retirement by men, one of the principal ways in which expansion in leisure time has been achieved in the UK is through increases in paid holiday entitlement. Historical evidence from the DfEE shows that the paid holiday entitlement for full-time, manual workers steadily increased over time, from a norm of three weeks or less in 1971 to a norm of four weeks or more in the late 1980s. The European Union's Working Time Directive has given added impetus to the increase in paid holiday entitlement, stipulating from November 1999 a minimum of four weeks' paid holiday entitlement a year. IDS (2000) and DfEE (2001) estimate an average, annual, paid holiday entitlement in the UK of 25 days excluding public holidays, with 24 days for men and 26 days for women.

Table 5.3 shows the distribution of paid holiday entitlements for full-time and part-time employees in 1995 (not counting public holidays) – i.e. prior to the UK's adoption of the EU Working Time Directive. The average entitlement for full-time employees was 23 days for men and 25 days for women, while for part-time workers the averages are 6 days for men and 14 for women. Perhaps the most remarkable part of Table 5.3 is the 4 per cent of full-time employees who have no paid holiday entitlement beyond statutory public holidays.

### Shiftwork and flexible working hours

One of the limitations of the standard neoclassical economic analysis of the allocation of time is that it concentrates on the quantitative allocation of time between work and leisure. However, in addition to significant changes in the quantities of work and leisure time, as reviewed above, there are also significant changes occurring in the flexibility of work and leisure time arrangements. These have an important role in the decisions of employers and the preferences of employees.

Table 5.3  Holiday entitlement, UK, 1995

| Days' entitlement per year* | Full-time employees (%) | Part-time employees (%) |
|---|---|---|
| 0 | 4.1 | 36.0 |
| 1–5 | 0.4 | 4.3 |
| 6–10 | 2.2 | 9.0 |
| 11–15 | 7.2 | 12.2 |
| 16–20 | 22.8 | 15.4 |
| 21–25 | 38.1 | 13.5 |
| 26–30 | 16.5 | 4.6 |
| 31+ | 8.7 | 5.0 |

Source: DfEE, National Statistics website, www.statistics.gov.uk. Crown copyright material is reproduced with the permission of the controller of HMSO.
* Not counting public holidays

Overtime and part-time working are two major expressions of flexibility of time allocation between work and leisure. However, flexibility is concerned not just with the quantities of work and leisure but also when they occur. An increasing proportion of the labour force is not working a standard, nine-to-five, Monday to Friday working week. Two of the most common forms of variation from the standard working week are shiftwork and flexible working hours (including flexitime, a compressed work week, and annualised hours). Hogarth et al. (2000) reported for the UK that 21 per cent of employees worked shifts, 24 per cent worked flexitime, 6 per cent worked compressed work weeks and 2 per cent worked annualised hours.

A key distinction between these non-standard work/leisure allocations is that whereas shiftwork is primarily the preference of the employer, flexitime is primarily the choice of the employee. An extreme demonstration of the demands of the modern service economy was reported by the Department for Education and Employment (DfEE 2000) with data on the extent of working on bank holidays – most likely a choice of the employer not the employee. In the period from December 1998 to August 1999 over 31 per cent of all full-time workers and nearly 29 per cent of part-time workers in the UK worked on at least one bank holiday. The occupations with the highest figures were 'personal and protection' services for full-time workers and 'selling' for part-time workers. In the Hogarth et al. (2000) report on work–life balance there was a considerable latent demand for more flexible work time arrangements by employees: 47 per cent of employees not using flexitime would have liked to do so; 35 per cent of employees not working a compressed work week would have preferred it; and 21 per cent of those not working annualised hours would have preferred them.

### Preferred work–leisure time allocations

Survey evidence has provided a consistent picture that the amount of work and leisure time being experienced is often not what individuals actually want. In the Institute of Management survey (Charlesworth 1996) 60 per cent of British managers found it difficult to find enough time to relax, for hobbies/interests and time for their partner. Another survey, commissioned by the Chartered Institute of Personnel and Development (Compton-Edwards 2001) researched a sample of 291 people who worked longer than 48 hours in a typical week in 1998 and continued to do so in 2000. The results suggest that most of such 'long hours' workers feel that they have struck the wrong work–life balance, 56 per cent saying that they have dedicated too much of their life to work; 54 per cent claiming that they suffered from mental exhaustion or always feeling drained and 43 per cent experiencing difficulty sleeping. Less than half the sample (47 per cent) claimed working long hours was entirely their own choice, with 43 per cent sometimes working long hours reluctantly and 10 per cent working long hours reluctantly most or all of the

*Table 5.4* Proportion of men and women who wish to reduce their working hours, UK, 1995

| Work time quintiles | % of women | % of men | Gross income quintiles | % of women | % of men |
|---|---|---|---|---|---|
| Lowest | 6 | 13 | Lowest | 9 | 11 |
| Second | 23 | 17 | Second | 24 | 25 |
| Third | 43 | 29 | Third | 41 | 31 |
| Fourth | 49 | 38 | Fourth | 50 | 41 |
| Highest | 57 | 50 | Highest | 57 | 43 |
| Whole sample | 28 | 35 | Whole sample | 28 | 35 |

Source: British Household Panel Survey (Gershuny 1996)

time. Clearly, even in this sample known to work long hours for years, work time is not always a matter of choice.

Gershuny (1996) reports evidence to show that there is a clear preference of those working the longest hours to reduce their working hours. Some 57 per cent of women in the top 20 per cent of income earners and of working hours wanted to reduce their working hours in 1994–5. Table 5.4 shows that as people move up the hierarchy of either income or working hours the preference for reducing working hours grows. The preference for reducing working hours in Table 5.4 rises more steeply for women than for men. Part of the reason for higher preferences of women for shorter working hours may be the length of time they also spend on domestic unpaid work outside the workplace.

### Unpaid work

Gershuny (1997) shows that although there has been a slight reduction in women's housework (cleaning, clothes washing, and cooking) time since 1961, there has been a sharp rise in time spent on shopping and domestic travel and perhaps more surprisingly, a massive rise in the amount of time both women and men spend on childcare. Even though family size has declined, Gershuny's evidence suggests that childcare time has almost doubled for both men and women in every category. He found that full-time employed women with children in 1995 appeared to devote more time to children than even non-employed mothers did in 1961.

Gershuny explains the rise in shopping and domestic travel time as due to the replacement of local shops by huge self-service stores in out-of-town sites that involve less cost to the retailers but more time from shoppers. He also discusses the reasons for the rise in childcare time:

> Children use all sorts of personal services – educational, medical, recreational – and as the scale of these facilities grows, their location becomes on average more distant from the child's own home. To these increasingly

remote facilities must be added another factor: the lapse in children's 'licence to roam'. In the UK in 1961, children were allowed a considerable degree of freedom to travel about unsupervised. But, as Meyer Hillman has documented, traffic danger and the perceived growth in child assault mean that children are now mostly constrained to travel to these remote facilities in the company of adults.

(Gershuny 1997: 57)

On the more positive side, however, Gershuny also attributes the rise in childcare time to an increasing commitment by parents to find 'quality time' with their children. Such time could more realistically be called leisure time rather than unpaid work time.

Overall though, Gershuny's evidence does suggest that in addition to increasing working hours there is also increasing time committed to other domestic chores, so they cannot simply be assumed to be constant.

### UK summary

The evidence for the UK suggests that the standard economic theory of work/leisure time decisions by individual employees being made in response to rates of pay is too simple. The main expectation from the standard theory (given an assumption that leisure is a normal good) – that a strong income effect will cause work time to contract as rates of pay rise in the long term – is not being realised in the period since the late 1980s in the UK, particularly for higher level, full-time occupations. Furthermore, individual preferences in work/leisure time allocations can often not be realised.

Gershuny (1999) attempts an overall summary of time allocations for the UK in the period 1961 to 1995, using data from time-budget studies. This presents trends for all people in the age band 20–60 years. The results for those in full-time employment are as follows:

- paid work time falling from 1961 to 1985, then rising from 1985 to 1995
- unpaid work time falling from 1961 to 1975, rising sharply from 1975 to 1985, then more or less constant from 1985 to 1995
- paid and unpaid work time combined falling from 1961 to 1985, then rising from 1985 to 1995.

The reason why leisure time has not expanded post-1985 for those in full-time employment is not necessarily that leisure is an inferior good (where, as incomes rise, less is demanded), although for some employees this may be the case. In practice the more persuasive evidence is that many preferences of employees, both for reduced work time and work at more flexible times, are being frustrated by labour market constraints. The economic theory that workers have a choice over their working hours is simply not supported by the evidence. If this is the situation in the UK, what is the position in other countries?

## International comparisons

In this section we examine the UK's allocation of time between paid work and leisure with two countries known to be more orientated to work time, the United States and Japan, and also with countries which have a lesser orientation to work time, in Europe.

### United States

Schor (1991) found that in the period 1969 to 1987, against all expectations, the United States had chosen to take all the benefits of productivity gains in more money rather than more leisure time. In fact, rather than working time being reduced over this period (as in the UK), it actually increased substantially.

> Since 1969 American workers have experienced a substantial rise in hours of work. The rise is very small for the population as a whole but if we look at people with jobs, it is quite substantial. The average employed person in America, excluding people who are under-employed or unemployed, increased his or her market hours over the period 1969 to 1987 by an average of about 160 hours a year, or by what I have referred to as the 'extra month of work'. For women, the increase in market hours was much larger, just over 300 hours a year. This has been brought about by a number of factors. Over the period there has been a substantial rise in the numbers of women in full-time jobs. Increasingly, these are career jobs which require both more hours of work per week and a more continuous labour force participation around the year than has conventionally been associated with female employment.
>
> Men also experienced an increase in their hours of work over this period by an average of about 100 hours. Around two thirds of the rise is accounted for by a larger fraction of the year that people are working and about a third of it is due to longer weekly hours. Increasingly, Americans can be described as overworked in what I would say is the technical rather than the popular sense of overwork. That is, increasing numbers of people say they are working more hours than they would like to and are willing to trade-off income in order to work fewer hours. A variety of polls in the last five years indicate that between 15 per cent and just over 50 per cent of workers feel this way, depending on the form of work time and income reduction proposed and the wording of the question.
>
> (Schor 1996: 6–7)

Schor's evidence, like the later evidence of the UK, is in direct contradiction to expectations from the neoclassical income/leisure trade-off model outlined earlier. One of the reasons Schor suggests is that rigidities in the labour market prevent people choosing to work the hours they would prefer. However, she suggests that the main factor explaining the unexpected decline in leisure time in the United States over this period is that the country has become enmeshed in what she calls 'the cycle of work and spend':

> The cycle of work and spend is an explanation for the following paradox: the United States has almost tripled its productivity level since the end of the Second World War. It has not used any of that increase in productivity to reduce working hours. Instead it has channelled it all into increases in income and in fact, not just income, but consumption. Consequently we have just about tripled the average goods and services that a person or a household consumes, but we have not given ourselves any more leisure.
> Why is this paradoxical? Economists typically think of leisure as a normal good, something that people will buy more of as they get richer. Certainly historically this has happened since the mid-nineteenth century. The fact that the USA has not done this since the Second World War despite substantial increases in productivity is therefore a paradox from the standard perspective. It also stands in great contrast to Western Europe where a much more significant fraction of productivity growth was channelled into reducing working hours.
>
> (Schor 1996: 12)

Schor argues that there is an economic incentive for employers to make existing workers work longer hours rather than take on new employees because there are a series of fixed costs (e.g. medical insurance, pension benefits) associated with taking on any employee. The more hours each employee works, the lower the cost per hour of such fixed costs. She also argues that a culture of long working hours has developed in American organisations. This culture gets stronger the higher people go up the jobs hierarchy. In effect, the only choice faced by those in high-ranking, well-paid jobs is to work long hours or not to work at all. This situation, she argues, is leading a significant minority of people to take the latter option and exit the formal labour market. This phenomenon is referred to as 'downshifting'.

Schor's interpretation of US evidence is challenged by Robinson and Godbey (1999), who argue that the survey evidence on which such interpretations are made exaggerate working hours, being based on ex-post perceptions of time spent. They prefer to use time-budget evidence, which records actual time spent. Unlike the UK, where the two sets of evidence are consistent (as we have seen), in the United States the conclusions of Robinson and Godbey (1999) differ from those of Schor (1996) for the long term. National time budget studies for 1965, 1975, 1985 and 1995 indicate that for those in employment there has been a continuous decline in working hours for men for the whole period, and a decline for women until 1985, followed by an increase from 1985 to 1995. This contrasts with the increase in work time that Schor reports.

Robinson and Godbey's explanation is that with increasing pressures on the use of time, at work and at leisure (a concept termed 'time deepening'), people are inclined to perceive increases in time at work when no real increases have occurred. There is therefore a gap between perceived (survey) hours of work and actual (time budget) hours of work, a gap which gets bigger the longer the actual hours worked. Robinson and Godbey (1999) estimate the gap averaged 4.9 hours a week for women and 4.8 hours a week for men in 1995, that is on average people perceived that they worked nearly 5 hours longer per week than they actually did.

Robinson and Godbey also estimate the trends from 1965 to 1995 in combined paid and unpaid work, results which for the latest decade show similar overall trends to Gershuny's UK data. They report that for employed women combined work time fell from 1965 to 1985 but then rose from 1985 to 1995 to exceed the level experienced in 1975. For employed men there was a similar trend, with a sharp fall from 1965 to 1975, then stability followed by a rise from 1985 to 1995, bringing work time back up to a level between the 1965 and 1975 averages. From 1985 to 1995 the rises in combined work time were 3.1 hours a week for women and 2.2 hours a week for men.

Corresponding estimates by Robinson and Godbey of changes in free time from 1985 to 1995 suggest a decline of 1.2 hours a week for employed women and an increase for employed men of 2.6 hours. The reconciliation of more hours of combined work time and more hours of free time for employed men lies in a reduction in obligated activities such as personal care, according to Robinson and Godbey's estimates. This is in contrast to the increase in obligated time commitments (particularly childcare) reported for the UK by Gershuny.

### Japan

Japan has traditionally had substantially higher working hours than either Britain or the USA. Table 5.5 shows the trend in working hours in the UK, United States and Japan from 1870 to 1970. In 1870, all three countries had remarkably similar working hours per year. Even by 1929, there was little difference between the three countries in terms of hours worked. The difference is that Japan has not seen the rapid decline in working hours in the post-war period (at least until 1970) that Britain and the United States have experienced.

If we examine Table 5.6 Britain seems to be closer to the position in Europe when it comes to the availability of leisure time than they are to the United States or Japan. The European worker is most different when it comes to paid holiday entitlement. Whereas 5 or 6 weeks are common in Europe, the Japanese worker takes only 9 days, and the American 16 days. In fact,

Table 5.5 Hours worked, UK, USA, Japan,
1870–1970

| | Annual hours worked | | |
|---|---|---|---|
| | UK | USA | Japan |
| 1870 | 2984 | 2964 | 2945 |
| 1929 | 2286 | 2342 | 2364 |
| 1950 | 1958 | 1867 | 2289 |
| 1970 | 1688 | 1754 | 2195 |

Source: OECD and Becker 1991

the Japanese have many more statutory holidays (20 days per year) than Europeans or Americans so that, in fact, Americans have the lowest number of paid holidays in total. Because Japanese workers often work at weekends the Japanese have the highest annual working hours at around 2100 hours per year in the 1990s, closely followed by the Americans at 1924 hours. The average for Europe is 1650, substantially below the other two major economic powers. Also, Table 5.6 shows that Europeans take more time off due to illness than the Japanese or Americans. This could be another indicator of a more leisurely approach to work.

Harada (1996) indicates the prevalence of a 'corporate warrior' culture in Japan as the main cause of the long working hours:

> They do not complain about working hours. Fighting stress and strain on all aspects of their job, they silently bear increasing overtime hours and long commuting time. These workers spend an amazing length of time at their jobs . . .
>
> In the finance and insurance industry, where considerable unpaid overtime occurs, 30% of the actual hours worked are unpaid overtime, as indicated by Ono (1991), bringing the annual hours worked for the industry to 2,500 hours. If this is divided by 250 working days, that

Table 5.6 Days off work, international comparisons, 1989

| | Japan | USA | UK | Germany | France |
|---|---|---|---|---|---|
| Weekends | 85 | 104 | 104 | 104 | 104 |
| National holidays | 20 | 9 | 8 | 11 | 8 |
| Paid holidays | 9 | 16 | 24 | 29 | 26 |
| Absences | 3 | 6 | 11 | 11 | 16 |
| Total | 117 | 138 | 147 | 155 | 154 |

Source: Nishi 1993, National Statistics website, www.statistics.gov.uk. Crown copyright material is reproduced with the permission of the controller of HMSO.

means 10 hours of work each day of work. People living in a large metropolis may require three hours of commuting time for the round-trip, leaving a meagre 10 hours for sleep, eating, bathing, and other daily living necessities. If we estimate that these workers spend no time what-soever doing household chores, that gives them free time at home total-ling a mere one hour per working day. This type of Japanese person is known for bringing work from the office home with him (it is mostly men). It is not unusual for this kind of person to carry home overtime work and to go to work on holidays. Almost all household chores and the raising of children is left up to the wife. Even if the wife is also maintain-ing a paid job, the responsibility for housework and taking care of the children rests entirely on her.

(Harada 1996: 38–39)

However, such corporate warriors tend to be the older generation. There are indications that the younger generation has much more interest in leisure and will not continue to work the long working hours traditionally associated with the Japanese economy.

### Europe

Although Britain has more leisure time than both the United States and Japan, within Europe Britain has the longest working hours. Table 5.7 shows

Table 5.7 Average total usual weekly hours worked by full-time employees, EU, 1999

| | Usual weekly hours of work, full-time employees | | |
| --- | --- | --- | --- |
| | All employees | Male | Female |
| Belgium | 38.4 | 39.1 | 37.7 |
| Denmark | 40.0 | 41.1 | 38.4 |
| Germany | 41.8 | 42.5 | 40.4 |
| Greece | 44.6 | 45.8 | 42.1 |
| Spain | 42.2 | 42.9 | 40.8 |
| France | 40.9 | 41.8 | 39.5 |
| Ireland | 42.1 | 44.1 | 38.6 |
| Italy | 40.5 | 41.9 | 37.9 |
| Luxembourg | 40.6 | 41.6 | 38.6 |
| The Netherlands | 41.0 | 41.4 | 39.3 |
| Austria | 41.9 | 42.1 | 41.5 |
| Portugal | 42.4 | 43.4 | 41.1 |
| Finland | 41.0 | 42.4 | 39.3 |
| Sweden | 41.3 | 41.9 | 40.4 |
| UK | 44.4 | 46.0 | 41.0 |
| EU average | 41.9 | 42.9 | 40.0 |

Source: Eurostat (1999) Labour Force Survey

the usual average weekly hours worked by full-time employees in the 15 countries of the European Union in 1999. The UK has the second highest working hours in Europe, just behind Greece and 2½ hours a week more than the EU average. Those EU countries with the lowest working weeks, Belgium, Denmark, Luxembourg, Italy and France, work around four hours a week less than the UK.

Figure 5.2 emphasises this discrepancy by showing the proportion of employees who usually worked over 48 hours per week in 1990, before the institutional constraint of the Working Time Directive was imposed. The UK has the highest proportion with the Netherlands the lowest.

Thus we see a clear difference between the United States, Japan and Europe in the availability of leisure time and, within Europe, Britain has shown trends in working time closer to the trend in the United States than in the rest of Europe. We now turn to the question of whether different countries have different preferences for leisure time on the basis of cultural differences in their ability to enjoy leisure time. In fact, some commentators have argued that this more leisurely situation in Europe is an expression of a different way of life in Europe.

According to Henzler (1992) Eurocapitalism is a different form of capitalism from that in North America and Japan. The American capitalist system is based on free markets and individual action; the Japanese system is much less individualistic than its US counterpart and is more of a corporate capitalist system. Henzler argues that Eurocapitalism is a form of social democratic capitalism:

> Eurocapitalism supports a social compact to which the great majority of our people subscribe . . . Although an actual written compact obviously does not exist, we Europeans explicitly accept our roles as members of society who must act responsibly within the bounds of that society. In return, we assume that society is, in the broadest sense, responsible for everyone in it. In this civic polity, jointly engaged in economic affairs, all sorts of people are bound together and responsible to one another.
>
> (Henzler 1992: 60)

The crucial question for Henzler is which of these capitalist systems will give its people the best quality of life. He argues that the European system will, and in no small part because of lower working hours and a greater emphasis on high quality leisure experiences:

> Europeans place a high value on quality of life. American and Japanese observers routinely comment on the pleasures of life in Europe, from affordable concerts to longer vacations to shorter working days. But achieving a decent quality of life for the largest number of people is a conscious social choice. For example theaters in Germany are heavily

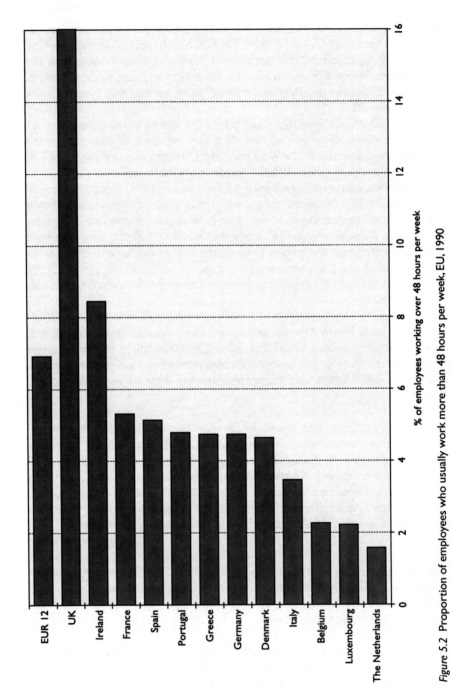

*Figure 5.2* Proportion of employees who usually work more than 48 hours per week, EU, 1990

Source: Eurostat 1992, cited in *Employment in Europe*, Commission of the European Communities, 1993

subsidised: ticket prices cover only about 30% of the cost; government picks up the rest. No one is eager for this largesse to disappear. This applies even more strongly to Germany's completely free university system and its generous health-care system.

If it is possible to supply these benefits and run the country's economic engine more productively at the same time, well and good. If products can be made even more competitive around the world, even better. But if the choice appears to lie between maintaining economic performance or quality of life, public opinion will tilt toward the latter. Higher return on equity is abstract. Reasonably priced theater tickets and affordable health care are tangible. And social cohesiveness is priceless.

(Henzler 1992: 62–63)

Scitovsky (1976) also argues that Europe is very different from the United States when it comes to preferences for work and leisure. Americans, according to Scitovsky, are much more work-centred than Europeans. This is due to a strong Puritan heritage backed up by an education system that is geared to the acquisition of production skills rather than consumption skills. Not only do Americans have less interest in leisure than Europeans, but also they lack appropriate consumption skills to allow them to fully enjoy their leisure time:

America's work ethic puts the earning of money ahead of the enjoyment of life. Every comparison of European and American work habits, among businessmen, professional people, administrative employees, and factory workers alike, shows that no matter whether we are driven by bosses or by internal compulsion, we always work harder, more persistently, more singlemindedly, and at a more relentless pace than the Europeans do. Our very much higher productivity, as shown by all the international comparisons, is one result of this difference; another result may well be our greater need for rest after work. Everybody, when exhausted, puts comfort ahead of pleasure . . .

Whereas the average European seeks status by showing off his expertise as consumer, displaying his knowledge of good but obscure and cheap restaurants, or demonstrating his ability to provide pleasant entertainment through unexpected and simple means, we Americans are more inclined to go in for austere ostentation, displaying our ability to spend a lot of money on goods distinguished from their cheaper counterparts mainly by their conspicuous expensiveness. In that way, we maintain our puritanical disdain for the frivolous matter of consumption, as if it were not dignified to aim at getting the lowest price, let alone to display skill at doing it.

(Scitovsky 1976: 210–211)

So it seems that Europe and Europeans are different. We pay more taxes so that government can provide a rich and varied leisure lifestyle for its citizens. Our education system gives us the skills to appreciate and enjoy culture and leisure. And we work less so that we have the time to enjoy our leisure. As a result, by American standards, we have a leisurely lifestyle that delivers a good quality of life.

## Conclusion

It was thought by many experts, including economists, that at the beginning of the twenty-first century we would be faced by a problem of having too much leisure time. However, for some countries in the world, most notably the United States and Britain, most people seem to be faced with decreasing leisure time. This does not, however, indicate that leisure is an inferior good because there is evidence that many would prefer to trade-off some of their income for more leisure time. Furthermore, many people would prefer to change the times at which they work and take leisure.

Such evidence casts doubt on the validity in practice of the income/leisure trade-off model. First, the choices are more complex (work, leisure, unpaid work, obligated time) and unpaid work and obligated time are not necessarily constant. Second, time allocations involve both the individual and the employer; and the individual's preferences are often overridden by employer decisions. Third, there are substantial labour market rigidities which prevent a continuity of choice for individual workers – they are faced with imperfect options such as working overtime to retain credibility in the workplace; and working unsocial hours or not at all. Fourth, market work, particularly over-time working, is not always compensated directly by an hourly wage rate. The income/leisure trade-off model is therefore too unconstrained – it assumes too much of the labour market.

The outcome of the constrained labour market is that many individuals in the UK, United States and Japan work for longer hours than they would ideally want, and possibly at times of the day and week that they would prefer not to work. But there are not feasible alternatives to this working arrange-ment and it is therefore a 'second best' solution which people get used to. It becomes a cultural and behavioural norm which is difficult to reverse. Both labour market rigidities and individual expectations conspire, therefore, to prevent the UK, United States and Japan approaching European norms in work and leisure time allocations.

As we become increasingly affluent, time becomes a more valuable com-modity. Yet in the richest societies, time has become increasingly scarce as long working hours, particularly for those earning most in the labour market, severely constrain the leisure time in which to enjoy this increasing affluence. The end result is the lack of correspondence of standard economic indicators with indicators of quality of life and well-being. Increasing economic wealth over recent decades has not, in many countries, led to increases in indicators of happiness and well-being. At least part of the explanation for this lies in the inability of the labour markets in these countries to allow people to express their preferences over their working hours.

## References

Becker, J. W. (1991) *The End of the Work Society*. Pijswijk, The Netherlands: Social and Cultural Planning Office.

Charlesworth, K. (1996) *Are Managers under Stress? A Survey of Management Morale*. Institute of Management Research Report, September. London: Institute of Management.

Compton-Edwards, M. (2001) *Married to the Job?* London: Chartered Institute of Personnel and Development.

Department for Education and Employment (DfEE) (1999) Overtime working. *Labour Market Trends* 107(4): 168.

Department for Education and Employment (DfEE) (2000) Bank holiday working. *Labour Market Trends* 108(8): 365.

Department for Education and Employment (DfEE) (2001) Holiday entitlement. *Labour Market Trends* 109(3): 139.

Gershuny, J. I. (1996) High income people want less work, ESRC Research Centre on Micro-Social Change Unpublished Paper. Colchester: University of Essex.

Gershuny, J. I. (1997) Time for the family. *Prospect* January: 56–7.

Gershuny, J. I. (1999) *Leisure in the UK across the 20th Century, Working Paper 99–3*. London: Institute for Social and Economic Research.

Gratton, C. and Taylor, P. D. (1985) *Sport and Recreation: An Economic Analysis*. London: E. and F. N. Spon.

Harada, M. (1996) Work and leisure in Japan. In C. Gratton (ed.) *Work, Leisure and the Quality of Life: A Global Perspective*. Sheffield: Leisure Industries Research Centre.

Henzler, H. (1992) The new era of Eurocapitalism. *Harvard Business Review* July–August: 57–68.

Hogarth, T., Hasluck, C. and Pierre, G. (2000) *Work–Life Balance 2000: Baseline Study of Work–Life Balance Practices in Great Britain*. London: DfEE.

Jenkins, C. and Sherman, B. (1981) *The Leisure Shock*. London: Eyre Methuen.

Incomes Data Services (IDS) (2000) *Hours and Holidays 2000*, IDS Studies 697, October. London: IDS.

Kodz, J., Kersley, B. and Strebler, M. (1999) *Breaking the Long Hours Culture*. Falmer, UK: Institute for Employment Studies, Sussex University.

Nishi, M. (1993) Emerging work and leisure time patterns in Japan. In J. R. Brent Ritchie and D. E. Howkins (eds) *World Travel and Tourism Review: Indicators, Trends and Issues*, vol. 3. Wallingford, UK: CAB International.

Ono, A. (1991) Working time in Japan: 200 hours longer than in statistics. *The Economist* B12: 74–7.

Robinson, J. P. and Godbey, G. (1999) *Time for Life: The Surprising Ways Americans Use their Time*, 2nd edn. University Park, PA: Pennsylvania State University Press.

Schor, J. B. (1991) *The Overworked American: The Unexpected Decline of Leisure.* New York: Basic Books.

Schor, J. B. (1996) Work, time and leisure in the USA. In C. Gratton (ed.) *Work, Leisure and the Quality of Life: A Global Perspective.* Sheffield: Leisure Industries Research Centre.

Scitovsky, T. (1976) *The Joyless Economy.* New York: Oxford University Press.

Vickerman, R. W. (1980) The new leisure society – an economic analysis. *Futures* 12(3): 191–200.

# Chapter 6

# Looking back

## Perspectives on the leisure–work relationship

A. J. Veal

## Introduction

To what extent are patterns of leisure behaviour influenced by, or even determined by, a person's work situation? In this chapter three research traditions which have addressed this issue are reviewed and their current relevance assessed. They are: first, the early work of Wilensky (1960) and Parker (1972, 1983) in devising typologies of work–leisure relationships; second, research on the relationships between leisure participation and occupation-based socio-economic groups; and third, the phenomenon of occupational communities. All three traditions largely faded from leisure studies during the 1980s and 1990s, squeezed out by more fashionable approaches and concerns, and often dismissed on the basis of incomplete or oversimplified representations of their essential nature. It is argued here that all three traditions provide a legitimate basis for current concerns in the study of leisure.

## Work–leisure relationships

Early empirical research on work–leisure relationships arose from investigations in industrial sociology and explored the extent to which workers were committed to work and the organisations that employed them, as opposed to concerns outside the work environment, including leisure. Thus research conducted by Dubin in the 1950s focused on the question of workers' 'central life interests' and, as indicated in Chapter 1, established that only a minority of industrial workers saw their work as the most important facet of their lives (Dubin 1956).

In the 1960s, American sociologist Harold Wilensky sought to theorise changing work–leisure relationships and observed that 'two major hypotheses' had been put forward by the critics of industrialism concerning the relationship between work and leisure in industrial society. These he described in the following classic passage.

The *compensatory leisure* hypothesis: In an up-to-date version the Detroit auto-worker, for eight hours gripped bodily to the main line, doing repetitive, low-skilled, machine-paced work which is wholly ungratifying, comes rushing out of the plant gate, helling down the super-highway at 80 miles an hour in a second-hand Cadillac Eldorado, stops off for a beer and starts a bar-room brawl, goes home and beats his wife, and in his spare time throws a rock at a Negro moving into the neighbourhood. In short, his routine of leisure is an explosive compensation for the deadening rhythms of factory life.

Engels also implies an alternative. The *'spillover' leisure hypothesis*: Another auto-worker goes quietly home, collapses on the couch, eats and drinks alone, belongs to nothing, reads nothing, knows nothing, votes for no one, hangs around the home and the street, watches the 'late-late' show, lets the TV programs shade into one another, too tired to lift himself off the couch for the act of selection, too bored to switch the dials. In short, he develops a spillover leisure routine in which alienation from work becomes alienation from life; the mental stultification produced by his labour permeates his leisure.

(Wilensky 1960: 544)

Although Wilensky did not directly attribute the first hypothesis to specific authors, it is notable that he attributed the second, 'spillover', hypothesis to Engels, and went on to relate it to the idea of the alienated worker and the class struggle. This, he argued, contrasted with the perspective of de Tocqueville, who saw alienation as a feature of 'mass society', in which individuals pursued material pleasures focused exclusively on the nuclear family, losing connections with the wider community – a 'false consciousness' perspective. Thus Wilensky sought to link the work–leisure relationship to questions of wider social and economic structure – an aspect which was largely lost in subsequent developments of his ideas in the leisure studies literature.

Wilensky went on to discuss two 'elaborations' of the above views of the work–leisure relationship, seemingly drawn from the literature of the time but not specifically attributed, namely the ideas of *segmentation* and *fusion*. The *segmentation* view saw an 'ever-sharper split' developing between work and leisure, resulting in 'interpersonal and intrapsychic strain and social instability' and weaker attachments to various spheres of private life, leading to 'stronger attachments to remote symbols of nation, race and class, which are expressed in hyper-patriotism, racism, extremist politics and fear of conspiracy' (Wilensky 1960: 545). Again a strong link can be seen with wider social and political issues. The *fusion* perspective saw work becoming more play-like and leisure becoming more work-like, although the examples given by Wilensky, of long coffee breaks and lunch hours, and card-games among shift-workers, are less than convincing. The negative consequences of this trend were portrayed, again somewhat unconvincingly, as a 'decline in creative autonomy, a general sense of oppression, and an increase in the anxious effort to conform' (Wilensky 1960: 546). Wilensky concluded that the 'issues remain obscure', but went on to say:

> It is apparent that these themes of social criticism centre on the major theoretical concerns of sociology – the attributes of social structure and their connexions, how one or another structural form emerges, persists, changes, how structure facilitates or hampers the efforts of men, variously located, to realise their strivings. More specifically, how does role differentiation arising in the economic order affect role differentiation in the community and society – ie. how do diverse institutional orders (economic, political-military, kinship, religious, education-aesthetic) maintain their autonomy and yet link up? What specific changes in work and leisure can be linked to changes in the class structure of the urban community? How do these changes affect the social integration of industrial society – the extent to which persons share common permanent definitions (values, norms, beliefs) of the roles they play?
>
> (Wilensky 1960: 546–7)

These comments, and later discussion on the need to combine research at the microlevel with 'big picture' research, were generally ignored by leisure researchers who subsequently drew on Wilensky's work. He addresses issues which, decades later, the field of leisure studies was accused of ignoring.

Also generally ignored by leisure scholars is the fact that Wilenksy's theoretical discussion of compensation/spillover and segmentation/fusion was not based on his own empirical research but was a preliminary and speculative summary of the views of other commentators, as he saw them. His own research, reported later in the same paper, in fact focused on the difference between employees with *careers*, who gained status from, and identified with, their work, and those *without careers*, whom he saw as largely alienated from their work. The career-orientated group would, he asserted,

> develop a 'pseudo-community' lifestyle characterised by many lightly held attachments ... The stronger their career commitments the more they will integrate leisure and work, but the majority of workers, those without careers, would withdraw further into family or neighbourhood localism.
>
> (Wilensky 1960: 558–9)

Again, the wider, negative, social implications of this social divide between an upwardly mobile, career-orientated elite and a non-mobile, alienated mass were discussed. The precise nature of a 'pseudo-community lifestyle' or 'neighbourhood localism' are not expanded on; thus even this empirically based contribution can be seen to be quite speculative and concerned primarily with broad social structural issues rather than with the minutiae of patterns of leisure participation.

Both Dubin's (1956) findings on the uninterested worker and Wilensky's (1960) observations on the non-career-orientated masses were confirmed in the 1960s 'Affluent Worker' study of British car-industry workers, conducted by Goldthorpe et al. (1968: 144), which found that the lack of job-orientation of affluent workers did not imply a corresponding 'leisure-orientation' in their lives. These male manual workers, who were often mobile, having moved city to secure a highly paid job,[1] did not necessarily enjoy an active social or leisure life: 'in the absence of many of their kin and of solidary local communities, the majority of our respondents were led to adopt a style of life which was decisively centred on the home and the conjugal family' (Goldthorpe et al. 1968: 154). The study did not, however, extend to an exploration of the detailed patterns of home-based leisure. Affluence meant rising housing standards and the study period also coincided with the advent of television, so, for men at least, being 'home and family centred' was not necessarily incompatible with being 'leisure-centred'. Thus we see that, even as the work–leisure dichotomy was being addressed by leisure researchers for the first time, the empirical evidence was suggesting that dividing life into two domains of work and leisure was an oversimplification – for most male workers there were at least three important domains, namely work, leisure and home/family.

British sociologist Stanley Parker, in his seminal study *The Future of Work and Leisure* (Parker 1972: 71, 99), and his later version, *Leisure and Work* (Parker 1983), elaborated Wilensky's typologies, as shown in Table 6.1, introducing a range of new terms and adding a third type of 'in-between' relationship, which he variously referred to as separateness, neutrality, containment, compartmentalisation and segmentation. But, while Wilensky at least speculates on the types of leisure which might flow from certain work–leisure relationships, Parker focuses almost entirely on the nature of the relationship itself, giving no clear indication of what specific leisure activities might flow from different types of relationship and different types of work. Further, Parker's exposition gives no explanations as to why particular work/leisure relationships arise – they just *are*. Wilensky's exposition arose from a concern about changes in the broader social structure brought about by industrialisation; his overall purpose was structural and analytical rather than prescriptive. Parker, while not ignoring such broader issues, puts more emphasis on the personal, philosophical dimension of work–leisure relationships: the choice between *segmentalism* and the *holistic* approach to life becomes largely a matter of personal philosophy. His discussion of broader issues is in the form of suggested policies to encourage a more holistic approach to work and leisure. Since he basically rejects the idea that leisure should be used as compensation for unpleasant, alienating or damaging work, his policy

Table 6.1 Wilensky and Parker: relationships between work and leisure

| General description of relationship | Wilensky | Parker 1971 and 1983 | | | Parker 1983 (additional terms used) |
| --- | --- | --- | --- | --- | --- |
| | Hypotheses | Individual level | Societal level | Philosophy | |
| Identity | Spillover/fusion | Extension | Fusion | Holism | Positive, extension, congruence, continuation, convergence, generalisation, integration, isomorphism, spillover |
| Contrast | Compensatory/ segmentation | Opposition | Polarity | ⎰ Segmentalism | Negative, dissimilar, opposition, compensation, competition, contrast, heteromorphism |
| Separateness | | Neutrality | Containment | | Neutrality, compartmentalisation, segmentation |

recommendations are largely concerned with humanisation of the workplace. Both Wilensky's and Parker's work can be seen as very much 'unfinished business', even in its own terms. Empirically the studies were quite limited, in terms of the numbers and range of people and occupations studied. While their theories implicitly promised a full outline of the relationships between types of work and types of leisure, in both cases the conclusions remained at a high level of generality. Nevertheless the ideas were influential and were seen as a key element of 'leisure theory' at the time. A considerable body of research on the theme of work/leisure relationships developed in the 1970s (see Zuzanek and Mannell 1983 for appraisal), but lost favour in the 1980s as a result of direct criticism and perceived loss of relevance.

The lack of theoretical rigour of leisure studies and its failure to connect with the concerns of mainstream social research of the time was subject to considerable comment, and Parker's work–leisure was a particular focus of the critique. Thus Moorhouse (1989) states:

> Parker . . . is unable or unwilling to suggest some actual causal line or major relation [between work and leisure], so we can be told: 'High involvement in work may be positively, negatively or neutrally related to high involvement in leisure', which is another way of saying there is *no* relation . . . What Parker claims to have revealed are some associations between 'work' and 'leisure' but even this is not really the case, for the evidence offered is very thin and contradictory, and even if it consisted of the reliable statistical associations Parker claims, correlation is far from causation, and all the academic labour required to turn what is in fact a typology of possibilities into hypotheses capable of being tested in reality remains all to be done.
>
> (Moorhouse 1989: 23)

Leisure studies researchers interested in theoretical issues tended to reject Parker's functionalist approach and his failure to connect satisfactorily with wider social theory (e.g. Rojek 1985: 87–97; Jarvie and Maguire 1994: 22). Neo-Marxist researchers, while welcoming Parker's focus on the centrality of work, rejected his functionalism and his failure to consider class relations and issues of freedom (Clarke and Critcher 1985: 16–22). Feminist researchers rejected Parker's approach because it failed to take account of the experiences of women not in the paid workforce and ignored the role of the family and children and the differences in the situation of men and women (Wearing 1999: 4–8). Some researchers shifted the focus from broad, structural-functional considerations and preferred a more individually orientated, social-psychological approach, in which work was just one influence on lifestyle (Rapoport and Rapoport 1975; Kelly 1983).

In addition to its neglect of women, both in and not in the paid work-force, the Wilensky/Parker approach to leisure analysis tended to ignore, by definition, other groups not in the paid workforce, including students, the retired and unemployed people. In his later book Parker (1983: 62–71) discusses the 'unwaged', including 'housewives', unemployed and retired people, but he examines these groups *before* outlining the work–leisure typology and so does not explicitly relate their situation to the typology. In fact, ideas such as segmentalism versus holism could readily be applied to the work of home and childcare undertaken primarily by women (Gregory 1982). Unwaged groups became of increasing policy interest in the 1980s and 1990s, so it is perhaps not surprising that Parker's bipolar work/leisure approach which had neglected these groups became marginalised in the leisure studies policy agenda.

As other chapters in this book indicate, the question of work–leisure relationships has returned as an issue in the 1990s, as a consequence of increasing working hours, casualisation of the labour market, the increased participation of women in the paid workforce and global competitive pressures being experienced by Western economies. Wilensky's discussion of work–leisure relationships in the 1960s arose from observed tendencies towards a polarisation of the workforce, into a career-orientated elite and a career-less, alienated mass. Such concerns have returned in Western economies in the 1990s (see Rojek's discussion of the 'Brazilianization thesis' in Chapter 3 in this volume). For example, in Australia, at the time of writing, the Australian Council of Trade Unions (ACTU) is seeking a ruling in the Australian Industrial Relations Commission concerning 'unreasonable hours' being imposed on increasing numbers of workers. As part of the preparation for the case the ACTU commissioned a study of the effects of unreasonable hours on 50 workers and their families. The accounts do not reveal a sense of alienation from work, but document the deleterious effects on health, family relationships and leisure of frequent, but often irregular, imposition of excessive working hours by employers. In an opening quotation in one of the chapters a miner draws attention to a '100 Years Ago' item in the local newspaper, reporting the celebrations of the achievement of the 10-hour working day by South Australian miners at the end of the nineteenth century: a hundred years later he was working 12½-hour shifts (Pocock et al. 2001: 17).

Thus the concerns raised by Wilensky are still with us. While the further refinement of the typology of work–leisure relationships offered by Parker has little to offer current debate, and his call for individuals to spontaneously adopt a 'holistic', balanced approach to work, leisure and the rest of life seems somewhat naive in the current environment, it is nevertheless true that large numbers of people in contemporary Western society appear to have failed to achieve such a balance. The work–leisure divide remains an issue.

## Socio-economic group

Empirical research relating leisure participation to occupation has a longer history than the work–leisure typologies discussed earlier. Thus, for example, as early as the 1930s, Lundberg et al. (1934: 100–1) examined the variation in time spent on various leisure activities by men and women in different occupational groups in the United States. Activities examined included eating; visiting; reading; entertainment; sports; listening to the radio; motoring; and visiting clubs. Occupations were divided into white collar; professional and executive; housewives; labour (blue-collar); unemployed; high school students; and college students. Variations between the groups were readily discernible, but not in the direction revealed by later studies; in Lundberg's study, blue-collar workers spent more time on a wider range of leisure activities than those in white-collar and professional jobs. The difference between this and the Wilensky/Parker work/leisure approach can readily be seen: both occupation and leisure activity are classified or measured 'objectively', or at least in a replicable manner, and the relationship is examined statistically.

An approach to the study of work–leisure relationships therefore emerged which involved relating patterns of leisure participation to *socio-economic group*, the hierarchical system of occupational classification devised by governmental statistical agencies and market research organisations. The socio-economic variable group can have as few as two categories – for example, 'white collar' and 'blue collar' – and as many as seventeen, as in the system originally devised by the UK Office of Population Censuses and Surveys. Typically, classification systems used in social research comprise four or five categories. Individuals in professional and managerial jobs are generally described as being in the 'higher' socio-economic groups and those in manual occupations are described as being in the 'lower' socio-economic groups – with a number of supervisory, clerical and skilled manual occupations being in the middle. These systems relate not only to the concept of *occupation* but also to *social class*, indeed, some forms of socio-economic classification are referred to as 'Social Class'.

One of the technical difficulties associated with the use of the socio-economic variable in the study of leisure behaviour can, paradoxically, be seen as an advantage over the work–leisure typology approach. In both approaches, individuals who are not in paid jobs are seemingly excluded from the analysis. However, with its social class dimension, socio-economic group has the advantage that unwaged individuals in a household with a waged 'main breadwinner' can be classified according to the socio-economic group of the breadwinner. This approach is clearly appropriate in representing the likely socio-economic situation of the individual household member and is advantageous in facilitating the classification of all members of a household, but clearly cannot be used if the focus of interest is the work experience of the individual. A further advantage of the socio-economic group approach is pragmatic: namely, that the variable is a standardised, 'routine' variable, widely used in social research and official statistics and relatively easily incorporated into questionnaires.

An early example of this type of research in the United Kingdom, was a government leisure participation survey of over 5000 respondents, which presented participation data related to six socio-economic groups (Sillitoe 1969: 46), but the particular measure of leisure participation used was somewhat idiosyncratic, so the study did not become a 'benchmark' for future studies. Reports of results from numerous subsequent surveys of leisure participation around the world have invariably included information on socio-economic group, and generally show it to have significant relationships with participation levels in a wide range of leisure activities (Cushman et al. 1996).

The empirical studies which use the socio-economic variable tend to concentrate on its 'social class' dimensions rather than its 'occupational' dimensions. That is, it is not the *type of work* that a person does that is of interest, but rather his or her social and economic *status*. There is an implicit, albeit simple, theoretical basis for this approach, namely that people in higher socio-economic groups have a distinctive educational background, and generally social background, which prompts them and equips them to engage in a certain range of leisure activities. Such ideas were later to be theorised by Bourdieu (1984) as 'habitus' and 'cultural capital'. They also tend to have a relatively high level of income which enables them to pursue a wide range of interests.

The primary motives of researchers in relating participation to this variable have therefore been twofold. First, the aim has been to explore *inequality* in participation – generally the research has shown that lower socio-economic groups participate less than higher socio-economic groups in a wide range of activities, with a few exceptions, such as television-watching. This lends support to arguments from critical theorists that fundamental inequalities in society are reflected and reproduced in leisure contexts (e.g. McKay 1990) and to arguments from reformists for public subsidy and/or direct public provision of a range of leisure activities on equity grounds. Second, the revealed patterns of inequality have been used in quantitative *demand forecasting* models, since future changes in the underlying socio-economic structure of the community, reflecting changes in the structure of the workforce and technology, can be predicted to lead to changes in overall leisure participation rates.

As regards the issue of inequality, the *embourgoisement* thesis suggests that the differences revealed by socio-economic group or social class analysis are diminishing over time. Actual empirical evidence in support of this assertion is limited, but British data on participation in sport and physical recreation over the decade 1987 to 1996, as shown in Figure 6.1, suggests that inequality

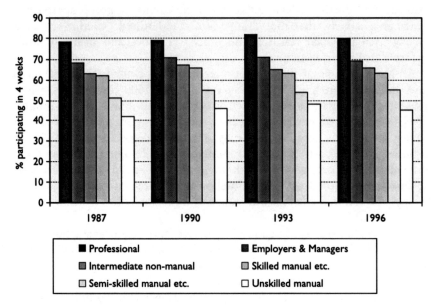

*Figure 6.1* Participation in sports, games and physical activities by socio-economic group, Great Britain, 1987–96

Source: based on data from Office for National Statistics 1997

in participation rates is pronounced, and that there was little change over the decade. It should, however, be noted that the two extreme groups, professionals and unskilled manual, account for only 3.4 per cent and 5.9 per cent of the workforce respectively; for the middle 90 per cent of the population the differences in participation rates are less marked, and fell somewhat over the decade. While this is an incomplete picture, based only on sport and physical recreation over a comparatively short time-period, it is at least not inconsistent with the *embourgoisement* thesis.

Roberts (1999: 86–7), however, argues that the 'class' element of socio-economic group is no longer important, that differences in patterns of leisure participation are influenced more by variations in levels of income and other variables, such as age, gender and family situation, than by socio-economic group. Thus, he implies, the differences shown in Figure 6.1 are largely due to the differing income levels of the various groups rather than class-based cultural differences. The fact that such differential participation rates are replicated in other areas, such as the arts (Gratton 1996: 117), reflects the fact that people in higher socio-economic groups engage in a wider range of activities, primarily, according to Roberts (1999), as a result of their higher incomes. If this were the case, it would follow that the lower levels of participation by members of lower socio-economic groups were due mainly to cost factors, so the state subsidies devoted over recent decades to various leisure services, notably the arts and sport, in order to reduce their cost to the user, should have led to a degree of equalisation in participation levels in these activities. But most analyses indicate that such measures have been substantially unsuccessful in achieving equality of outcomes.

While the available data are incomplete, it is therefore plausible to suggest that there remain significant differences in tastes, preferences and behaviour patterns between socio-economic groups which appear to be related to education and culture as well as income. The relative influences of education, occupation, income, gender, age, family situation, ethnicity, commercial pressures and personal and group lifestyle choices in shaping leisure behaviour patterns are, however, still to be fully explored empirically with an adequate database. In any case it is likely that these influences are fluid and unpredictable and are not subject to firm 'laws'. Such conclusions present challenges for research aimed at exploring inequality but even more so for research aimed at demand forecasting, since successful forecasting relies on stable, predictable relationships.

## Occupational communities

Research on leisure among members of occupational communities has been neglected in the three decades since the publication of the best-known leisure-orientated study of its type, Salaman's (1974) *Community and Occupation*. While occupational communities are often thought of in spatial terms, as relatively geographically isolated communities dominated by a single firm or industry, Salaman specifically excludes such communities from consideration in his study. Instead, he deals with occupational communities which have the following 'defining components'.

> First, members of occupational communities see themselves in terms of their occupational role: their self-image is centred on their occupational role in such a way that they see themselves as printers, policemen, army officers or whatever, and as people with specific qualities, interests and abilities. Second, members of occupational communities share a reference group composed of members of the occupational community. Third, members of occupational communities associate with, and make friends of, other members of their occupation in preference to having friends who are outsiders, and they carry work activities and interests into their non-work lives.
>
> (Salaman 1974: 21)

Salaman reviews existing research on shipbuilders, police, fishermen and jazz musicians and presents results of his own studies of architects and railway workers. These case studies emphasise the social context of leisure behaviour and thus complement the above work–leisure relationship studies and socio-economic group research, which tend to focus on the individual as the unit of analysis. For some occupations, the physical and social work environment and/or the constraints imposed by the occupation lead to friends and non-family associates of the worker being primarily from the same workplace or profession. And for some this can lead to the adoption of particular patterns of leisure behaviour.

Research on occupational communities is unlikely to displace socio-economic group as the 'standard' way to take account of a person's occupation in leisure studies. Such research does, however, raise a number of interesting issues of contemporary interest. First, the strength of the occupational or workplace culture may be a relevant factor in examining trends towards, and gradual acceptance of, working longer hours, particularly unpaid hours. Second, one of the most common constraints on leisure noted by Salaman occurs among those occupations where shiftwork is common. As we move towards the '24-hour society' (Kreitzman 1999) more and more people are working 'unsocial hours', and there has been some research on the implications of shiftwork for leisure and leisure services (themselves large employers of 'unsocial hours' workers) (Roberts 1999: 58–60). Finally, to return to Wilensky's concern with an alienated 'mass', and the widespread perception of a decline in community (Putnam 2000), it would seem that certain occupational cultures are able to resist this trend, providing the individual with social networks beyond the family.

## Conclusion

Contemporary social and economic trends suggest that the relationship between work and leisure is as important as ever. This review has indicated that a careful examination of past research on work–leisure relationships reveals a body of material which can provide a basis for future research in the area. In research on work–leisure typologies there was a supposition that paid work influenced leisure and that the individual should seek to achieve a satisfactory balance between the two spheres. In research on socio-economic group leisure activity is generally seen as a dependent variable with socio-economic group and other variables, such as age, gender and education, being the independent, influencing, variables. In research on occupational communities a more rounded and flexible approach is taken to studying human experience, but the work relationship still takes pride of place. Each of these approaches offers important insights into the relationship between leisure participation and the rest of life, but each also has its limitations. It would seem that research combining aspects of each of these approaches may be the way forward. In the early 1980s Zuzanek and Mannell (1983: 340) called for research on occupational culture and 'lifestyle orientation', the latter being concerned with 'active socio-cultural mechanisms of social and cultural integration of work and leisure experiences in people's lives'. Similar calls to focus on the multidimensional concept of lifestyle, rather than the bivariate examination of work and leisure alone, have been made by others (e.g. Chaney 1987; Durantye 1988; Moorhouse 1989: 31; Veal 1989, 1993) and more recently it has been suggested that leisure researchers should focus on the concept of *culture* to capture the potentially reflexive relationship between leisure and other domains, such as work, family, education and community (e.g. Wynne 1998; Rojek 2000).

## Note

1 Growing up in rural south-west England in the 1950s I can attest to the 'El Dorado' status of the car factories of London and the Midlands at the time. It was rumoured that unskilled workers on the production line earned as much as £20 a week, more than double the wage of other manual workers at the time. But it was still a time of post-war housing shortages, so the prospect of whole families actually being able to move to 'the smoke', a daunting proposition at the best of times, was remote.

## References

Bourdieu, P. (1984) *Distinction: A Social Critique of the Judgement of Taste*. London: Routledge.

Chaney, D. (1987) Review of Rojek's *Capitalism and Leisure Theory* and Clarke and Critcher's *The Devil Makes Work*. *Sociological Review* 35(1): 200–2.

Clarke, J. and Critcher, C. (1985) *The Devil Makes Work: Leisure in Capitalist Britain*. London: Macmillan.

Cushman, G., Veal, A. J. and Zuzanek, J. (eds) (1996) *World Leisure Participation: Free Time in the Global Village*. Wallingford, UK: CAB International.

Dubin, R. (1956) Industrial workers' worlds: a study of the 'central life interests' of industrial workers. *Social Problems* 3(3): 131–42.

Durantye, M. (1988) Towards multidisciplinary research on leisure and lifestyles: an holistic approach. Paper presented to the World Leisure and Recreation Association Congress, *Free Time, Leisure and Society*, Lake Louise, Canada, May.

Goldthorpe, J. H., Lockwood, D., Bechefor, F. and Taylor, P. (1968) *The Affluent Worker: Industrial Attidtudes and Behaviour*. London: Cambridge University Press.

Gratton, C. (1996) Great Britain. In G. Cushman, A. J. Veal and J. Zuzanek (eds) *World Leisure Participation: Free Time in the Global Village*. Wallingford, Oxon: CABI Publishing.

Gregory, S. (1982) Women among others: another view. *Leisure Studies* 1(1): 47–52.

Jarvie, G. and Maguire, J. (1994) *Sport and Leisure in Social Thought*. London: Routledge.

Kelly, J. R. (1983) *Leisure Identities and Interactions*. London: Allen and Unwin.

Kreitzman, L. (1999) *The 24 Hour Society*. London: Profile.

McKay, J. (1990) Sport, leisure and social inequality in Australia. In D. Rowe and G. Lawrence (eds) *Sport and Leisure: Trends in Contemporary Popular Culture*. Sydney: Harcourt, Brace, Jovanovich.

Moorhouse, H. F. (1989) Models of work, models of leisure. In C. Rojek (ed.) *Leisure for Leisure*. London: Macmillan.

Office for National Statistics (1997) *General Household Survey 1996*. London: Stationery Office.

Parker, S. (1972) *The Future of Work and Leisure*. London: Paladin.

Parker, S. (1983) *Leisure and Work*. London: Allen and Unwin.

Pocock, B., van Wanrooy, B., Strazzari, S. and Bridge, K. (2001) *Fifty Families: What Unreasonable Hours are Doing to Australians, their Families and their Communities*. Melbourne: Australian Council of Trade Unions.

Putnam, R. D. (2000) *Bowling Alone: The Collapse and Revival of American Community*. New York: Simon and Schuster.

Rapoport, R. and Rapoport, R. N. (1975) *Leisure and the Family Life Cycle*. London: Routledge and Kegan Paul.

Roberts, K. (1999) *Leisure in Contemporary Society*. Wallingford, Oxon: CABI Publishing.

Rojek, C. (1985) *Capitalism and Leisure Theory*. London: Tavistock.

Rojek, C. (2000) *Leisure and Culture*. London: Macmillan.

Salaman, G. (1974) *Community and Occupation: An Exploration of Work/Leisure Relationships*. London: Cambridge University Press.

Sillitoe, K. K. (1969) *Planning for Leisure* (Government Social Survey SS 388). London: HMSO.

Veal, A. J. (1989) Leisure, lifestyle and status: a pluralistic framework for analysis. *Leisure Studies* 8(2): 141–54.

Veal, A. J. (1993) The concept of lifestyle: a review. *Leisure Studies* 12(4): 233–52.

Wearing, B. (1998) *Leisure and Feminist Theory*. London: Sage.

Wilensky, H. L. (1960) Work, careers and social integration. *International Social Science Journal* 12(4): 543–60.

Wynne, D. (1998) *Leisure, Lifestyle and the New Middle Class*. London: Routledge.

Zuzanek, J. and Mannell, R. (1983) Work–leisure relationships from a sociological and social psychological perspective. *Leisure Studies* 2(3): 327–44.

# Part II

# Quality of life and work and leisure

# Chapter 7

# Work, leisure, time-pressure and stress

*Jiri Zuzanek*

## Introduction

The questions of whether people living in modern societies work longer or shorter hours or have gained or lost free time, and the implications of such trends, have been at the centre of sociological, social political and social economic discussion since the 1930s. John Maynard Keynes, in his essay 'Economic possibilities for our grandchildren', contemplated the future of humanity after the anticipated resolution of the economic problem of 'scarcity' and observed:

> For the first time since his creation, man will be faced with his real, his permanent problem – how to use his freedom from pressing economic cares, how to occupy his leisure, that science and compound interest will have won for him.
>
> (Keynes 1972 [1931]: 366–8)

According to the optimistic forecasts of the 1950s and 1960s, fewer working hours and greater access to leisure were expected to bring considerable social, psychological, cultural and health benefits. Many of these hopes were dashed in the 1980s and 1990s when the tenor of the intellectual debate shifted from leisure to 'burnout', 'work overload', 'multiple role conflict', 'time famine' and 'stress'. Some believe, however, that the negative trends of the 1980s and 1990s are only temporary setbacks on the path to a more 'time-affluent' society.

There appears to be genuine disagreement on whether the amount of working time has declined or increased since the early 1980s, whether people feel more or less pressed for time, and whether they face greater emotional, psychological and social challenges than in the not-so-distant past. This chapter addresses six major issues. First, have people in Western societies gained or lost leisure time in recent years? Second, are *subjective* feelings of increased time pressure rooted in *objective* time-use trends? Third, what are the relationships between time pressure and emotional well-being? Fourth, what is the association between time pressure and psychological stress? Fifth, what are the effects of time pressure and psychological stress on health? Sixth, how can the negative effects of time pressure and stress on health be countered? The chapter draws particularly on analyses of time-use and population health data collected by Statistics Canada (see Table 7.1) but also on findings from other countries reported in the literature. In the concluding section, an attempt is made to summarise the findings and draw some research and policy conclusions.

## More work – less leisure? Historical views on trends in work and leisure time

According to Lundberg, Komarovsky and McInerny, authors of the bench-mark 1930s publication *Leisure: A Suburban Study* (1934: 4), leisure time had been increasing since the end of the nineteenth century and seemed 'destined to an even more rapid increase in the near future'. Thirty years later, simply on the basis of extrapolated trends of the time, Fourastié (1965) predicted that, by 1985, people in most industrial societies would work only one-third of their life, the length of the working week would not exceed 30 hours, and 12 weeks of vacation would be guaranteed. Similarly, in the United States, in the mid-1960s, the National Commission on Technology, Automation and Economic Progress predicted that, by 1985, the working week would decline to 22 hours or paid vacations would extend to 25 weeks (quoted in Kraus 1971: 464).

In the 1970s, however, the mood with regard to the future of work and leisure turned more sombre. Linder (1970) observed that people in modern societies led increasingly hectic rather than more leisurely lives. Twenty years

*Table 7.1* Time-use and population health surveys, Canada, 1981–90

| Survey | Year conducted | Time conducted | Sample size | Age-range | Area sampled |
|---|---|---|---|---|---|
| National Time Use Pilot Survey | 1981 | Sept.–Oct. | 2,685 | 15+ | 14 urban areas |
| General Social Survey – Time-use (GSS) | 1986 | Nov.–Dec. | 9,946 | 15+ | Nationwide |
| General Social Survey – Time-use (GSS) | 1992 | All year | 9,815 | 15+ | Nationwide |
| General Social Survey – Time-use (GSS) | 1998 | All year | 10,748 | 15+ | Nationwide |
| National Population Health Survey (NPHS) | 1994–5 | | 17,626 | 12+ | Nationwide |
| US National Health Interview Survey (NHIS) | 1990 | | 31,868 | 19+ | USA |

later, Juliet Schor claimed, in *The Overworked American*, that, if present trends continued, by the end of the twentieth century Americans would be spending as much time at their jobs 'as they did back in the nineteen twenties' (Schor 1991:1). The historic preference of employers for longer working hours, gender inequalities and the addictive nature of consumption contributed, she argued, to a vicious 'work-and-spend' cycle resulting in a 'time squeeze' for both men and women.

Yet not all researchers agree. Robinson and Godbey, in *Time for Life: The Surprising Ways Americans Use their Time* (1997), argue that Americans now work less and have more free time than they did in the mid-1970s and that 'free time is likely to increase even more in the future' (Robinson and Godbey 1997: 5). Gershuny (2000) suggests that, in the long run, modern societies will resume their move towards leisure.

How can we reconcile these findings? Can questions about the changing amounts of paid work and leisure be answered with any certainty? The analyses of Canadian time-use trends reported in Table 7.2 suggest that, for the employed part of Canada's population, the total combined paid and unpaid workload has been increasing since the early 1980s. But, contrary to popular belief, this *did not* result in less hours of free time, which declined between 1981 and 1986, but then remained relatively stable from 1986 to 1998. After 1986 the expansion of paid and unpaid work was accommodated not at the expense of leisure time but primarily by a reduction of almost half an hour per day in the time spent in personal needs and continuing education. In light of these findings, the interesting question is: how did the changes in time-use affect Canadians' psychological perception of time pressure?

*Table 7.2* Trends in time-use, Canada, 1981–98

|  | 1981 | 1986 | 1992 | 1998 |
|---|---|---|---|---|
| *Time-use, based on time-diariess* | *Minutes per day (Employed population, aged 20–64)* | | | |
| Paid and unpaid workload | 491 | 541 | 557 | 566 |
|   Paid work, including travel | 323 | 397 | 392 | 387 |
|   Travel to and from work | 34 | 33 | 31 | 33 |
|   Overtime/second job | – | 3 | 4 | 6 |
| Domestic work, family care, shopping | 167 | 142 | 165 | 179 |
| Study, continuing education | 13 | 8 | 5 | 5 |
| Personal needs (sleep, meals, personal care) | 601 | 592 | 576 | 566 |
| Voluntary organisations, religious activities | 11 | 9 | 12 | 10 |
| Free time (watching TV, social leisure, reading) | 325 | 283 | 291 | 293 |
| Physically active leisure (sports, outdoors) | 20 | 21 | 25 | 33 |
| Hobby | 12 | 7 | 7 | 6 |

Sources: GSS – see Table 7.1

Note: All data reported here are weighted, save data for 1981

## What makes people feel 'time crunched'?

Numerous polls conducted in the United States and other industrialised nations indicate that people reported higher levels of time pressure in the 1980s and 1990s than they did in previous decades. According to Robinson (1993), more US people responded that they were 'always rushed' in 1985 than in 1975 or 1965. Bond et al. (1998) reported that the proportion of Americans who felt that they 'never had enough time' to get everything done on the job rose from 40 per cent in 1977 to 60 per cent in 1997. Canadian General Social Survey data demonstrate that, in 1992, 45 per cent of the population aged 20 years or over felt more rushed than they did 'five years ago' (Zuzanek and Smale 1997). These and similar findings have attracted researchers' attention to the relationship between *subjective* perceptions of time pressure ('time crunch') and trends in the *actual* use of time. Some researchers have begun to ask whether the apparent increases in feelings of time pressure were due to longer hours of paid and unpaid work or were driven by the general speeding-up of life in a media and computer-dominated world. The answers to these questions have varied.

For Schor (1991: 8), overwork and the feelings of time pressure that plague many Americans 'spring from a combination of full-time male jobs, the expansion of housework to fill the available hours, and the growth of employment among married women'. The consumerist treadmill and long-hour jobs form, according to Schor, an insidious cycle of *work and spend*. For Robinson and Godbey (1997: 25) the heightened sense of time pressure is not necessarily grounded in an actual lack of free time, but rather it is a psychological response to the general 'speeding up' of modern life. They suggest that we have become victims of our exceedingly high aspirations and that the problem of 'time famine' is, in most instances, 'a perceptual problem'. Bertman (1998) observes:

> Driven by the momentum of technologies operating at the speed of the light, our social speedometer has continued to climb. Like the crew of the Starship Enterprise, 'boldly going where no man has gone before', we are now nearing the velocity called 'warp speed'.
>
> (Bertman 1998: 3)

Time crunch has also been associated with a greater 'fragmentation' of time in modern societies: rapid change-over from one activity to another, according to Peters and Raaijmakers (1998: 426), adds significantly to the feeling of time crunch.

An alternative explanation suggests that growing publicity given to the issue of time pressure may reflect the specific life cycle and professional circumstances of the reporters and commentators who have made time crunch an issue for pubic debate. According to Gershuny (2000: 74), 'the vehemence and wide visibility of the current "running-out-of-time" argument may relate to the specific life-circumstances of the writers on this subject and perhaps to some degree to their readers'. Implicit in Gershuny's observation is yet another concern, namely that respondents' greater willingness to report high levels of time pressure is a result of an 'echo-chamber effect'. In an environment where misrepresented research findings are cited repeatedly, they 'start to carry the weight of unquestioned truth' (Loftus et al. 1995).

In an attempt to resolve this controversy we turn to the survey evidence and focus on three interrelated issues:

- the relationship between the hours of work and perceived experience of time pressure
- the incidence of perceived time pressure across population groups
- other factors contributing to higher levels of time pressure.

These issues are now discussed in turn.

### Heavier workloads – higher levels of time pressure!

Analyses of Canadian data show that there is an apparent relationship between respondents' *hours of paid work* and their levels of *perceived time pressure*. In 1998 some 88 per cent of respondents working over 50 hours per week reported feeling rushed on an almost daily basis. For respondents working under 30 hours per week this figure was only 53 per cent. As shown in Table 7.3, the 'composite index of time pressure' for employees working under 30 hours per week is 45 points on a 100-point scale, but for employees working 40 to 50 hours it is 61 points, and for employees working in excess of 50 hours it is 65 points.

It has been suggested, for example by Greenhaus and Parasuraman (1987), that the effects of paid and unpaid work on time pressure and stress should not be examined separately but jointly. According to Joner and Fletcher (1993), research on the interface between work and family suggests that these two domains are functionally interdependent and the events in one sphere impinge on the other. Not surprisingly, the association between respondents' *combined paid and unpaid workloads* and *perceived time pressure* is positive. As shown in Table 7.3, 89 per cent of those with combined workloads in excess of 12 hours per day reported feeling 'rushed' almost daily compared with only 52 per cent of those with combined workloads of fewer than 8 hours per day. The relationship between amount of *free time* and sense of being pressed for time is, as expected, inverse to the relationship between time crunch and the amount of work. Only half of respondents reporting more than 7 hours of free time per day felt rushed on an almost daily basis, compared to 85 per cent of respondents with fewer than 3 hours.

*Table 7.3* Feelings of time pressure by gender and workload, Canada, 1998

| | Time pressure index* (1–100) Mean scores | % rushed daily or few times a week |
|---|---|---|
| Total population | 52.2 | 66.6 |
| Men | 51.1 | 64.9 |
| Women | 53.2 | 68.3 |
| Estimated weekly hours of paid work | | |
| 0 to 30 hours | 44.8 | 53.3 |
| 30.1 to 40 hours | 58.8 | 79.7 |
| 40.1 to 50 hours | 61.1 | 81.5 |
| 50.1 hours or more | 65.5 | 88.3 |
| Combined load of paid and unpaid work per day | | |
| 8 hours or less | 45.1 | 51.9 |
| 8.1 to 10 hours | 55.8 | 73.6 |
| 10.1 to 12 hours | 56.7 | 78.3 |
| 12.1 hours or more | 63.8 | 88.7 |
| Amounts of free time per day (including travel) | | |
| 3 hours or less | 61.3 | 84.7 |
| 3.01–5 hrs | 55.5 | 73.8 |
| 5.01–7 hrs | 50.5 | 65.2 |
| 7.01–9 hrs | 46.5 | 54.6 |
| 9.01 hours or more | 43.8 | 48.3 |

Source: GSS – see Table 7.1

* A 12-item measure based on questions that asked respondents, among other things: how rushed they felt compared to five years ago; how often they felt rushed at the time of the survey; whether they worried about not spending enough time with family and friends; if they felt stressed because of lack of time; and whether they did not have time for fun anymore (range = 0–100; Alpha = 0.76)

In general, analyses of the relationships between time pressure and participation in daily activities do not support the proposition that non-working activities, in particular leisure, contribute substantially to the feelings of time pressure. Even leisure activities most susceptible to time pressure, such as social and physically active pursuits, were not accompanied by feelings of 'time crunch' as much as paid or unpaid work activities. In sum, feelings of time pressure seem to be rooted primarily in *contracted* and *committed* rather than *discretionary* time, that is in paid work, family obligations and, possibly, voluntary work.[1]

### Time pressure and different social groups

Another interesting question with regard to time pressure is whether the rising levels of 'time crunch' affect the entire population equally or are more pronounced in specific occupational and life cycle groups. As shown in Table 7.4, during the 1990s, feelings of 'time crunch' rose faster among Canada's middle-aged, employed and parental population than among the non-employed and non-parental population. And levels of time pressure increased more steeply for employees working in excess of 40 and 50 hours per week than for employees working fewer than 30 hours. Time-use data suggest that modern societies may be becoming increasingly polarised along time-pressure lines, with some groups exposed to considerably higher levels of time pressure than others.

This trend has been observed by a number of authors (e.g. Hinrichs et al. 1991; Gershuny 2000). According to Tremblay and Villeneuve (1998), the seeming stabilisation of the average length of the work week in Canada and in the United States during the 1980s and 1990s masks a profound transformation in the distribution of working hours. The proportions of employees working short hours (under 30 hours per week), and long hours (in excess of 50 hours per week), have increased at the expense of employees working 30 to 40 hours. A similar trend has been found in the Netherlands by Knulst and van den Broek (1998) and in France by Dumontier and Pan Ke Shon (1999).

*Table 7.4* Changes in perceived time pressure between 1992 and 1998

| | Time pressure index (1–100) | | |
| --- | --- | --- | --- |
| | *1992* | *1998* | *% change* |
| *Total population* | 49.8 | 52.2 | 4.8 |
| Men | 48.6 | 51.1 | 5.1 |
| Women | 50.9 | 53.2 | 4.5 |
| *Life cycle group* | | | |
| Student, single, 18–24 years old | 57.2 | 59.4 | 3.8 |
| Single, unemployed, 18–34 years | 45.5 | 48.0 | 5.5 |
| Single, employed, 18–34 years | 55.3 | 59.7 | 8 |
| Married, employed, 25–44 years, no children | 55.9 | 60.4 | 8.1 |
| Married, employed, 25–44 years, child =<11 | 59.6 | 66.1 | 10.9 |
| Married, homemaker, 25–44 years, child =<11 | 55.8 | 60.8 | 9 |
| Divorced/separated, 25–44 years | 64.4 | 68.8 | 6.8 |
| Married, employed, 45–64 years, child <25 | 56.5 | 58.2 | 3 |
| Married, employed, 45–64 years, empty nest | 50.4 | 53.4 | 5.9 |
| Retired/housekeeping, 65+ years | 29.6 | 31.9 | 7.7 |
| *Estimated paid workload (hrs/wk)* | | | |
| 0 to 30 hours | 51.1 | 53.3 | 4.3 |
| 30.1 to 40 hours | 54.9 | 58.8 | 7.1 |
| 40.1 to 50 hours | 55.9 | 61.1 | 9.3 |
| 50.1 hours or more | 60.7 | 65.5 | 7.9 |

Source: GSS – see Table 7.1

*Choice and control over time*

Although feelings of time pressure have increased particularly for employees working long hours, the Canadian data show that, between 1992 and 1998, virtually *all groups* of Canada's population experienced increases in perceived time pressure, the proportion who reported feeling rushed every day or a few times a week growing from 64 per cent to 67 per cent between 1992 and 1998.

Factors *other* than the length of paid and unpaid work may, however, be at the root of feelings of time pressure, including the amount of choice and interest people have in what they are doing; their level of control over time and the activity they engage in; and the extent to which their time is fragmented by frequent 'switch-overs' from one activity to another. As Table 7.5 shows, feelings of time pressure among employed respondents are affected more strongly by the lack of discretion over one's job and a sense of low level of control over one's life than by the length of paid working hours. The length of paid and unpaid working hours is thus an important, but not the sole, determinant of subjectively felt time pressure. Lack of choice, interest, and control over working and non-working time, and a rapid change-over of activities contribute significantly to elevated levels of time crunch.

## Work overload, time pressure and emotional well-being

Relatively few authors have addressed the question of how work overload and feelings of time pressure affect *emotional well-being* (Robinson and Godbey 1997; Barnett 1998; Lehto 1998). Table 7.6 presents correlation coefficients between measures of emotional well-being (job satisfaction, life satisfaction, etc.) and working hours and feelings of time pressure. The results suggest that longer hours of paid work, while negatively associated with work–family balance and leisure, are, paradoxically, positively associated

*Table 7.5* Relationships between feelings of time pressure, paid workload and psychological state, Canada, 1994

|  | Feeling of time pressure (taking on too many things – 1–6) | |
|  | Pearson 'r' | Beta |
| --- | --- | --- |
| Estimated hours of paid work | 0.07 | 0.08 |
| Decision latitude at work | -0.13 | -0.14 |
| Mastery | -0.09 | -0.13 |

Source: NPHS – see Table 7.1

Notes:
Controlled for respondent's age, gender, and education.
Composite measure based on skill requirements and the amount of decision-making freedom at work.
Controlled for respondent's age, gender, education and the day of the week (workday).

with job satisfaction, although the relationship is weak (r = 0.04 (GSS) and 0.06 (NPHS))[2]. This relationship may seem surprising at first, but it has been observed by other researchers, including Barnett (1998). Subjective feelings of time pressure, on the other hand, are negatively associated with *all* aspects of emotional well-being.

Additional analyses (not reported in the tables) suggest that a positive relationship between the length of paid work time and job satisfaction is stronger for employees in white-collar, management and professional positions than for those in blue-collar occupations. Managers and professionals, who typically work long hours, usually like their jobs and report high levels of job satisfaction. Not surprisingly, in the 1988–9 Experience Sampling Method survey, which focused on white collar and management personnel, the correlation between respondents' paid working hours and job satisfaction was strongly positive (r = 0.43).

It is clear that work overload and feelings of time crunch are negatively associated with respondents' emotional well-being, in particular satisfaction with the balance of work–family life and the use of non-working time. The difference between the effects of long hours of paid work and subjective sense of time pressure on job satisfaction is due to the dissimilarity of the two concepts. People can work long hours without feeling 'time crunched' if they have freely chosen their work and are interested in it. People working shorter hours, on the contrary, may feel time-stressed if they are not interested in what they are doing and have little control over their work. Consequently, the presence or absence of feelings of 'time crunch' emerges from our analyses as a better predictor of respondents' emotional well-being than the length of paid working hours.

*Table 7.6* Relationships between workload, perceived time pressure and well-being, Canada, employed population, 1994, 1998

| Source | | Estimated weekly hours of paid work | Feelings of time pressure[a] |
|---|---|---|---|
| | | Pearson 'r' | |
| GSS 1998 | Job satisfaction | 0.04 | -0.2 |
| | Life satisfaction | Ns | -0.28 |
| | Satisfaction with work–family balance | -0.17 | -0.38 |
| | Satisfaction with the use of non-working time | -0.07 | -0.37 |
| | Perceived stress | 0.11 | 0.49 |
| NPHS 1994 | Job satisfaction | 0.06 | -0.05 |
| | Feeling happy | -0.01 | -0.05 |

Sources: GSS and NPHS – see Table 7.1

Note: [a] GSS = Composite index (1–100) NPHS = Taking on too many things

## Time pressure and psychological stress

Another issue that attracts the attention of researchers and policy-makers is the relationship between work overload, time pressure and psychological stress (Karasek and Theorell 1990; Lehto 1998). As indicated earlier, analyses of this relationship may be complicated by the fact that stress is often conceptualised by researchers differently. For the purposes of this analysis the focus is on self-assessed or *psychological stress* rather than the more traditional measurement of stress involving a summation of objective 'stressors', such as work overload, family conflicts, and financial and health problems.

Analyses of the 1998 GSS data show a robust correlation of 0.49 between the subjective sense of time pressure and psychological stress, as shown in Table 7.7. This association remains significant and substantial even when hierarchical regression procedures are used to control for respondents' employment status, age, gender, education and spouse's weekly hours of paid work (beta = 0.51).[3]

Similarly to time pressure, for most respondents psychological stress is associated with paid work and to a lesser extent with family or financial concerns. According to the 1998 GSS data presented in Table 7.7, 43 per cent of respondents identified paid work as the main source of psychological stress – more than twice as many as mentioned family concerns (19 per cent); financial concerns were mentioned by 12 per cent of respondents and 'general concerns' by just 5 per cent. Among employees working 50 hours or more, over 75 per cent listed work as the major source of psychological stress, but for those working 8 to 35 hours per week this figure was halved to 39 per cent.

It goes without saying that, due to the very design of the survey instruments, respondents impute their own interpretations onto the concepts of *time pressure* and *psychological stress*. There are, however, certain similarities between these two notions. Both refer to excessive demands on human

*Table 7.7* Sources of stress, Canada, 1998

|  | Work | Family | Finances | General concerns |
|---|---|---|---|---|
|  | % | % | % | % |
| Total population | 43.3 | 19.0 | 12.1 | 4.7 |
| Men | 55.1 | 10.6 | 13.3 | 3.7 |
| Women | 34.8 | 25.1 | 11.2 | 5.4 |
| Employed population | 63.0 | 12.7 | 11.4 | 4.3 |
| Estimated paid workload |  |  |  |  |
| 8–35 hrs/wk | 39.1 | 18.6 | 13.5 | 5.4 |
| 35.1–40 hrs/wk | 59.6 | 13.2 | 12.4 | 4.1 |
| 40.1–50 hrs/wk | 69.1 | 10.2 | 9.2 | 5.1 |
| 50.1 hrs/wk | 75.4 | 7.8 | 8.5 | 3.4 |

Source: GSS – see Table 7.1

resources. Perceived time pressure results from excessive demands on time, while psychological stress is born out of excessive demands on human capacity to deal with the physical and emotional challenges of work and life in general. Time pressure appears as the more situational of the two concepts. Feelings of time pressure are, to a degree, a reflection of circumstances outside of the respondent's control, such as long hours of paid work, limited choice and control over job tasks and fragmentation of time due to conflicting demands of paid work and family obligations. Psychological stress, on the other hand, implicitly includes an admission of the insufficiency of an individual's personal psychological resources to deal with these outside pressures. Consequently, psychological stress seems to carry stronger negative connotations with regard to respondents' mental health (see pp. 135). Perceived time pressure may 'feed' feelings of stress, but psychological stress affects human mental and emotional defences more directly and decisively.

## Work overload, time pressure, stress and health

Public concerns with the rising levels of time pressure have been fuelled, from the very beginning, by an awareness of the potential links between time pressure, psychological stress and *mental* and *physical health*. Researchers have pointed out that time pressure resulting from work overload and multiple role conflicts contributes to higher levels of stress and that continuous exposure to stress, in turn, contributes to mental health disorders, cardiovascular deficiencies and other health problems.

The *policy relevance* of the 'time crunch–stress–health' link has been recognised in a number of policy and research documents prepared by, and for, the Canadian government. A report on public policy research summarises concerns with regard to time as follows:

> Little is known about the implications of time crunch on the short-term and long-term well-being of individuals and society. Time pressure can be expected to have not only an immediate impact on productivity and absenteeism at work for time-pressed workers, but is also likely to have longer-term effects on the *health* of individuals and to influence their decisions to have children and how these children are raised.
>
> (Policy Research Initiative 1996)

In an often-quoted study on Type A behaviour, Friedman and Rosenman (1974) concluded that elevated competitiveness, a sense of time urgency, aggressiveness and self-imposed stress, typical of Type A personalities, expose individuals to a heightened risk of cardiovascular disease. A follow-up study showed that Type A men were twice as likely to have clinical coronary heart disease and twice as likely to die from heart attacks as were the less competitive and stressed Type B respondents (Rosenman and Friedman

1983). Similarly, in a case-controlled study, Alfredsson et al. (1982) reported that individuals in occupations characterised by a hectic work tempo and low level of control over work had an increased risk of myocardial infarction.

A 1997 Finnish Quality of Working Life Survey showed that 69 per cent of employees reporting *high* levels of time pressure frequently experienced fatigue, 50 per cent complained of exhaustion, 45 per cent had sleeping problems and 19 per cent felt depressed (Lehto 1998). Analyses of Canadian and Dutch time-use data also found that feelings of time pressure contribute to insomnia and lower levels of self-assessed health (Zuzanek and Beckers 1998). According to Cooper and Cartwright (1994), in the United Kingdom almost half of all premature deaths can be attributed to lifestyle and stress-related illnesses, and the American Institute of Stress identified stress as a contributing factor in 75 to 90 per cent of all illnesses. Robinson and Godbey (1997) report that people who feel rushed rate their health lower than those who do not. The stress that accompanies 'sped-up' styles of life, the authors continue, is a major cause of early death. In Japan, similar concerns have resulted in a public debate over the phenomenon of 'karoshi', which is translated as 'sudden death from overwork' (Nishiyama and Johnson 1997).

There are sceptics, however, who dispute the effects of time pressure on health and specifically on cardiovascular diseases. Gleick (1999) contends that three decades of attention from cardiologists and psychologists have failed to produce any 'carefully specified and measurable set of character traits that predict heart disease,' or to demonstrate that people who change their Type A behaviour will actually lower their risk of heart disease. 'If the Type "A" phenomenon made for poor medical research,' Gleick continues, 'it stands nonetheless as a triumph of social criticism' (Gleick 1999: 17–20).

Can time-use and population health surveys shed new light on these disputed issues? The answer to this question is a qualified one. To date, few time-use surveys have been used to examine relationships between time pressure, stress and health in any detail. National population health surveys are rich in health-related information, but usually short on questions dealing with time-use and time pressure. To complicate the situation, the effects of time pressure and stress on health are often indirect, and a paucity of longitudinal studies makes it difficult to establish the direction of causality between time pressure, work overload, stress and physical health.

Given these limitations, the analyses below are focused on a few questions that may contribute to a better understanding of the key links and components in the complex 'time pressure–stress–health' relationship. The questions addressed are:

- How do work overload and time pressure affect health?
- What are the effects of psychological stress on mental and physical health?

- What factors can counter the negative effects of work overload and psychological stress on health?

### Relationships between work overload, time pressure and health

The analyses summarised in Table 7.8 indicate that the relationships between hours of paid work and health, although weak, are positive rather than negative. Heavier paid workloads appear to be associated with above average levels of self-assessed mental health and fewer sleeping problems rather than the other way around. These relationships are confirmed by multivariate analyses controlling for respondents' employment status, age, gender, and education.

The positive association between the length of the working hours and health should not be interpreted, however, as an indication that longer hours of paid work contribute to better health. The direction of causality in this instance is, most likely, the opposite. Put simply, healthier people are more willing and likely to work longer hours.

*Perceived* time pressure, on the other hand, clearly has an overall negative effect on respondents' physical and, particularly, mental health.

*Table 7.8* Relationships between workload, time crunch, stress and health, Canada, 1994, 1998

|  |  | Paid workload | Feelings of time pressure | Stress |
|---|---|---|---|---|
| Source |  |  | Pearson 'r' |  |
|  |  | Paid work on the diary time (min) | Composite index (1–100) | Psychological stress (1–5) |
| GSS 1998 | Self-assessed health (1-5) | 0.04 | -0.13 | -0.13 |
|  | Satisfaction with health | 0.03 | -0.2 | -0.21 |
|  | Sleeping problems | -0.14 | 0.19 | 0.17 |
|  |  | Estimated weekly hours of paid work | Taking on too many things | Chronic stress |
| NPHS 1994 | Physical health conditions | 0.02 | -0.09 | -0.18 |
|  | Self-assessed health | 0.06 | -0.07 | -0.22 |
|  | Mental health | 0.08 | -0.15 | -0.4 |
|  | Use of anti-depressant drugs | -0.03 | 0.06 | 0.13 |

Sources: GSS and NHPS – see Table 7.1

In general, the effects of *work overload* and *perceived time pressure* on health resemble the effects of these two dimensions of time squeeze on respondents' emotional well-being, as discussed above. Longer hours of paid work are associated with above average levels of health, while a subjective sense of time pressure affects health outcomes negatively. The effects of prolonged hours of work seem to 'kick in' and begin to affect respondents' health only when 'internalised' as acute feelings of time pressure.

### Relationship between psychological stress and health

The data presented in Table 7.8 suggest that psychological stress has a direct *negative* effect on respondents' health. Correlations between perceived psychological stress and self-assessed health, satisfaction with health and sleeping problems are -0.13, -0.21 and 0.17 respectively. When controlled for age, education, and gender, the respective betas are -0.22, -0.16 and 0.18.

According to the 1994 NPHS study, which uses a different definition of stress than the GSS or NHIS, chronic stress has a strong negative impact on human health, with the correlation between the two being -0.40, as shown in Table 7.8. For self-assessed health the correlation is -0.22, for major physical health conditions -0.18, and for the use of anti-depressant drugs 0.13 (Table 7.9). These relationships are confirmed by multivariate analyses that control for employment status, gender, age and education, where the respective betas are -0.41, -0.23, -0.20 and 0.18.

As indicated earlier, the effects of work overload on health are often indirect. Work overload begins to impinge upon respondents' health only when prolonged hours of paid and unpaid work result in psychologically acute feelings of time famine, time deficiency, or time crunch. These feelings, in turn, contribute to emotional strains and psychological stress that subsequently impact on mental and possibly physical health.

## Countering the effects of time pressure and stress on health

The final question to be addressed in this chapter concerns measures that might alleviate the negative effects of time pressure and stress on health. If perceived time pressure and stress have negative effects on health, as most survey evidence seems to suggest, what are the remedies available to reduce the magnitude of such impacts? Some of the possible countervailing measures mentioned in the literature include: organisational restructuring of the workplace (greater decision latitude and skill requirements); greater social support at and outside of work; development or strengthening of desirable personality dispositions (mastery, self-esteem, hardiness); and time-management competency and participation in leisure activities, particularly in physically active leisure (Lazarus and Folkman 1984; Kobasa et al. 1985;

Wethington and Kessler 1986; Karasek and Theorell 1990; Coleman and Iso-Ahola 1993; Spector and O'Connell 1994).

Analyses of GSS data shown in Table 7.9 indicate that participation in sporting activities is positively associated with self-assessed health (r = 0.13). The beta for this relationship when employment status, age, gender and education are controlled for, is 0.13. In the Canadian NPHS study, the correlation between a composite measure of physically active leisure and self-assessed health is 0.13 (beta = 0.13) for the employed population. Analyses of the US NHIS data show an almost identical relationship.

The effects of physically active leisure on *mental health* are less clear. According to the NPHS data, the association between participation in physically active leisure and mental health (lack of distress and depression) is *weak* (r = -0.02; beta 0.04).

The findings about the ability of sporting and outdoor activities to reduce the negative effects of time pressure and stress on health are also inconclusive. The GSS and NPHS data indicate that participation in physically active leisure has little effect on stress (the respective 'r' values are -0.03 and 0.00), while US NHIS data suggest that participation in sporting and outdoor activities may be associated with *higher* rather than *lower* levels of psychological stress (r = 0.05). Nor is there sufficient support for the proposition that leisure participation 'buffers' negative effects of stress on health (Coleman and Iso-Ahola 1993). Physically active leisure does not seem to carry stronger

*Table 7.9* Relationships between participation in physically active leisure, personality dispositions, time competency and health, Canada, USA, 1990–8

| Source | Measures of physically active leisure, personality dispositions, time competency | Self-assessed health (1–5) | Mental health | Stress[a] |
|--------|---------------------------------------------------------------------------------|---------------|---------------|--------|
| | | Pearson 'r' (Employed population) | | |
| GSS 1998 (Canada) | Composite index of physically active leisure | 0.13 | | -0.03 |
| | Sense of belonging to the community | 0.16 | | -0.05 |
| NHIS 1990 (USA) | Composite index of physically active leisure | 0.16 | | 0.05 |
| NPHS 1994 (Canada) | Composite index of physically active leisure | 0.13 | -0.02 | ns |
| | Mastery | 0.23 | 0.36 | -0.33 |
| | Self-esteem | 0.24 | 0.3 | -0.17 |
| | Social support | 0.08 | 0.18 | -0.18 |

Sources: GSS, NPHIS, NPHS, see Table 7.1

Note: [a] GSS/NPHIS: psychological stress, GSS: chronic stress beneficial health effects for people under stress than for those who are not stressed (see also Iwasaki and Mannell 2000).

In general, the survey evidence provides support for the proposition that physically active leisure contributes to better physical health, but lends little support to the stress-reducing capacity of leisure. The assessment of the impact of leisure participation on mental health requires additional attention.

The survey evidence, however, does lend solid support to the proposition that positive psychological dispositions, such as mastery (perceived control of one's life), self-esteem and social support, have positive effects on both mental and physical health and, in some instances, effectively 'buffer' the health-damaging effects of stress. The correlation between mastery and self-assessed health in the 1994 NPHS is 0.23, and between self-assessed health and self-esteem 0.24. The association between mental health and dispositions of mastery, self-esteem and social support is even stronger. These relationships remain significant in multivariate analyses, when controlled for employment status, age, gender and education.

The positive impact of an improved organisational environment at work on physical and mental health has found only limited support in our analyses, but this may be due to the relative paucity of work-related information in most surveys.

The relationships between leisure participation, personality dispositions, social support, and health are complex. Direct and indirect influences often point in different directions. For example, longer hours of watching television are associated with lower ratings of self-assessed health (negative effect), as well as lower levels of psychological stress (beneficial effect). The impact of sporting activities on health and stress is, however, different. Higher levels of sporting activity contribute to higher levels of both physical health and stress. The important question is, how much of the positive effect is offset by the negative one, or to put it differently, what is the *balance sheet* of the conflicting effects?

A balanced lifestyle is in many regards the key to moderating the stress–health relationships. Unfortunately the concept of *lifestyle balance* is poorly conceptualised in the research literature and the available methodological tools for its study are inadequate. In summary, the survey evidence about the negative effects of time crunch and psychological stress on health is compelling. We appear to be at a loss, however, on how to effectively cope with this challenge. Concerns with the ways to counter the negative effects of time pressure and stress on health require more research attention.

## Conclusion

The analyses reported in this chapter demonstrate that subjective feelings of time pressure are primarily embedded in heavy loads of paid and unpaid work and, to a lesser extent, are associated with the 'speeding-up' of non-work activities, such as voluntary work or social leisure. Survey evidence further shows that work overload and a subjective sense of time pressure contribute to feelings of emotional deficiency and stress and that these, in turn, negatively affect mental and physical health. In short, high levels of perceived 'time crunch' are psychologically and behaviourally consequential, and should not be dismissed as simple 'echo-chamber' phenomena. It should not be surprising, for example, that 90 per cent of the women surveyed in a 1992 US Gallup poll said that the costs of combining work and motherhood are too high (quoted in Noor 1994).

The effects of time pressure and psychological stress on health are often indirect and incremental. There is considerable anecdotal evidence that marital conflicts and family dissolution frequently start with arguments about shared time responsibilities. Once put into motion, these conflicts carry with them significant negative implications for spousal and children's emotional life and mental health (Spitze and South 1985; Presser 2000). In the long run, emotional strains born out of time crunch can, similar to the proverbial straw that breaks the camel's back, severely impair human health.

Much of current research literature focuses on *individual coping strategies* in dealing with the effects of time pressure and psychological stress on health. The development of positive personality dispositions, greater access to social support, improved time-management competency and participation in active leisure have all been shown to contribute positively to physical or mental health, or both. The above analyses suggest, however, that the effectiveness of these strategies may vary for different population groups. Participation in physically active leisure can, surprisingly, have fewer beneficial effects for people who are pressed for time and psychologically stressed than for those who are not (see Zuzanek et al. 1998). For the 'overworked' the preferred remedy may lie not in leisure participation but in gaining greater control over time and life and in strengthening personality dispositions such as mastery and self-esteem.

There is growing awareness among researchers and policy-makers that individual coping strategies and lifestyle modifications alone are not sufficient to offset the negative impacts of time pressure and psychological stress on health. Most pressures faced by people in modern societies are social or *structural*. They are embedded in the competitive demands of globalised economies, changing workplace environments, value orientations emphasising rapid material gains and conformity with standardised and fast forms of expression prevalent in popular culture. As mentioned in an earlier article (Zuzanek et al. 1998), in today's society, practising 'yoga' is paradoxically a *symptom* rather than a *remedy* for stress.

It is clear that improvements in human health are predicated not only on individual coping or medical advances, but also upon improved socio-economic conditions. As suggested by Frank (1995: 162), the major determinants of human health status, particularly in countries at an advanced stage of socio-economic development are not medical care inputs and utilisation, but cultural, social, and economic factors.

Traditional economic solutions to the improvement of social conditions have, however, often relied on strategies that are laden with time and psychological strains, and that have contributed to the 'polarisation' of societies along time pressure lines. Bennett Berger (1963: 27), in an article published in the 1960s, argued that we are all victims of a compromised attempt to bridge the 'leisure' ideals of Ancient Greece and those of the Protestant work ethic. The situation today is no different. The desired equilibrium of *economic* and *time prosperity* appears to be no closer now than it was before (see Garhammer 1998). We long for the comforts of the *Gemeinschaft*-like relationships without abrogating the material and cultural aspirations typical of a *Gesellschaft*-type mass society.[4] We may have blurred traditional class lines between the 'haves' and 'have-nots' at the 'lower-to-middle' end of the social continuum, but we have created new 'have' and 'have-not' divides with regard to time that are fraught with tensions.

The relationships between stress, health and lifestyles need to be addressed from a broader social as well as *cultural* perspective (Marmot 1981; Wilkinson 1986; Evans et al. 1994). If, at the individual level, a balanced lifestyle is the key to countering the negative effects of time pressure and psychological stress on health, then at the societal level the key notions for changing the stress–health imbalance are a socially functional *division of labour* and a culturally sustainable *rhythm of collective life*. Durkheim (1912), Halbwachs (1925), Lynd and Lynd (1929; 1937), Sorokin (1943), Luhmann (1982) and Zerubavel (1985) all discussed extensively the role of the social division of labour and collective rhythms of life, such as calendar time, work schedules and rites of passage, in serving economic needs as well as the needs of social solidarity and spiritual and cultural development.

The fragmentation of time that was identified in the above analyses as one of the main sources of time pressure is socially imposed and culturally sanctioned in today's society, but it is neither an inevitability nor a cultural imperative. The solutions to the problems of 'social arrhythmia' addressed in this chapter are not entirely out of humanity's reach. After all, as suggested by Frank (1995: 163), many propositions advanced by researchers, such as reduction of work overload, securing of time for relaxation, greater control over one's time or increased social support, coincide with the conventional wisdom and desires of lay culture. Technological and economic progress should and *need not* clash with the goals of social solidarity, cohesion, and human development. Let us hope that the desired lifestyle equilibrium will occur not by default as a result of mounting conflicts, but rather by design, as a result of a gradual change in social policies and cultural values.

## Acknowledgements

The author would like to thank Dr Roger Mannell and Lisa Wenger for their assistance in preparing this chapter and the Canadian Institute for Health Information for supporting the analysis of data that form part of this chapter.

## Notes

1 For a discussion of the concept of contracted and committed time see Robinson and Godbey (1997: 11).
2 All correlations reported in this chapter are significant at the 0.05 level, unless otherwise stated.
3 Betas reported in this chapter are controlled for respondents' employment status, age, gender and education, unless otherwise stated.
4 Terms of *Gemeinschaft* (community) and *Gesellschaft* (society) were used by Ferdinand Toennies (1855–1936) to contrast a genuine form of living together surviving in rural areas with superficial and mechanical relationships typical of modern urban and industrial settings. See Toennies (1963 [1887]).

## References and further reading

Alfredsson, L., Karasek, R. A. and Theorell, T. (1982) Myocardial infarction risk and psychosocial work environment: an analysis of the male Swedish working force. *Social Science Medicine* 16(2): 463–7.
Barnett, R. C. (1998) Toward a review and reconceptualization of the work/family literature. *Genetic, Social, and General Psychology Monographs* 124(2): 125–82.
Berger, B. M. (1963) The sociology of leisure. In E. O. Smigel (ed.) *Work and Leisure: A Contemporary Social Problem*. New Haven, CT: College and University Press.
Bertman, S. (1998) *Hyperculture: The Human Cost of Speed*. Westport, CT: Praeger.
Bond, J. T., Galinsky, E. and Swanberg, J. E. (1998) *The 1997 National Study of the Changing Workforce*. New York: Families and Work Institute.
Coleman, D. and Iso-Ahola, S. E. (1993) Leisure and health: the role of social support and self-determination. *Journal of Leisure Research* 25(2): 111–28.
Cooper, C. L. and Cartwright, S. (1994) Healthy mind, healthy organization: a proactive approach to occupational stress. *Human Relations* 47(4): 455–71.
Coverman, S. (1989) Role overload, role conflict, and stress: addressing consequences of multiple role demands. *Social Forces* 67(4): 965–82.
Dumazedier, J. (1967) *Toward a Society of Leisure*. New York: Free Press.
Dumazedier, J. (1975) Introduction. *Society and Leisure* 7(1): 7–19.
Dumontier, F. and Pan Ke Shon, J-L. (1999) Thirteen years later: less constrained time, more free time. *INSEE Premiere* 675: 1–5.
Durkheim, E. (1954 [1912]) *The Elementary Forms of Religious Life*. New York: Free Press.
Evans, R. G., Barer, M. L. and Marmor, T. R. (1994) *Why are Some People Healthy and Others Not? The Determinants of Health of Populations*. New York: Aldine de Gruyter.
Fourastié, J. (1965) *Les 40000 Heures*. Paris: Robert Laffont.

Frank, J. W. (1995) Why 'Population Health'? *Canadian Journal of Public Health* 86(3): 162–4.

Friedman, M. and Rosenman, R. H. (1974) *Type A Behavior and your Heart.* New York: Alfred A. Knopf.

Garhammer, M. (1998) Time pressure in modern Germany. *Society and Leisure* 21(2): 327–52.

Gershuny, J. (2000) *Changing Times.* New York: Oxford University Press.

Gleick, J. (1999) *Faster: The Acceleration of Just about Everything.* New York: Pantheon.

Greenhaus, J. H. and Parasuraman, S. (1987) A work–nonwork interactive perspective of stress and its consequences. *Journal of Organizational Behavior Management* 8: 37–60.

Halbwachs, M. (1925) *Les Cadres sociaux de la memoire.* Paris: Albin Michel.

Hinrichs, K., Roche, W. and Sirianni, C. (eds) (1991) *Working Time in Transition.* Philadelphia, PA: Temple University Press

Hochschild, A. R. (1997) *The Time Bind.* New York: Metropolitan.

Iwasaki, Y. and Mannell, R. C. (2000) The effects of leisure beliefs and coping strategies on stress–health relationships: a field study. *Leisure/Loisir* 24(1–2): 3–57.

Joner, F. and Fletcher, B. (1993) An empirical study of occupational stress items to survey respondents. *Journal of Applied Psychology.* 77(5): 623–8.

Karasek, R. and Theorell, T. (1990) *Healthy Work: Stress, Productivity and the Reconstruction of Working Life.* New York: Basic Books.

Keynes, J. M. (1972 [1931]) Economic possibilities for our grandchildren. In *The Collected Writings of John Maynard Keynes, Volume 9: Essays in Persuasion.* London: Macmillan.

Knulst, W. and van den Broek, A. (1998) Do time-use surveys succeed in measuring 'busyness'? Some observations of the Dutch case. *Society and Leisure* 21(2): 563–72.

Kobasa, S. C., Maddi, S. R., Pucetti, M. C. and Zola, M. A. (1985) Effectiveness of hardiness, exercise and social support as resources against illness. *Journal of Psychosomatic Research* 29(2): 525–33.

Kraus, R. (1971) *Recreation and Leisure in Modern Society.* New York: Appleton-Century-Crofts.

Lazarus, R. S. and Folkman, S. (1984) *Stress, Coping and Appraisal.* New York: Springer.

Lehto, A-M. (1998) Time pressure as a stress factor. *Society and Leisure* 21(2): 491–512.

Linder, S. B. (1970) *The Harried Leisure Class.* New York: Columbia University Press.

Loftus, E. F., Milo, E. M. and Paddock, J. R. (1995) The accidental executioner: why psychotherapy must be informed by science. *Counseling Psychologist* 23(1): 300–9.

Luhmann, N. (1982) *The Differentiation of Society.* New York: Columbia University Press.

Lundberg, G. A., Komarovsky, M. and McInerny, M. A. (1934) *Leisure: A Suburban Study.* New York: Columbia University Press.

Lynd, R. S. and Lynd, H. M. (1929) *Middletown: A Study in Contemporary American Culture.* New York: Harcourt, Brace.

Lynd, R. S. and Lynd, H. M. (1937) *Middletown in Transition: A Study in Cultural Conflicts.* New York: Harcourt, Brace.

Marmot, M. G. (1981) Culture and illness: epidemiological evidence. In M. J. Christie and P. G. Mallet (eds) *Foundations of Psychosomatics*. Chichester: Wiley.

Maslach, C. (1982) *Burnout: The Cost of Caring*. New York: Prentice-Hall.

Nishiyama, K. and Johnson, J. V. (1997) Karoshi – death from overwork: occupational health consequences of Japanese production management. *International Journal of Health Services* 27(4): 625–41.

Noor, N. M. (1994) Children and well-being: a comparison of employed and non-employed women. *Work and Stress* 8(1): 36–46.

Peters, P. and Raaijmakers, S. (1998) Time crunch and the perception of control over time from a gendered perspective: the Dutch case. *Society and Leisure* 21(2): 417–34.

Policy Research Initiative (1996) *Growth, Human Development and Social Cohesion* (Draft Interim Report). Ottawa: Policy Research Initiative.

Presser, H. B. (2000) Nonstandard work schedules and marital instability. *Journal of Marriage and the Family* 62(1): 93–110.

Rifkin, J. (1987) *Time Wars: The Primary Conflict in Human History*. Toronto: Simon & Schuster.

Robinson, J. P. (1993) Your money or your time. *American Demographics* November: 22–6.

Robinson, J. P. and Godbey, G. (1997) *Time for Life: The Surprising Ways Americans Use their Time*. University Park, PA: Pennsylvania State University Press.

Rosenman, R. H. and Friedman, M. (1983) Relationship of Type A behavior pattern to coronary heart disease. In H. Selye (ed.) *Selye's Guide to Stress Research*, Volume 2. New York: Scientific and Academic Editions.

Russell, B. (1935) *In Praise of Idleness and Other Essays*. London: Allen & Unwin.

Schor, J. B. (1991) *The Overworked American: The Unexpected Decline of Leisure*. New York: Basic Books.

Sorokin, P. A. (1943) *Sociocultural Causality, Space, Time*. Durham, NC: Duke University Press.

Spector, P. E. and O'Connell, B. J. (1994) The contribution of personality traits, negative affectivity, locus of control and Type A to the subsequent reports of job stressors and job strains. *Journal of Occupational and Organizational Psychology* 67(1): 1–11.

Spitze, G. and South, S. (1985) Women's employment, time expenditure, and divorce. *Journal of Family Issues* 6(3): 307–29.

Toennies, F. (1963 [1887]) *Community and Society*. New York: Harper & Row.

Tremblay, D-G. and Villeneuve, D. (1998) De la réduction a la polarisation des temps de travail; des enjeux de société. *Society and Leisure* 21(2): 399–416.

Wethington, E. and Kessler, R. C. (1986) Perceived support, received support, and adjustment to stressful events. *Journal of Health and Social Behavior* 27(1): 78–89.

Wilensky, H. (1961) The uneven distribution of leisure: the impact of economic growth on free time. *Social Problems* 9(1): 32–6.

Wilkinson, R. G. (1986) Socio-economic differences in mortality: interpreting the data and their size and trends. In R. G. Wilkinson (ed.) *Class and Health*. London: Tavistock.

Zerubavel, E. (1985) *The Seven Day Circle: The History and Meaning of the Week*. New York: Free Press.

Zuzanek, J. and Beckers, T. (1998) Changing valuations of the perceived importance of leisure, family, and work in Canada and the Netherlands: a comparative and across-time analysis. In *Abstracts of the XIV World Congress of Sociology, Montreal*. Madrid: International Sociological Association.

Zuzanek, J. and Smale, B. J. A. (1997) More work – less leisure? Changing allocations of time in Canada, 1981–1992. *Society and Leisure* 20(1): 73–106.

Zuzanek, J., Robinson, J. P. and Iwasaki, Y. (1998) The relationships between stress, health, and physically active leisure as a function of life-cycle. *Leisure Sciences* 20(2): 253–75.

# Chapter 8

# Stress and working parents

*Barbara Schneider, Alisa M. Ainbinder and Mihaly Csikszentmihalyi*

## Parents and stress: an overview

Over the past few decades, the number of dual-earner families in the United States has increased substantially (Waite and Nielsen 2001). In 1949, the percentage of working parents with children under the age of 18 was 10 per cent; in the mid-1990s it was over 60 per cent (Bronfenbrenner 1996). When both parents are employed, it is assumed that there are likely to be emotional costs for the adults and the children (Hochschild 1997). One of the personal costs often associated with work for men and women is job stress, that is, role demands originating in the workplace that cause individuals to feel tense, anxious and lacking in self-esteem and confidence (Kahn 1980). Job-related stress, however, is only one type of stress that working couples experience. Balancing the demands of work and family, maintaining a healthy marriage, and providing adequate care for one's children are just a few of the many demands that create stress for dual-career couples (Hill et al. 2001). Thus, stress that most working families experience is evident in a variety of situations and is likely to affect other relationships at work and at home.

Stress is viewed as a complex emotion, much like excitement, that individuals experience everyday (Wheaton 1999). Commonly regarded as a negative emotion, when individuals are highly stressed they can be expected to feel anxious and tense (Monat and Lazarus 1991).[1] Extreme levels of perceived stress have shown to be related to physical problems and general feelings of depression (Taylor 1991). Everyone experiences stress, especially individuals in certain jobs and those who have multiple responsibilities (Link et al. 1993). One of the common assumptions about stress is that, among working families, particularly mothers, it occurs frequently and is of such intensity that it is reaching near crisis proportions.

Although scholars view stress as likely to be experienced by individuals at various levels every day, few studies have looked at stress over the course of a day or week or in a variety of different situations (special issue of the *American Psychologist* on Stress and Coping, 55, 2000). In a review of thousands of studies conducted on stress, several scholars regrettably conclude that stress has yet to be investigated with a methodology that is longitudinal, process-oriented, and constructed within an ipsative-normative research design (Somerfield and McCrae 2000; Tennen et al. 2000). The methods commonly used in studying stress, such as journals or time diaries, often rely on time-elapsed recall. Critics argue that these methods may erroneously estimate the stress levels an individual is likely to experience throughout the day.

We suspect that stress is more of an ongoing experience, and that individuals have internalised coping mechanisms to deal with routine and non-routine stressful life experiences at home and at work. This is not to say that all individuals experience stress minimally. We do suspect that stress varies among individuals and is likely to be associated with particular types of jobs, perceptions of work, hours worked, and family structure and dynamics. Assuming that most mothers and fathers have stress in their lives, it becomes particularly important to examine those individuals with high levels of stress compared to those who have lower stress levels.

In this chapter, we study the stress levels of working couples at work, home and in leisure. We investigate how high and low stress mothers and fathers perceive their experiences of work and leisure as well as relationships with their spouse and children. To understand how stress is experienced and how it affects others in the family, we use data obtained from the Alfred P. Sloan 500 Family Study, which includes survey information, time diary data (i.e., the Experience Sampling Method or ESM) and intensive interviews.

## Stress: an ongoing phenomenon

In the first half of the twentieth century, stress was conceptualised primarily as a response to adverse internal or external stimuli (Cannon 1932; Selye 1952). An individual was 'acted upon' and responded to these actions biologically and psychologically. Stress was conceived as a negative force that was personally destructive. This perspective changed with the early work of Lazarus and his colleagues (Deese and Lazarus 1952; Lazarus and Eriksen 1952; Eriksen et al. 1952; Lazarus et al. 1952) who showed that, under equally stressful circumstances, there were tremendous variations in responses to stress. These results were particularly valuable because they began to deconstruct the effects of stress, demonstrating that individuals react differently to stress-inducing experiences.

Since the late 1970s, there has been a continuing interest in developing holistic theories that better encompass more of the observed complexities of human behaviour (Garièpy 1995). Today, few would examine stress strictly from a biological or psychological perspective. Stress is commonly viewed as developing and occurring on a macrolevel (e.g., between the individual and the environment), as well as on the microlevel (e.g., within the individual and between the individual's established beliefs and the new beliefs required as a result of these environmental interactions).

By definition, stress is a process, that is,

> a particular relationship between the person and the environment that is appraised by the person as taxing or exceeding his or her resources and endangering his or her well-being.
>
> (Lazarus and Folkman 1984: 19)

Stress is not conceptually meaningful unless it is examined within context, and studied with careful attention to individual variations. As explained by Lazarus (1993), the experience of stress involves cognitive, emotional, physiological, and social processes, the combination and activation of which depend upon how 'the person and environment interact' as well as what a person is 'thinking and doing' (Lazarus 1993: 236, 241) – that is, how she or he is appraising the situation at the moment a potential stressful encounter unfolds.

Even though most investigators working on stress-related research have moved from thinking about stress as the response of an individual to a specific stimulus to viewing it as an ongoing interactive process, little empirical evidence has shown this to be the case. While researchers from diverse academic fields have theoretically challenged the earlier biological perspectives, they themselves have infrequently studied stress from their own rich and complex perspective. As Thoits (1995) points out, life events, chronic strains, and daily hassles are different areas of stress research; yet few investigators have looked at how these domains are related to and interact with each other. One explanation for this is that researchers have often lacked a methodology that would allow them to determine how stress is experienced daily and what types of variation in stress occur when individuals face a particularly challenging life event such as the death of a spouse, or the chronic strain of caring for a disabled child.

Our work uses the Experience Sampling Method, which allows us to view stress in the context of an individual's life and to look at stress in relation to other emotions. In our analyses, we begin by showing the relationship between stress and other emotions. Second, we discuss how stress is experienced over the course of a typical week. Third, we describe the relationship between different levels of stress and various work and family characteristics. Finally, we examine how stress is experienced by mothers and fathers at home.

## Method

The data for this study are taken from the 500 Family Study of the Alfred P. Sloan Center on Parents, Children, and Work, which obtained information from mothers, fathers and their children. Relying on surveys, qualitative interviews, and the Experience Sampling Method, this is one of the few studies where stress is examined in combination with other emotions across a variety of contexts both individually and within couples.

The sample consists of 204 families in which both the mother and father were employed and had children under the age of 18 living at home. Participants were drawn from eight middle- and upper-middle-class communities throughout the United States and were solicited through local public elementary schools and high schools. For each family, all parents residing in the household and at least one child participated in the study.

## Procedures

Parents of both teenagers and kindergarteners were administered a survey, a time diary form (referred to as the ESM), and intensive interviews. Parents of teenagers were given slightly different versions of the instruments than parents of kindergarteners. Each instrument included questions that were appropriate for the age of the children in the family. Adolescents also completed surveys, in-depth interviews, and the ESM. This analysis focuses on parents' responses to the ESM and the survey.

### Experience Sampling Method

The ESM is a time-diary instrument developed by Mihaly Csikszentmihalyi (Csikszentmihalyi and Larson 1984; Csikszentmihalyi 1997). The ESM examines several different dimensions beyond more conventional time diaries as used by Robinson and Godbey (1997). In addition to determining how individuals spend their time and what activities they are engaged in, the ESM is designed to examine an individual's subjective interpretations of his or her emotional states during the day. The ability to capture subjective interpretations as they occur throughout the day is particularly valuable for studying emotions such as stress, as it is possible to determine one's overall feelings of stress as well as specific instances when stress increases or decreases.

The ESM is a week-long data collection process during which participants are asked to wear wristwatches that are pre-programmed to beep eight times each day. Watches are set to beep at random times in each two-hour block during participants' waking hours, with the restriction that no two signals be less than 30 minutes apart. Signalling schedules are modified slightly in cases where participants are typically awake for substantially fewer or greater than 16 hours each day. When beeped an individual describes his or her feelings at that exact moment, overcoming the problem of time-elapsed recall. The emotion is recorded as it is experienced naturally, not experimentally induced as in a laboratory.

In the 500 Family Study, to the extent that it was possible, members of the same family were put on identical signalling schedules. In response to the signals, participants were asked to complete a self-report form in which they answered a number of open-ended and scaled questions about their location, activities, companions, and psychological states at the moment they were signalled. A number of Likert and semantic-differential scales were used to assess participants' psychological states. Trained coders, using detailed schemes, coded the open-ended responses. Inter-rater reliabilities on the ESM coding ranged from 0.79 to 0.95. For a more detailed description of this methodology, as well as several descriptions of its validity and reliability, see Csikszentmihalyi and Larson (1987) and Csikszentmihalyi and Schneider (2000).

### Surveys and interviews

The surveys were specifically designed to learn how working families are coping with their lives. To gain information about work and family life, surveys administered to parents and teenage children included demographic information as well as items pertaining to home, work, and school experiences, and views about self. The in-depth interviews explored many of the survey topics in greater detail, trying specifically to understand how families cope with the stress and demands of two working parents with children under the age of eighteen in the household. For this chapter, we specifically focus on the relationship between levels of stress and husbands' and wives' occupational status, educational background, job type, attitudes toward work, job satisfaction, and marital satisfaction.

## Results

### Experiencing stress

Using ESM beep responses obtained over the course of a week, we computed a mean level of stress for each individual. In our first analysis, we examine the relationship between stress and other emotions, including relaxation, enjoyment, self-esteem, feeling good, feeling strong, feeling happy, and feeling excited.

As shown in Table 8.1, stress is negatively correlated with the positive emotional states of happiness, enjoyment, and feeling good and strong. The highest negative relationship is found between stress and relaxation, whereas the least negative correlation is found for excitement. These results seem valid since individuals who are stressed are likely to feel uncomfortably anxious with themselves. They are also likely to feel slightly excited, although we would expect that higher levels of excitement would occur when they are engaged in activities that are more pleasurable. Finally, we find that stress is

*Table 8.1* Correlations of stress and emotion[a]

|  | Stress[b] | Relax | Enjoy | Good | Strong | Happy | Excited | Self-esteem |
|---|---|---|---|---|---|---|---|---|
| Stress | 1.00 | -0.54** | -0.35** | -0.31** | -0.25** | -0.42** | -0.11** | -0.31** |
| Relax |  | 0.46** | 0.40** | 0.28** | 0.48** | 0.20** | 0.38** |
| Enjoy |  |  | 0.48** | 0.39** | 0.56** | 0.46** | 0.48** |
| Good |  |  |  | 0.50** | 0.54** | 0.40** | 0.79** |
| Strong |  |  |  |  | 0.63** | 0.54** | 0.53** |
| Happy |  |  |  |  |  | 0.53** | 0.50** |
| Excited |  |  |  |  |  |  | 0.37** |
| Self-esteem |  |  |  |  |  |  |  | 1.00 |

Notes: **p<0.01

[a] Based on 17,094 ESM beep-level responses of 395 parents who are employed (204 fathers and 191 mothers).
[b] Stress, relax, enjoy, and good are on a scale of 0–3. Strong, happy, excited are on a scale of 1–7. Self-esteem is a composite of expectations, control, success and good based on a scale of 0–3.

highly negatively correlated with self-esteem, suggesting that, even when experienced positively, stress contributes to a negative sense of self.

Recognising that stress is an ongoing phenomenon, we investigated whether there were variations in mothers' and fathers' stress throughout the week. Figure 8.1 shows that, in a typical week, for both mothers and fathers, stress is at the lowest on the weekends and rises during the weekdays, peaking on Mondays and Thursdays. Stress begins to decline on Friday, and this decline continues through Saturday, which is the least stressful day of the week. Significantly less stress is experienced on Saturday when compared to either Friday (p<0.001, t = 9.80) or Sunday (p<0.001, t = -5.97). The higher levels of stress experienced by mothers and fathers on Sunday in comparison to

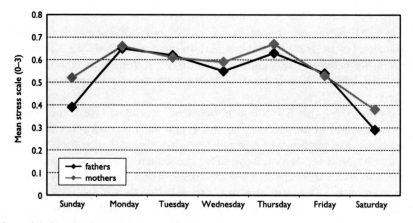

*Figure 8.1* Average stress levels across the week

Saturday may indicate that, by end of the weekend, families are beginning to think about their commitments and responsibilities for the week ahead.

There is no gender effect for stress during the workweek. Men and women have nearly similar levels of stress from Monday to Friday. At the weekend, this pattern changes and men experience significantly less stress than women (on Sunday $p<0.001$, $t = -4.01$ and on Saturday $p<0.001$, $t = -3.56$). This may be because on the weekends mothers tend to engage in more childcare responsibilities and household chores than fathers. In additional analyses, we found that mothers are less relaxed on the weekends, and report performing significantly greater numbers of household tasks than their husbands.

## High and low stress

When stress is aggregated by person and compared across persons there are few differences. A very different picture emerges when we categorise mothers and fathers as having either high or low stress.[2] Examining the times that mothers and fathers were stressed, we found that 60 per cent reported being 'not at all stressed', whereas 13 per cent reported being stressed most of the time. The mean stress for parents overall was 0.56 on a scale where, '0' is 'not at all stressed', '1' is a 'little bit stressed', '2' is 'somewhat stressed' and '3' is 'very stressed'. This is a fairly low average, which might suggest that dual-career parents are not as stressed in their daily lives as they or others think they are. However, other qualitative data obtained in our study seemed to indicate that these results may be obscuring significant differences in stress among the sample. Interviews and survey data suggested that some of the parents in our study experience stress with a higher frequency and intensity than the mean stress level would indicate.

To investigate this hypothesis, we divided the sample into those below the mean (hereafter known as the 'low stress' group) and those above or equal to the mean (hereafter known as the 'high stress' group).[3] Dividing the sample in this way revealed several important distinctions between the groups. The high stress group shows higher mean levels of stress at work and with their spouse. This group also seems to experience more work–family conflict, more anger about work, and to be more depressed overall than the low stress group.

Examining the two groups using standard demographic measures few differences were found between the two groups. Those in high and low stress groups did not differ by gender, race or ethnicity, whether they had children under the age of 6, or lived in a reconstituted family.[4] Surprisingly, there also was no difference in educational attainment. Individuals with a graduate degree were as likely to be in the high stress group as those who were college graduates, or had a high school diploma. Religion also did not differentiate the groups. Low and high stress individuals were as likely to see themselves as either religious or non-religious and attended religious services at the same frequency.

Turning to the work variables, one of the most unexpected findings was that the high and low stress groups were not differentiated by whether they held a full- or part-time job. It is often assumed that part-time work is associated with lower stress, especially for mothers. This did not appear to be the case for our sample. The only work-related measures that showed differences between the two groups were income, hours worked, and length of time at current job.

## Stress and work characteristics

As shown in Table 8.2, overall stress increases with income. However, there is not a significant difference among income groups – that is, those with higher

*Table 8.2* Demographic characteristics of mothers and fathers currently employed[a]

|  | Stress level[b] | | | |
|---|---|---|---|---|
|  | Average stress (N = 394) | High stress (N = 171) | Low stress (N = 223) | t[c] |
| Total family income | | | | |
| <50,000–80,000 | 0.49 (0.36) | 0.86 (0.29) | 0.28 (0.16) | -12.40*** |
| 80,001–100,000 | 0.56 (0.34) | 0.89 (0.21) | 0.29 (0.13) | -15.30*** |
| 100,001–150,000 | 0.58 (0.42) | 0.91 (0.35) | 0.27 (0.16) | -11.74*** |
| Over 150,000 | 0.61 (0.46) | 1.00 (0.40) | 0.29 (0.16) | -13.54*** |
| Average | 0.56 (0.41) | 0.93 (0.34) | 0.28 (0.15) | -25.21*** |
| Hours of work[d] | | | | |
| 1–37 hours | 0.66 (0.52) | 1.07 (0.50) | 0.40 (0.33) | -7.88*** |
| 38–45 hours | 0.70 (0.50) | 1.08 (0.38) | 0.34 (0.29) | -11.09*** |
| 46–50 hours | 0.76 (0.59) | 1.23 (0.49) | 0.42 (0.39) | -9.12*** |
| 51 or more hours | 0.76 (0.61) | 1.18 (0.57) | 0.36 (0.30) | -7.77*** |
| Average | 0.72 (0.55) | 1.13 (0.48) | 0.38 (0.33) | -17.75*** |
| Years at job[d] | | | | |
| 0–5 years | 0.71 (0.54) | 1.10 (0.44) | 0.42 (0.40) | -9.66*** |
| 5+–15 years | 0.75 (0.54) | 1.13 (0.48) | 0.39 (0.29) | -12.09*** |
| 15+ years and over | 0.70 (0.61) | 1.24 (0.59) | 0.35 (0.27) | -8.44*** |
| Average | 0.73 (0.55) | 1.14 (0.49) | 0.39 (0.33) | -17.62*** |

Notes: ***$p < 0.001$

[a] The total number of parents is 394. One person is missing data on stress and could not be included in this analysis.
[b] Mean level of stress overall was 0.56 (scale is from 0 to 3). Columns indicate mean level of stress within each type of stress classification. Standard deviation is in parentheses. High stress people were those whose overall stress level was equal to or above the mean. Low stress people were those whose overall stress level was below the mean.
[c] Column indicates the t-value for each row. High stress individuals were compared to low stress individuals.
[d] Mean level of stress was calculated when at work. The mean level of stress at work overall is 0.73 (scale is from 0 to 3).

incomes were no more likely to have higher stress than those with lower incomes. Rather, what we find is that, within each income bracket, there are individuals who experience stress differently.

With respect to hours of work, the median is 41.5 hours, and there are no significant differences in median hours worked among high and low stress individuals.[5] Longer hours do not necessarily produce greater work stress. As with income, there are significant differences between the high and low stress groups by each category of hours worked. This pattern is repeated with years at current job. The mean length of time at one's job is nine years. For high stress individuals, the longer one has been at one's job, the more work stress one experiences. For low stress individuals, length at job is inversely related to stress, although these differences are not significant. However, within each category of length at job, we again find a significant difference between the high and low stress groups.

Moving beyond demographics, we next examined whether high and low stress mothers and fathers had different experiences doing work at home and different thoughts about work. As shown in Figure 8.2, results follow the expected pattern. High stress mothers and fathers are twice as likely as low stress mothers and fathers to spend three or more hours a week working at home on the weekends. On weekday evenings, high stress mothers and fathers are likely to spend almost 15 per cent more time doing three or more hours of work at home. These differences in time allocations suggest that stress and working at home are related, a conclusion often drawn in the media.

As shown in Figure 8.3, high stress mothers and fathers are much more likely to feel drained, exhausted and angry than low stress mothers and fathers. High stress mothers and fathers are nearly two and half times more likely than low stress mothers and fathers to say that they feel drained. They are twice as likely to report that they are exhausted. This is particularly the case for high stress fathers who reported feeling exhausted most of the time. Finally the high stress mothers and fathers are one and half times as likely as low stress mothers and fathers to say they feel angry. Medical research has linked high stress to high blood pressure and other physiological effects (Taylor 1991). These results suggest that stress may have deleterious social and psychological consequences as well.

As expected, these long hours and negative emotions take a toll, and we find that work and family relations suffer. Figure 8.4 shows that high stress individuals are nearly twice as likely as low stress individuals to think about work when with their families. At the same time, when thinking about work, these high stress parents are more likely to feel guilty about not spending more time with their families. High stress parents are also the most likely to report having higher work and family conflict. This may be the result of the working conditions that high stress individuals experience. High stress mothers and fathers are more likely than low stress mothers and fathers to

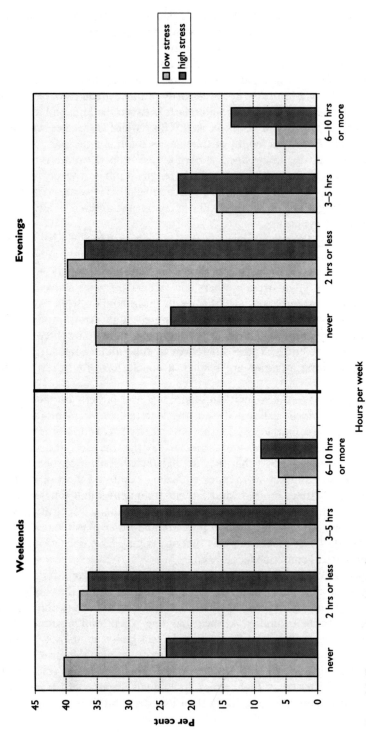

*Figure 8.2* Time spent working at home

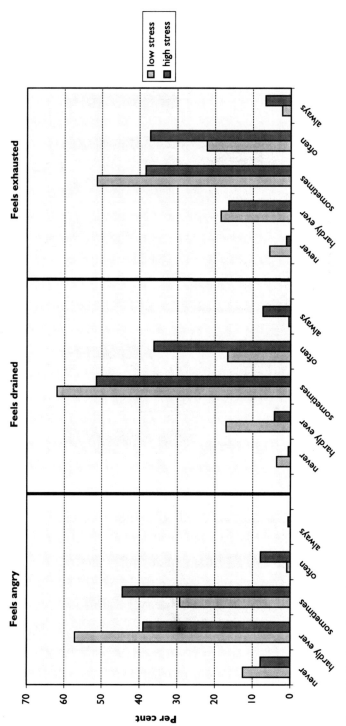

Figure 8.3 Feelings after work

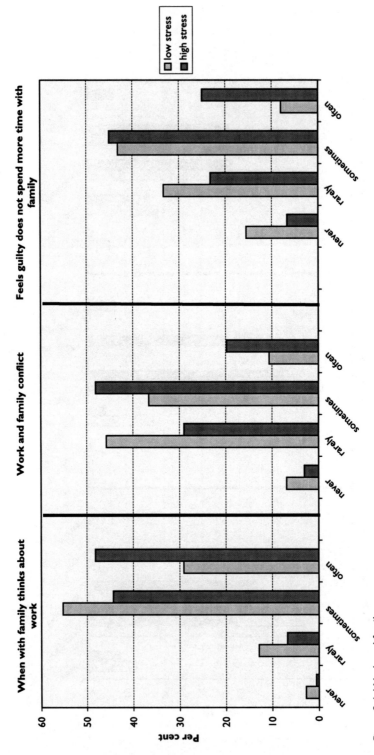

Figure 8.4 Work and family

work on short notice. High stress fathers in particular are significantly more likely than others to work on short notice. Finally, both high stress mothers and fathers are more likely than their low stress counterparts to bring work home in order to keep up with job demands.

## Stress at work

In our next analysis (Table 8.3) we examined how stressed individuals were at work when interacting with co-workers, clients, supervisors, and when alone. Only for low stress fathers do we find a significant difference in stress in different social situations at work. For low stress fathers, the most stressful time is interacting with their supervisors. This is also the situation for high stress mothers, although it is not significant in relation to time spent with others. On the other hand, low stress mothers and high stress fathers show similar patterns. They both report the lowest stress when interacting with their supervisors and have substantially higher stress when with co-workers and clients or when alone. But again there are no significant differences within categories. What these results seem to suggest is that, at least with respect to relationships, stress remains fairly constant, with the exception of stress experienced by low stress fathers.

Transitions from home to work and work to home can be perceived as stressful. In the media, mothers and fathers are often seen frantically trying to get their children ready for school and themselves out of the door. Contrary to this image, we find that leaving for work does not significantly increase one's stress level, with one exception. High stress mothers seem to be the most stressed all the time and their first work beep is higher than all other groups. (The mean home-to-work stress level for high stress mothers was 0.72, and their mean stress level from work-to-home was 0.49.)[6] Everyone appears to look forward to coming home and stress appears to decrease when leaving work for home. This is particularly the case for high stress fathers, as shown in Figure 8.5. Low stress mothers and fathers have the least fluctuation in their stress levels when making these home-to-work and work-to-home transitions.

## Stress at home

Being at home is less stressful than being at work regardless of whether one has high or low stress (home = 0.46, work = 0.73, t = 7.87, p<0.001). Stress appears to decrease the most for high stress fathers whereas high stress mothers have the highest stress level when at home. (Home stress: low stress fathers 0.20, low stress mothers 0.25, high stress fathers 0.68 and high stress mothers 0.86. Work stress: low stress fathers 0.34, low stress mothers 0.44, high stress fathers 1.16 and high stress mothers 1.15).

Investigating this further, we compared stress levels at home for couples

Table 8.3 Experiences of stress when at work

| | Overall average[a] | Low stress fathers | Low stress mothers | High stress fathers | High stress mothers | F[b] |
|---|---|---|---|---|---|---|
| Alone | 0.76 (0.64) | 0.37 (0.37) | 0.48 (0.53) | 1.21 (0.52) | 1.15 (0.63) | 69.36*** |
| With co-workers | 0.75 (0.68) | 0.35 (0.40) | 0.45 (0.46) | 1.22 (0.67) | 1.07 (0.70) | 45.42*** |
| With supervisor | 0.80 (0.80) | 0.71 (0.78) | 0.27 (0.39) | 1.11 (0.78) | 1.26 (0.88) | 4.24** |
| With clients/pupils | 0.73 (0.71) | 0.34 (0.50) | 0.46 (0.50) | 1.23 (0.80) | 0.94 (0.61) | 14.51*** |
| Average | 0.76 (0.67) | 0.37 (0.43)[c] | 0.45 (0.50) | 1.22 (0.63) | 1.09 (0.67) | 126.13*** |

Notes: **p<0.01*** p<0.001

[a] Columns indicate mean level of stress within each type of stress classification when participants were at work. Standard Deviation is in parentheses.
[b] Column indicates the F-value for each row (low and high stress mothers and fathers are being compared).
[c] There is a significant difference (p<0.05) among social situations at work for low stress fathers (F = 2.62).

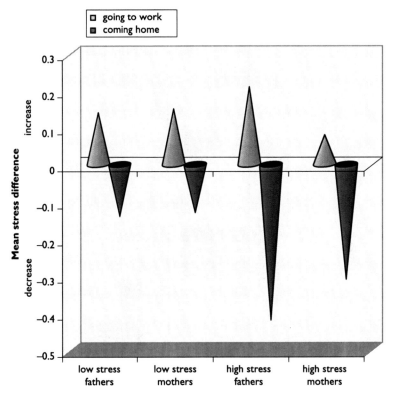

*Figure 8.5* Increases and decreases in stress

(Table 8.4) categorising couples into those that were both highly stressed, those who were low stressed and those couples where one spouse was highly stressed.[7] We then examined these couples when they were with their spouse, their children, their children and their spouse, and when they were alone.

Overall there is little variation in stress by social relationships. The only significant difference among and between these groups occurs when high stress couples are with their spouse and their children. We find that stress significantly decreases for these couples in these situations. In contrast, on the individual level in other analyses, we found that stress increases for high stress mothers when they are with their children (high stress mothers: with children 0.94, with spouse 0.72, alone 0.83). Here we find that the presence of a spouse, at least in a couple situation, seems to moderate stress levels.

Our earlier analyses show that high stress mothers and fathers in comparison to low stress mothers and fathers are more likely to work longer hours on weekends and at home, and to think about work at home. It could be that when they spend time together with their children, this family time becomes more precious and enjoyable. When high stress mothers are with

Table 8.4 Social experiences of stress when at home for couples

| | Overall average[a] | Low stress couples N = 61 | Split stress couples N = 71 | High stress couples N = 46 | F[b] |
|---|---|---|---|---|---|
| Home | 0.47 (0.31) | 0.23 (0.15) | 0.47 (0.21) | 0.79 (0.31) | 83.10*** |
| With spouse | 0.43 (0.49) | 0.23 (0.37) | 0.48 (0.41) | 0.72 (0.51) | 14.66*** |
| With children | 0.50 (0.45) | 0.22 (0.20) | 0.52 (0.44) | 0.83 (0.46) | 33.33*** |
| With family[c] | 0.45 (0.42) | 0.24 (0.28) | 0.50 (0.41) | 0.65 (0.48)[d] | 14.66*** |
| Alone | 0.47 (0.36) | 0.23 (0.21) | 0.46 (0.23) | 0.82 (0.41) | 57.56*** |

Notes: *** $p<0.001$

[a] Mean level of stress was calculated by who the couple was with when at home. Standard deviation is in parentheses.
[b] Column indicates the F-value for each row (low, split and high stress couples are being compared).
[c] 'Family' is defined as being with one's spouse and child/ren.
[d] There is a significant decrease ($p<0.05$) in mean stress level of high stress couples when with their family compared to their overall stress level at home ($t = -2.01$).

their children they are involved in many childcare and household tasks, and perhaps feel particularly tense and anxious. In comparison, we find that when high stress mothers are with their spouse their stress levels decline (stress does not vary for high stress fathers when they are with their spouse, children or alone). It may be that the worries of work for fathers and mothers and the drudgery of childcare and housework for mothers have less salience to these couples when they are engaged together with their children.

To learn more about the social relationships of these couples we examined their perceptions of their relationships with each other. These items were taken from the parent surveys. Table 8.5 shows that in all instances low stress couples have a more positive view of their married lives and seem the most satisfied with their spouse.

*Table 8.5* Couples' perceptions of relationship with spouse

|  | Overall average[a] | Low stress N = 60 | Split stress N = 67 | High stress N = 45 | F[b] |
|---|---|---|---|---|---|
| Partner and I understand each other | 3.65 (0.94) | 3.81 (0.84) | 3.70 (0.79) | 3.34 (1.18) | 3.45* |
| Not happy with personality of partner | 1.97 (0.94) | 1.77 (0.77) | 1.96 (0.85) | 1.19 (0.18) | 3.61* |
| Happy with role responsibilities | 3.95 (0.88) | 4.18 (0.76) | 3.95 (0.72) | 3.66 (1.13) | 4.85** |
| Unhappy about financial position | 2.32 (1.04) | 1.96 (0.91) | 2.44 (1.02) | 2.61 (1.11) | 6.25** |
| Needs not being met by relationship | 3.04 (1.14) | 2.68 (1.09) | 3.03 (1.04) | 3.53 (1.19) | 7.87*** |
| Happy with how manage leisure activities | 3.47 (0.96) | 3.88 (0.85) | 3.45 (0.88) | 2.94 (0.96) | 14.23*** |
| Unhappy with how handle parent role responsibilities | 1.99 (0.91) | 1.61 (0.73) | 2.16 (0.91) | 2.24 (0.99) | 8.96*** |
| Overall: satisfied with relationship with partner | 4.42 (0.88) | 4.63 (0.66) | 4.47 (0.74) | 4.04 (1.20) | 6.28** |

Notes: *p <0.05 **p<0.01 ***p<0.001
[a] Relationship perception was calculated as mean agreement for the couple on each relationship statement on a scale from 1 to 5 ('1' indicates 'strongly disagree' and '5' indicates 'strongly agree'). Standard deviation is in parentheses.
[b] Column indicates the F-value for each row (low, split and high stress couples are being compared).

It is important to point out that on most of these items, individuals were more likely than not to agree positively with the statements. However, the fact that levels of stress point to differences among couples suggest that stress may be contributing to marital discord. For every item, the pattern is the same with low stress couples giving the most positive response, followed by split stress couples, and with high stress couples being the most negative. The greatest difference among the couples concerns how their lives are managed outside of work. High stress couples are the most dissatisfied with this aspect of their lives. The next most problematic situation is the parenting role with high stress couples being almost twice as negative about how their spouse handles their responsibilities as a parent. Financial concerns were another area of high disagreement. The smallest disagreements among the couples were with their respective partners more generally, suggesting that by and large these couples were more positive toward their spouse than their role relationship with that person.

## Stress and leisure

We then examined whether high and low stress individuals also have different experiences of leisure. Our definition of leisure was based on within-day diary responses to the question, 'What are you doing?' (e.g., playing computer games, shopping at the mall). Voluntary activities were then collected into a general leisure category. Parents engaged in leisure activities approximately 18 per cent of their time with low stress individuals spending slightly more of their time in leisure (18 per cent as compared to 16 per cent for high stress individuals). Figure 8.6 shows the per cent of total activity time spent engaged in leisure by each leisure category for both high and low stress individuals.

Although it was not unexpected to find 'television watching' as the most popular leisure activity (approximately 4 per cent of the total activity time and 24 per cent of the total leisure time, with reading being a close second at approximately 4 per cent of the total activity time and 23 per cent of the total leisure time), we were surprised at the low percentage of time respondents engaged in hobbies or active leisure (such as practising an instrument or doing an art project). Interestingly, the average percentage of time spent doing each of these activities did not vary significantly across low and high stress groups or gender. Low stress individuals, however, spend more time watching television (4.8 per cent compared to 3.6 per cent of the time) with high stress mothers watching the least amount of television (3 per cent of the time) and low stress fathers watching the most amount of television (5.6 per cent of the time). In terms of gender, low and high stress mothers read slightly more than they watch television whereas low and high stress fathers watch television more than they read.

Low and high stress parents did not differ in the amount of time they spent

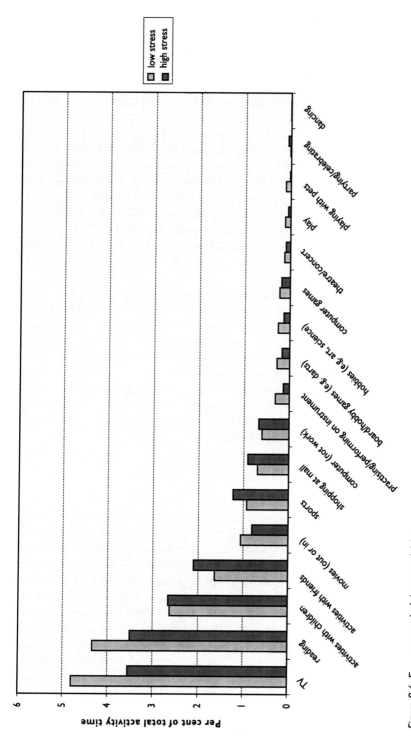

Figure 8.6 Engagement in leisure activities

in leisure. As expected, we also found that for each leisure activity the mean stress score of high stress individuals remains significantly higher than that of low stress individuals. In other words, leisure does not seem to erase the higher level of stress reported by high stress individuals. Still, we wondered if leisure pursuits might have more psychological benefit for high stress as compared to our low stress individuals because they provide safer, more relaxing opportunities compared to work situations.

To determine whether leisure activities did lower stress and improve mood, we compared the low and high stress group by their mean z-scores. Findings indicated that pursuing leisure activities decreased mean z-score stress more for the high stress than the low stress group, but the difference was only significant when respondents were engaged in more passive and solitary leisure activities, that is, when watching movies ($p<0.001$, $t = 4.284$), television ($p<0.001$, $t = 5.298$), or reading ($p<0.001$, $t = 3.486$). There were no significant differences in mean z-score for mood. In other words, neither group reported higher relative well-being than the other group when engaged in leisure.

Nevertheless, at home, being engaged in leisure activities does have some benefits for both high and low stress parents when compared to other types of non-leisure pursuits. For example, the mean z-score stress when watching television was significantly less than when cooking, personal caretaking (e.g., getting dressed), or house cleaning (for the low stress group $p<0.001$, $F = 14.71$ and for the high stress group $p<0.001$, $F = 30.60$). The same pattern held true for reading as compared to other home activities (for the low stress group $p<0.001$, $F = 11.80$ and for the high stress group $p<0.001$, $F = 21.57$). This suggests that making specific time for leisure activities at home is important for working parents.

## Stress and dual-career couples: a synopsis

These findings suggest that parents may not be as stressed as some have claimed. Stress when examined in relation to other emotions behaves quite predictably. Stress is negatively related to relaxation, feeling happy, good, strong, and enjoying oneself. However, the relationship between stress and excitement is relatively low in comparison to other emotions. We suspect that some stress is associated with seeking challenging activities. It may be that the threshold for engaging in challenging activities is a slight increase in stress, where one is not entirely sure of what will happen. Thus, some stress may not be entirely negative and maybe a reasonable response when attempting tasks that involve some uncertainty.[8] On the other hand, high levels of stress, sustained over time demonstrate a lack of control of over one's activities and a sense of frustration. We suspect that it is the balance between stress, control, and challenge that creates greater feelings of enjoyment and self-satisfaction.

What was less predictable was the lack of variation in stress by gender, income or level of education, at least among individuals in this sample. It was only when we divided our sample into high and low stress groups that more expected patterns of behaviour were evident. High stress individuals, for example, show more work–family conflict, that is, they are more likely to feel guilty about not spending enough time with their family and unhappy with their role as partner and parent.

In the case of high stress women, they appear to fit the image of the 'harried' worker. What is perhaps most disconcerting is that they do not have the benefit of 'moderating' stress that others experience when being at home. This seems particularly troublesome, as they may be less likely to have the opportunity to recover from the daily hassles of their jobs and the demands of their households. Perhaps the greatest challenge for researchers working with stress is to find those activities and situations that precipitate stress and those that enhance recovery toward a state of equilibrium.

What our results show is that it is not the job itself that creates stress. Stress does not appear related to whether one is a doctor, banker or teacher, or whether one earns $70,000 or $150,000 a year. It may be that job performance standards and responsibilities permeate all aspects of the workforce. The stockbroker and the nurse both appear to be internalising the demands of their work and it is this internalisation that appears related to feelings of stress, that is, the feeling that they have to work at home on the weekends or in the evenings or thinking about work when at home. Both high stress mothers and fathers feel physically drained and exhausted. And not surprisingly, less positive relationships at home between husband and wife are related to high levels of couple stress. These results seem to suggest that stress is less structurally determined and more personally and relationally situated.

## Notes

1 In our current related work, we find that stress declines in intensity when an individual gains a sense of control over a situation and experiences a decrease in feelings of frustration.

2 The average number of beeps responded to was 43 beeps per person over the course of seven days. There was not a significant difference between the number of beeps answered by high (43.24) or low (41.09) stress individuals. Mothers tended to respond to more beeps (45.61) than fathers (41.09).

3 Among participants in the sample, 223 individuals were identified as having low stress and 171 were identified as having high stress.

4 In preliminary analyses, we did find that single employed mothers (women who have been separated, divorced, single or widowed) are significantly more stressed than married employed mothers ($t = 2.01$, $p<0.05$).

5 Even though men work at a mean of 43.7 hours a week and women a mean of 34.8, there were no gender effects for stress.

6 Home-to-work stress was calculated as follows. First, we selected all beeps that occurred when mothers and fathers were leaving home and going to work. Then each of these home stress beeps was subtracted from each of the corresponding

work stress beeps. Next, stress scores were aggregated on the person level. Thus, each person had a mean stress transition score for leaving home and going to work. The same procedure was followed to calculate going home from work.

7   There was no gender difference among the split couples: 35 of the fathers had high stress whereas 36 of the mothers reported high levels of stress.

8   In some additional analyses we found that slightly elevated levels of stress were positively associated with enjoyment and excitement.

## References

Bronfenbrenner, U. (1996) *The State of Americans: This Generation and the Next.* New York: Free Press.

Cannon, W. B. (1932) *The Wisdom of the Body.* New York: W. W. Norton.

Csikszentmihalyi, M. (1997) *Finding Flow: The Psychology of Optimal Experience.* New York: Harper and Row.

Csikszentmihalyi, M. and Larson, R. (1984) *Being Adolescent: Conflict and Growth in the Teenage Years.* New York: Basic Books.

Csikszentmihalyi, M. and Larson, R. (1987) Validity and reliability of the experience-sampling method. *Journal of Nervous and Mental Disease* 175: 526–36.

Csikszentmihalyi, M. and Schneider, B. (2000) *Becoming Adult: How Teenagers Prepare for the World of Work.* New York: Basic Books.

Deese, J. and Lazarus, R. S. (1952) The effects of psychological stress upon perceptual-motor performance. *United States Air Force Human Resources Research Center Research Bulletin no. 52–19,* v. 15.

Eriksen, C. W., Lazarus, R. S. and Strange, J. R. (1952) Psychological stress and its personality correlates. *Journal of Personality* 20: 277–86.

Garièpy, J. (1995) The evolution of a developmental science: early determinism, modern interactionism, and new systemic approach. *Annals of Child Development: A Research Annual* 11: 167–222.

Hill, J. E., Hawkins, A. J., Ferris, M. and Weitzman, M. (2001) Finding an extra day a week: the positive influence of perceived job flexibility on work and family life balance. *Family Relations* 50: 49–58.

Hochschild, A. R. (1997) *The Time Bind: When Work Becomes Home and Home Becomes Work.* New York: Metropolitan.

Kahn, R. L. (1980) Conflict, ambiguity and overload: three elements in job stress. In D. Katz, R. L. Kahn and J. S. Adams (eds) *The Study of Organizations: Findings from Field and Laboratory.* San Francisco, CA: Jossey-Bass.

Lazarus, R. S. (1993) Coping theory and research: past, present, and future. *Psychosomatic Medicine* 55: 234–47.

Lazarus, R. S. (2000) Toward better research on stress and coping. *American Psychologist* 55: 665–73.

Lazarus, R. S. and Eriksen, C. W. (1952) Effects of failure stress upon skilled performance. *Journal of Experimental Psychology* 43: 100–5.

Lazarus, R. S. and Folkman, S. (1984) *Stress, Appraisal, and Coping.* New York: Springer.

Lazarus, R. S., Deese, J. and Osler, S. F. (1952) The effects of psychological stress upon performance. *Psychological Bulletin* 49: 293–317.

Link, B. G., Lennon, M. C. and Dohrenwend, B. P. (1993) Socioeconomic status and depression: the role of occupations involving direction, control, and planning. *American Journal of Sociology* 98: 1351–87.

Monat, A. and Lazarus, R. S. (1991) Stress and coping: some current issues and controversies. In A. Monat and R. S. Lazarus (eds) *Stress and Coping*, 3rd edn. New York: Columbia University Press.

Robinson, J. P. and Godbey, G. (1997) *Time for Life*. University Park, PA: Pennsylvania State University Press.

Selye, H. (1952) *The Story of the Adaptation Syndrome*. Montreal: Acta.

Somerfield, M. R. and McCrae, R. R. (2000) Stress and coping research: methodological challenges, theoretical advances, and clinical applications. *American Psychologist* 55: 620–5.

Taylor, S. E. (1991) Health psychology: the science and the field. In A. Monat and R. S. Lazarus (eds) *Stress and Coping*, 3rd edn. New York: Columbia University Press.

Tennen, H., Affleck, G., Armeli, S. and Carney, M. A. (2000) A daily process approach to coping: linking theory, research, and practice. *American Psychologist* 55(6): 626–36.

Thoits, P. A. (1995) Stress, coping, and social support processes: where are we? What next? *Journal of Health and Social Behavior* (extra issue): 53–79.

Waite, L. J. and Nielsen, M. (2001) The rise of the dual worker family: 1963–1997. In R. Hertz and N. Marshall (eds) *Working Families*. Berkeley, CA: University of California Press.

Wheaten, B. (1999) Social stress. In C. S. Aneshensel and J. C. Phelan (eds) *Handbook of the Sociology of Mental Health*. New York: Kluwer Academic/Plenum Publishers.

# Chapter 9

# Work, leisure and well-being

*John T. Haworth*

## Introduction

The chapter summarises current perspectives on work, leisure and well-being, and highlights a range of measures of well-being and enjoyment. A model is presented focusing on the influence of characteristics of situations and persons on well-being, and the pivotal role played by enjoyment. The chapter concludes with the recognition that research is embedded in broader processes influencing well-being, work and leisure.

The relationship between work, leisure, social structure and well-being is of considerable concern. Work has been with us a long time. Tools made to a common pattern have been discovered 2 million years old. Some anthropologists argue that interaction with the physical and social environment (work) led to the development of both tools and the organism, stimulating our evolution (Ingold 2000). Work can be considered central to human functioning. Both Marx and Freud extolled the potential importance of work for the individual and society. The historian of work, Applebaum (1998), states that 'The work ethic is the human ethic'. Kohn and Schooler (1983) indicate that where work has substantive complexity there is an improvement in mental flexibility and self-esteem.

Yet stress in employment is viewed as a major problem. Many individuals experience long hours of work, increasing workloads, changing work practices and job insecurity. Many have to change jobs more frequently, and increasing numbers of people are forced to spend periods without jobs. This 'flexibilisation' of work patterns is seen to have advantages for those who can enhance their CVs and employment potential, while creating greater uncertainty and stress for those facing the possibility of redundancy with less personal, social, cultural and financial resources. In the United Kingdom there is a socio-economic class divide in access to such resources (ESRC Future of Work Programme: Taylor 2001, 2002). But there are also indications that in a minority of organisations a new work ethic is emerging, emphasising a 'reasoned wellness'.

Research into leisure is becoming increasingly important. While leisure as traditionally conceived has not been able to substitute for the lack of work opportunities for unemployed people, it has been able to ameliorate the negative psychological symptoms caused by unemployment. For retired people, keeping active, including active leisure pursuits, is seen as the main way of enhancing well-being for the financially secure. Employed people are also found to benefit from both active and passive leisure.

The diversity of lifestyles and relationships between work and leisure is an important feature of technological societies, particularly for women, who have multiple work, leisure and family roles, though also for men who are now finding themselves in this position. Leete (2000) in *Working Time* states that much work by women, including childrearing, was done in the home, but that consumerism now drives women out to work and still do childrearing. Gershuny (2000) advocates that we should take the path chosen by the Nordic countries where males do not work excessively long hours, and share the domestic work more equally. This allows both partners to develop their careers, and also allows time to engage in enjoyable leisure consumption, which can aid well-being and create jobs. Yet if 'globalisation' is not managed well, such policies will be difficult to implement.

## Employment

Employment is the source of much work. Here the wage relationship provides traction for people to engage in work, which they may or may not find enjoyable. Jahoda (1982) claims that employment automatically provides five categories of experience which are important for well-being. These are time structure, social contact, collective effort or purpose, social identity or status, and regular activity. Considerable research has shown the importance of these categories of experience for well-being (see Haworth 1997 for a summary). They have been incorporated in the nine environmental factors proposed by Warr (1987) as important for well-being.

Jahoda (1982) emphasises that in modern society it is the social institution of employment which is the main provider of the five categories of experience. While recognising that other institutions may enforce one or more of these categories of experience, Jahoda stresses that none of them combine them all with as compelling a reason as earning a living. Jahoda does recognise that the quality of experience of some jobs can be very poor and emphasises the importance of improving and humanising employment. Jahoda also emphasises the important influence the institution of employment has on shaping thought and behaviour. She considers that since the industrial revolution employment has shaped the form of our daily lives, our experience of work and leisure, and our attitudes, values and beliefs. Jahoda (1986) agrees that human beings are striving, coping, planning, interpreting creatures, but adds that the tendency to shape one's life from the inside-out operates within the possibilities and constraints of social arrangements which we passively accept and which shape life from the outside-in. A great deal of life consists of passively following unexamined social rules, not of our making but largely imposed by the collective plans of our ancestors. Some of these rules meet basic human needs, even if we become aware of them only when they are broken by, for example, the enforced exclusion from an institution as in unemployment. Jahoda regards dependency on social institutions not as good or bad but as the *sine qua non* of human existence.

## Leisure

It has long been accepted that it is difficult to define work and leisure. At one time an activity can be considered by a person as work, another time as leisure. Iso-Ahola (1997) and Iso-Ahola and Mannell (Chapter 10 in this volume) recognise that many people are stressed because of financial difficulties and the dominance of work, and that leisure is used for recuperation from work. The result is a passive leisure lifestyle and a reactive approach to personal health. They argue on the basis of considerable research that active leisure is important for health and well-being. Iso-Ahola (1997) states that participation in both physical and non-physical leisure activities has been shown to reduce depression and anxiety, produce positive moods, and enhance self-esteem and self-concept, facilitate social interaction, increase general psychological well-being and life satisfaction, and improve cognitive functioning. Of course, leisure is not a panacea. If it is used as avoidance behaviour in order not to face up to something that has to be done, it can increase stress. However, many people fail to discover active leisure.

Stebbins (1992, 1997; see also Chapter 11 in this volume) argues that an optimal leisure lifestyle includes both serious and casual leisure. His extensive studies of *serious leisure* activities, such as astronomy, archaeology, music, singing, sports, and career volunteering, show that it is defined by six distinguishing qualities. These are the occasional need to persevere at it; the development of the activity as in a career; the requirement for effort based on specialised knowledge, training or skill; the provision of durable benefits or rewards; the identification of the person with the activity; the production of an ethos and social world. It also offers a distinctive set of rewards, satisfying as a counterweight to the costs involved.

## Work–life balance

Primeau (1996) argues that it is not possible to say what is a healthy work–life balance. He suggests that occupational psychologists should examine the range of affective experiences that occur during engagement in one's customary round of occupations in daily life. He sites an important example being research into enjoyable, challenging ('flow') experiences in daily life. Lewis (2001, seminar 2 www.wellbeing-esrc.com, 2003) notes that the issue of work–life integration is a major topic in government and employer discussions in the United Kingdom. Managing multiple work and non-work (especially family) roles can be very stressful, but can also create opportunities for multiple sources of satisfaction and well-being. Organisational change occurring in response to globalisation can create higher workloads, and psychological pressures to work long hours to show commitment. Organisations may also privilege male definitions of commitment and competency based on the assumed separation of the public and private spheres (Rapoport et al. 2002). Information technology can enable work to be done in almost any situation, creating pressures and opportunities. Currently, there is considerable research interest in Europe in the transitions that young working couples make into family life (see www.workliferesearch.org/transitions). A report on 'The Future of Work-life Balance' (Taylor 2001) from the ESRC-funded Future of Work Programme advocates the need to address work pressures and dissatisfactions experienced by both men and women in paid employment. The report notes significant class differences in Britain in access to basic minimum rights for time off.

## Well-being

The societal changes outlined previously are accompanied by a resurgence of interest in the study of well-being. This is particularly the case in the United States, where a new focus on 'Positive Psychology' is concerned with factors leading to well-being, positive individuals and to flourishing corporations and communities (Kahneman et al. 1999; special edition of the *American Psychologist*, January 2000; Snyder and Lopez 2000; website www. positivepsychology.org). Proponents of positive psychology see it as concerned with how normal people might flourish under benign conditions – the thriving individual and the thriving community. Positive Psychology changes the focus of psychology from preoccupation with repairing the worst things in life to building the best things in life. In the United States, the field of Positive Psychology at the subjective level is about positive experience: well-being, optimism, hope, happiness and flow. At the individual level it is about the character strengths, such as the capacity for love and vocation, courage, interpersonal skill, aesthetic sensibility, perseverance, forgiveness, originality, future-mindedness and genius. At the group level it is about the civic virtues and the institutions that move individuals toward better citizenship: leadership, responsibility, parenting, altruism, civility, moderation, tolerance, and work ethic.

In Europe, a World Data Base of Happiness Research is freely available on the Internet at http://www.eur.nl./fsw/research/happiness. In the United Kingdom, Layard (2003) has given a series of lectures on happiness, which can be accessed at the website cep.lse.ac.uk. The Cabinet Office has produced a report on life satisfaction (Donovan et al. 2002). The study of well-being is now a key element in the Economic and Social Research Council's Lifecourse, Lifestyle, and Health Thematic Priority 2000.

A series of seminars has been funded by the ESRC on 'Wellbeing: social and individual determinants' (Haworth et al. 2001–2002). Reports can be found on the website www.wellbeing-esrc.com. Research into subjective well-being emphasises the need to understand the complex interplay between social, personal and environmental factors, and the need to develop new theories and methods of research. This subject, though receiving a great deal of contemporary interest, is by its nature trans-disciplinary, with many disciplines playing their part in determining the processes and circumstances that generate well-being in individuals, groups, communities and societies. The seminar series aims to generate research interest in the processes and circumstances that facilitate well-being (including positive mental and physical health) in different individuals, groups, communities and societies. The objective is not to replace, but provide an alternative to, and to complement, the overwhelming harm-based focus of much social scientific research into health. Well-being offers a paradigm that allows those in the academic, policy and user fields to focus on positive outcomes, and how best to realise them.

Yet the investigation of well-being is very much marginalised in comparison with the investigation of stress and ill-health. The US Positive Psychology programme is very praiseworthy, and will stimulate much needed research in other countries as well as in the United States. The programme could be enhanced by the study of the influence of social institutions on behaviour and well-being, as instigated by Jahoda (1982). Prilleltensky (2001) argues from extensive studies undertaken in Canada and Australia that wellness is achieved by the simultaneous and balanced satisfaction of personal, interpersonal and collective needs. The 'Wellness Promotion Unit' in the Psychology Department at the Victoria University, Melbourne, works with communities and government to promote healthy behaviour and prevent problems, as opposed to treating the problem after the damage has been done.

## Quantitative measures of well-being

Well-being can be studied using both quantitative and qualitative measures. The continued development of quantitative measures parallels the increasing sophistication of concepts of well-being. The work of Bradburn and Caplovitz (1965) and Herzberg (1966) indicated that negative and positive well-being are not on the same continuum, and that different factors may influence each aspect. The need to recognise the multifaceted nature of subjective well-being has also been advocated by Brief et al. (1993). Diener (2000) advocates that researchers need to use measures of both pleasant and unpleasant affect, since both are major components of affective well-being which often correlate with different variables. He notes that good life events and extroversion tend to correlate with pleasant emotions, whereas neuroticism and negative life events covary more strongly with negative emotions. He also recognises that subjective well-being is not a sufficient condition for mental health. It is recognised that well-being may have many components, and that what we view as important may be culturally determined. In his concept of mental health from a Western perspective, Warr (1987) advocates the measurement of affective well-being, competence, autonomy, aspiration and integrated functioning. However, it is the measure of affective well-being (outlined later), which has received the greatest empirical attention by Warr and colleagues.

When people are asked about their psychological well-being they typically refer to two types of evaluations. One is concerned with affective states such as the degree to which they experience feelings that are pleasant. The other is related to cognitive states such as satisfaction (Argyle 1987). In a review of subjective well-being, Diener (2000) notes that early research usually relied on only single self report items, whereas recent measures often contain multiple items. Bradburn (1969) developed a single item measure of happiness which asked 'Taking all things together, how would you say things are these days – would you say that you are very happy, pretty happy or not too happy?' Andrews and Withey (1974) asked respondents 'How do you feel about your life as a whole?' Respondents were provided with a seven-point response scale ranging from *delighted* to *terrible*. Single item measures of well-being are useful and still used today. They allow a person to make a general judgement about a particular facet of their well-being. It is recognised, however, that it is also useful to assess emotions and satisfaction by questions which tap a number of related aspects.

A life satisfaction scale developed by Warr et al. (1979) includes eleven items which refer to different aspects of the respondents' everyday life and their environment. The sum of the scores to the eleven items constitutes a measure of an individual's total life satisfaction. A twelfth and final item on the scales asks respondents to rate their life as a whole at the present moment. All items in the life satisfaction scale are answered using seven-point scales, ranging from *extremely dissatisfied* (1) to *extremely satisfied* (7).

Warr (1987, 1990) has devised a series of scales to measure affective well-being on three principal axis: the 'pleasure axis' (measuring displeasure to pleasure) the 'anxiety–contentment' axis and the 'depression–enthusiasm' axis. The scales can be administered to measure affective well-being in work or in leisure. The pleasure axis contains single item measures of enjoyment, satisfaction and happiness, with answers ranging in five stages from e.g. (5) I could not be happier to (1) I am not at all happy. This measure is similar to the one used by Bradburn (1969). Warr terms these 'narrow band' measures in that they index pleasure without specific reference to level of arousal. The other two axes are 'broad band' measures, which measure pleasure from negative to positive and include level of arousal. They are based on more sophisticated analyses of emotion (e.g. Watson and Tellegen 1985). They measure the frequency of occurrence of a range of positive and negative mood states including tense, uneasy, worried, calm, contented, and relaxed (measuring the anxiety–contentment axis), and depressed, gloomy, miserable, cheerful, enthusiastic and optimistic (measuring the depression–enthusiasm axis).

While Warr (1990) notes that the anxiety–contentment and depression–enthusiasm measures are likely to be intercorrelated in practice, rather than independent, they can distinguish between different facets of well-being in different groups. For example, individuals at higher occupational levels reported significantly more job-related enthusiasm, but also reported experiencing more anxiety at work than individuals of lower occupational level.

## Enjoyment

In discussing Positive Psychology, Seligman and Csikszentmihalyi (2000) distinguish between pleasure and enjoyment. They note that

> Pleasure is the good feeling that comes from satisfying homeostatic needs such as hunger, sex, and bodily comfort. Enjoyment on the other hand, refers to the good feelings people experience when they break through the limits of homeostasis – when they do something that stretches them beyond what they were – in an athletic event, an artistic performance, a good deed, a stimulating conversation. Enjoyment, rather than pleasure, is what leads to personal growth and long term happiness.
>
> (Seligman and Csikszentmihalyi 2000: 12)

Csikszentmihalyi has long considered enjoyment to play a pivotal role in well-being (Csikszentmihalyi 1975, 1982, 1991, 1993, 1999; Csikszentmihalyi and Csikszentmihalyi 1988). In a pioneering study, Csikszentmihalyi (1975) set out to understand enjoyment in its own terms and to describe what makes an activity enjoyable. He found that when artists, athletes and creative professionals were asked to describe the best times experienced in their favourite activities they all mentioned a dynamic balance between opportunity and ability as crucial. Optimal experience, or 'flow' as some of the respondents described it, could be differentiated from states of boredom, in which there is less to do than what one is capable of, and from anxiety, which occurs when things to do are more than one can cope with.

Csikszentmihalyi and Csikszentmihalyi (1988) report several in-depth accounts of flow and its importance for subjective well-being. They summarise the main dimensions of enjoyable flow as:

- intense involvement
- clarity of goals and feedback

- deep concentration
- transcendence of self
- lack of self-consciousness
- loss of a sense of time
- intrinsically rewarding experience
- balance between skill and challenge.

Csikszentmihalyi (1991: 36) notes that in the flow state, action follows upon action according to an internal logic that seems to need no conscious intervention by the actor. He expresses it as a unified flowing from one moment to the next in which he is in control of his actions, and in which there is little distinction between self and environment, between stimulus and response, between past, present and future. It is considered that flow can be obtained in almost any activity, with the goals of activities serving as mere tokens that justify the activity by giving it direction and determining rules of action. Csikszentmihalyi emphasises that flow activities need not be active in the physical sense, and that among the most frequently mentioned enjoyable activities are reading and being with other people. He also recognises that the flow experience is not good in an absolute sense, and that whether the consequences of any particular instance of flow is good in the larger sense needs to be discussed in terms of more inclusive social criteria. Burglary, for example, can be a flow experience.

Flow has also been extensively investigated using the Experience Sampling Method. Respondents answer questions about activity and subjective states on short scales in a diary several times a day in response to signals from a pre-programmed device such as a watch or radio pager. Several such studies are reported in Csikszentmihalyi and Csikszentmihalyi (1988). The defining characteristic of flow in these studies is a balance between skill and challenge. An important development of the three-channel model of flow (anxiety, flow, boredom) proposed by Csikszentmihalyi (1975) was made by Massimini and Carli (1988) by using the level of challenge as well as the skill challenge ratio (e.g. greater, equal and less) to give more differentiated models. A four-channel model showed that people were found to report the most positive subjective states when challenge and skills were in balance and when both were above the mean levels for the week of testing. Csikszentmihalyi and Csikszentmihalyi (1988: 260) note that when both challenges and skills are below what is customary for a person, it does not make sense to expect a person to be in flow, even if the two variables are perfectly balanced.

Dividing challenge into high, medium and low, and skill into greater, equal and less gives an even more differentiated model. Massimini and Carli (1988) in a study of teenage students in a classical lyceum in Milan found that when challenges and skill were both high (flow), respondents were concentrating significantly more than usual, they felt in control, happy, strong, actively involved, creative, free, excited, open, clear, satisfied and wishing to be doing the activity at hand. A study of adolescents in UK training schemes by Haworth and Evans (1995) also found that positive subjective states occurred more frequently when high challenges were met with equal skills. However, when Massimini and Carli (1988) analysed data from a sample of American adolescent students in Chicago, this showed that while some positive states were associated with high challenge activities being met with equal skill (flow), other positive subjective states were associated with moderate challenge where skill was higher. Similar results have been found for a sample of British college students by Clarke and Haworth (1994). High challenges met by equal skill are not then always the primary locus of positive subjective states.

The studies by Clarke and Haworth (1994) and by Haworth and Evans (1995) also showed that activities described as highly challenging with skill equal were highly enjoyable about only half of the times. Further, these studies showed that high enjoyment could be experienced when individuals engaged in activities which were described as only of a low challenge, such as watching TV. It is important to note, however, that high enjoyment was more often associated with high challenge met with equal skill (flow). Also, when high challenge met with equal skill is found to be enjoyable this seems to be beneficial for well-being. In the study of college students by Clarke and Haworth (1994) subjects who had flow experiences which were highly enjoyable were found to score significantly higher on several standard questionnaire measures of psychological well-being (Goldberg 1978; Warr et al. 1979; Warr 1990) than subjects who did not experience flow as highly enjoyable. The enjoyable flow group also experienced more happiness, relaxation, and interest, on average, as measured by the ESM, than those who did not experience flow as highly enjoyable. Thus enjoyable flow seems to be important for psychological well-being, though this requires further validation.

Enjoyable flow experiences come from a wide range of activities. In the study of young people by Haworth and Evans (1995) highly enjoyable flow experiences were most frequently associated with the job, followed by listening to music. Csikszentmihalyi and LeFevre (1989) in an ESM study, found, contrary to expectations, that the vast majority of flow experiences, measured as perceived balanced skill–challenge experiences above the person's average level, came when people were at work rather than in free time. A study by Haworth and Hill (1992) of young adult white-collar workers shows similar results.

A small study of working women by Allison and Duncan (1987, 1988) used a questionnaire they devised to measure enjoyable flow:

> When I stop to think about it I realise that an important part of this state of mind is enjoyment. I get so involved in what I am doing that I almost forget about time. When I experience this state of mind, I feel really free from boredom and worry. I feel like I am being challenged or that I am

very much in control of my actions and my world. I feel like I am growing and using my best talents and skills; I am master of my situation.

(Csikszentmihalyi and Csikszentmihalyi 1988: 121)

Respondents were asked how often in a week they experienced a similar state of mind, selecting from 1 (not at all), 2 (once a week), 3 (several times a week), 4 (every day), 5 (several times a day). They were also asked to indicate whether these experiences occurred in work or leisure and give a brief description of the types of activities which gave rise to these experiences. The results showed work to be the primary source of flow for professional workers, whereas for blue-collar women it was leisure. The greatest source of flow in leisure was found to be in interpersonal relationships for both groups, particularly those with children. Using a similar questionnaire, a study of male and female office workers by Bryce and Haworth (2002) showed flow to be associated with well-being. Results also emphasised the importance of interpersonal relationships for flow in women. This is consistent with previous research indicating the importance of social interaction in leisure for women, arguably resulting from gender demands (Deem 1986; Green et al. 1990; Shaw 1994; Samuel 1996).

## A model of well-being

An influential model of the influence of characteristics of situations and persons on well-being has been proposed by Warr (1987, 1999). Warr (1987) identified nine 'situational' factors, or Principal Environmental Influences (PEIs) important for well-being, measured on several dimensions. These factors are opportunity for control, environmental clarity, opportunity for skill use, externally generated goals, variety, opportunity for interpersonal contact, valued social position, availability of money, and physical security. These features of the environment are considered to interact with characteristics of the person to facilitate or constrain psychological well-being or mental health. Warr produced a classification of 'enduring' personal characteristics which interact with situational factors on mental health. These person factors include baseline mental health, demographic factors such as age and gender, values, and abilities. Baseline mental health includes several features often considered as elements of personality, such as neuroticism, self-confidence, hardiness and locus of control.

The nine factors have been devised in the light of considerable research into both jobs and unemployment, which Warr (1987) summarises. Research conducted at Manchester University (summarised in Haworth 1997), shows strong associations between each of the nine Principal Environmental Influences and measures of mental health, and also discriminates between patterns of PEIs important for well-being in different occupational groups. Bryce and Haworth (2003) have also shown that the influence of control on well-being can operate by different pathways in males and females.

An important development of the model, proposed by Haworth (1997: see Figure 9.1) is the inclusion of the role of enjoyment in well-being. In line with research into enjoyment (e.g. Csikszentmihalyi and Csikszentmihalyi 1988; Clarke and Haworth 1994; Haworth and Evans 1995; Bryce and Haworth 2002), the model suggests that enjoyment and situational factors are conjoined, and that enjoyment can give rise directly to well-being. Research into a small group of female clerical workers by Haworth et al. (1997), used questionnaires developed at Manchester (Haworth 1997) to measure the PEIs, standard scales to measure well-being, and a standard measure of locus of control (Rotter 1966), which is the degree to which an individual feels that behavioural outcomes are due to personal effort (internal locus of control) rather than to chance (external locus of control). The Experience Sampling Method was also used over a period of one week to measure positive subjective states, including enjoyment. The results, illustrated in Figure 9.1, showed, in line with previous research, that several of the PEIs were associated with measures of well-being. Also in line with previous research, locus of control was associated with measures of well-being, with internal locus of control individuals having better scores. Internal locus of control individuals had better scores on several PEIs; and also greater levels of enjoyment, interest and control, and wished to be doing activities more, than external locus of control individuals, measured over the week of the study. Path analysis showed that for some measures of well-being, locus of control had a greater indirect effect on well-being through the PEIs than a direct effect. The study suggested that enjoyment and feelings of control might enhance locus of control, which in turn may lead to enhanced well-being either directly or through greater access to PEIs.

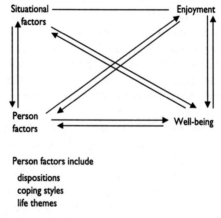

Figure 9.1 A model of well-being

Rotter (1966, 1990) emphasises that locus of control is a learned expectancy, rather than a fixed trait. Feist et al. (1995) suggest that dispositions such as optimism can filter perceptions of daily experience, and that daily experience can in turn influence dispositions. Furnham and Steele (1993) also note that while locus of control beliefs may influence experience, the reverse may also be true. They suggest that positive successful life experiences probably increase internal locus of control beliefs through optimistic attributions. These may increase confidence, initiative and positive motivation, and thus lead to more successful experiences. Rotter (1982) indicates the possible importance of 'enhancement behaviours', which he viewed as 'specific cognitive activities that are used by internals to enhance and maintain good feelings'. However, Uleman and Bargh (1989) also indicate the importance of subconscious processes in well-being, and Merleau-Ponty (1962) in his Embodiment theory of consciousness indicates the importance of both non-reflective and reflective interactions in Being (see Haworth 2000). Conceivably, positive subjective states could influence person factors, such as dispositions, coping styles and life themes, through both reflective and non-reflective interactions. In turn, person factors could influence well-being directly, or indirectly through access to situational factors important for well-being. The model can be investigated in both work and non-work situations, using the questionnaires given in Haworth (1997). Qualitative methods, including interviews, accounts, observation, and ethnographic studies (Haworth 1996; Crossley 2000) can be used to investigate particular aspects in greater detail. Warr (2001, seminar 1 www.wellbeing-esrc.com) makes the important point that in investigating well-being in employment it is also necessary to link this with the investigation of performance, seeking benefits in both areas.

## Conclusion

As noted in Haworth (1997) our postmodern condition is characterised by diversity, uncertainty, and threats and opportunities. Our conceptions of how we come to know and understand things are undergoing significant change. Traditional views, which conceive perception as being a representation of pre-given, objective, properties of the world, are being challenged. In *The Embodied Mind*, Varela, et al. (1991) see cognition not as representation of the world but as embodied action. Perception and our knowledge of the world are considered to be generated by our interaction with the world which takes on a specific form due to the nature of our bodies and our individual and social experiences in the particular culture in which we live. Truths and ideas are thus cultural objects, rather than absolute certainties. Yet this does not detract from their organising force, and they may give a firm focus to action and thought (see Haworth 2000). Social science research can produce information useful for the endeavour of enhancing well-being, including performance. But it is not knowledge which is universally applicable. Instead, it has to be used with an understanding of particular situations. It may also be the case, as Perri 6 (2002) (www.wellbeing-esrc.com seminar on Research and Policy for Wellbeing) has strongly argued, that recommendations for enhancing well-being in one social group may impinge on the well-being of another social group, and that there will be some degree of conflict which will need to be handled by negotiation and compromise.

Similarly, when considering work and leisure, research can be valuable in providing information and perspectives for both understanding and policy making. Research shows the importance of social institutions for both facilitating and constraining human endeavour in work and leisure. Major issues such as the balance between paid work and the rest of life, require global, national, and local perspectives on the role of social institutions in creating satisfactory work and leisure in agreed economic frameworks. Research is also crucial in monitoring the distribution of resources available for work and leisure in different groups in society, whether these are analysed by class, age, gender, ethnicity or location. Equally important in societies characterised by diversity, is research into the experiences and motivations of individuals with varying work and leisure lifestyles. Recognising the diversity of human experience and requirements, and the social and temporal nature of human endeavour, means there is no one correct policy for work and leisure. In rapidly changing societies, time is needed for social practices to meet new requirements. Research can inform transitions, but does not supplant the role of negotiation.

## References

Allison, M. T. and Duncan, M. C. (1987) Women, work and leisure: the days of our lives. *Leisure Sciences* 9: 143–62.

Allison, M. T. and Duncan, M. C. (1988) Women, work and flow. In M. Csikszentmihalyi and I. S. Csikszentmihalyi (eds) *Optimal Experience: Psychological Studies of Flow in Consciousness*. Cambridge: Cambridge University Press.

*American Psychologist* (2000) 55 special edition.

Andrews, F. M. and Withey, S. B. (1974) Developing measures of perceived life quality: results from several national surveys. *Social Indicators Research* 1: 1–26.

Applebaum, H. A. (1998) *The American Work Ethic and the Changing Work Force: A Historical Perspective*. Westport, CT: Greenwood Press.

Argyle, M. (1987) *The Psychology of Happiness*. London: Methuen.

Beck, U. (2000) *The Brave New World of Work*. Oxford: Blackwell with Polity.

Bradburn, N. M. (1969) *The Structure of Psychological Well-being*. Chicago: Aldine.

Bradburn, N. M. and Caplovitz, D. (1965) *Reports of Happiness*. Chicago: Aldine.

Brief, A. P., Butcher, A. H., George, J. M. and Link, K. E. (1993) Integrating bottom-up and top-down theories of subjective well-being: the case of health. *Journal of Personality and Social Psychology* 64: 646–53.

Bryce, J. and Haworth, J. T. (2002) Wellbeing and flow in a sample of male and female office workers. *Leisure Studies* 21: 249–63.

Bryce, J. and Haworth, J. T. (2003) Psychological wellbeing in a sample of male and female office workers. *Journal of Applied Social Psychology* 33(3): 565–85.

Clarke, S. G. and Haworth, J. T. (1994) 'Flow' experience in the daily lives of sixth form college students. *British Journal of Psychology* 85: 511–23.

Crossley, M. (2000) *Introducing Narrative Psychology*. Buckingham: Open University Press.

Csikszentmihalyi, M. (1975) *Beyond Boredom and Anxiety*. San Francisco, CA: Jossey-Bass.

Csikszentmihalyi, M. (1982) Towards a psychology of optimal experience. In L. Wheeler (ed.) *Review of Personality and Social Psychology*, vol. 2. Beverley Hills, CA: Sage.

Csikszentmihalyi, M. (1991) *Flow: The Psychology of Optimal Experience*. New York: Harper Perennial.

Csikszentmihalyi, M. (1993) *The Evolving Self*. New York: HarperRow.

Csikszentmihalyi, M. (1999) Flow. In A. E. Kazdin (ed.) *Encyclopedia of Psychology*, vol. 3. New York: Oxford University Press.

Csikszentmihalyi, M. and Csikszentmihalyi, I. S. (1988) *Optimal Experience: Psychological Studies of Flow in Consciousness*. Cambridge: Cambridge University Press.

Csikszentmihalyi, M. and LeFevre, J. (1989) Optimal experience in work and leisure. *Journal of Personality and Social Psychology* 56(5): 815–22.

Deem, R. (1986) *All Work and No Play? The Sociology of Women and Leisure*. Milton Keynes: Open University Press.

Diener, E. (2000) Subjective well-being: the science of happiness and a proposal for a national index. *American Psychologist* 55(1): 34–43.

Donovan, N., Halpern, D. and Sargeant, R. (2002) *Life Satisfaction: The State of Knowledge and Implications for Government*. London: Strategy Unit, Cabinet Office, Downing Street.

Feist, G. J., Todd, E., Bodner, T. E., Jacobs, J. F., Miles, M. and Tan, V. (1995) Integrating top-down and bottom-up structural models of subjective wellbeing: a longitudinal investigation. *Journal of Personality and Social Psychology* 68: 138–50.

Furnham, A. and Steele, H. (1993) Measuring locus of control: a critique of general, children's, health and work related locus of control questionnaires. *British Journal of Psychology* 84: 443–79.

Gershuny, J. (2000) *Changing Times: Work and Leisure in Postindustrial Society*. Oxford: Oxford University Press.

Goldberg, D. P. (1978) *Manual for the General Health Questionnaire*. Windsor: National Foundation for Educational Research.

Green, E., Hebron, S. and Woodward, D. (1990) *Women's Leisure, What Leisure?* London: Macmillan.

Haworth, J. T. (1996) *Psychological Research: Innovative Methods and Strategies*. London: Routledge.

Haworth, J. T. (1997) *Work, Leisure and Well-being*. London: Routledge.

Haworth, J. T. (2000) The embodied mind and wellbeing. *Consciousness and Experiential Psychology* 5: 14–19.

Haworth, J. T. and Evans, S. (1995) Challenge, skill and positive subjective states in the daily life of a sample of YTS students. *Journal of Occupational and Organisational Psychology* 68: 109–21.

Haworth, J. T. and Hill, S. (1992) Work, leisure and psychological well-being in a sample of young adults. *Journal of Community and Applied Social Psychology* 2: 147–60.

Haworth, J. T., Jarman, M. and Lee, S. (1997) Positive psychological states in the daily life of a sample of working women. *Journal of Applied Social Psychology* 27: 345–70.

Haworth, J. T., Hart, G. and Curtis, S. (2001–2002) ESRC seminar series 'Wellbeing: situational and individual determinants' 2001–2002 www.wellbeing-esrc.com.

Herzberg, F. (1966) *Work and the Nature of Man*. Chicago: World Publishing.

Ingold, T. (2000) *The Perception of the Environment*. London: Routledge.

Iso-Ahola, S. (1997) A psychological analysis of leisure and health. J. T. Haworth (ed.) *Work, Leisure and Well-being*. London: Routledge.

Jahoda, M. (1982) *Employment and Unemployment: A Social Psychological Analysis*. Cambridge: Cambridge University Press.

Jahoda, M. (1986) In defense of a non-reductionist social psychology. *Social Behaviour* 1: 25–9.

Kahneman, D., Diener, E. and Schwarz, N. (1999) *Well-Being: The Foundations of Hedonic Psychology*. New York: Russell Sage Foundation.

Kohn, M. and Schooler, M. (1983) *Work and Personality: An Enquiry into the Impact of Social Stratification*. Norwood, NJ: Ablex.

Layard, R. (2003) Happiness: has social science a clue? A series of three lectures which can be accessed at the website cep.lse.ac.uk.

Leete, L. (2000) History and housework: implications for work hours and family policy in market economies. In L. Golden and D. M. Figart (eds) *Working Time: International Trends, Theory and Policy Perspectives*. London: Routledge.

Lewis, S. (2001) Work–life integration. ESRC seminar series 'Wellbeing: situational and individual determinants' 2001–2002 www.wellbeing-esrc.com Work, employment, leisure and wellbeing.

Lewis, S. (2003) The integration of paid work and the rest of life. Is post-industrial work the new leisure? *Leisure Studies* 22(4): 343–55.

Massimini, F. and Carli, M. (1988) The systematic assessment of flow in daily experience. In M. Csikszentmihalyi and I. S. Csikszentmihalyi (eds) *Optimal Experience*. Cambridge: Cambridge University Press.

Merleau-Ponty, M. (1962) *Phenomenology of Perception*. London: Routledge and Kegan Paul.

Perri 6 (2002) Sense and solidarities: a neo-Durkheimian institutional theory of wellbeing and its implications for public policy. ESRC seminar series 'Wellbeing: situational and individual determinants' 2001–2002 www.wellbeing-esrc.com Research and Policy for Wellbeing.

Prilleltensky, I. (2001) Personal, relational, and collective Well-being: an integrative approach. ESRC seminar series 'Wellbeing: situational and individual determinants' 2001–2002 www.wellbeing-esrc.com Wellbeing: interaction between person and environment.

Primeau, C. A. (1996) Work and leisure: transcending the dichotomy. *American Journal of Occupational Therapy* 50: 569–77.

Rapoport, R., Bailyn, L., Fletcher, J. and Pruit, B. (2002) *Beyond Work–Family Balance: Advancing Gender Equity and Work Performance*. San Francisco, CA: Jossey-Bass.

Rotter, J. B. (1966) Generalised expectancies for internal versus external control of reinforcement. *Psychological Monographs* 80 (whole no.): 609.

Rotter, J. B. (1982) *The Development and Application of Social Learning Theory*. New York: Praeger.

Rotter, J. B. (1990) Internal versus external locus of control of reinforcement: a case history of a variable. *American Psychologist* 45(4): 489–93.

Samuel, N. (1996) *Women, Family and Leisure in Contemporary Society*. Wallingford, UK: CAB International.

Seligman, M. E. P. and Csikszentmihalyi, M. (2000) Positive psychology: an introduction. *American Psychologist* 55(1): 5–14.

Shaw, S. M. (1994) Gender, leisure and constraint: towards a framework for the analysis of women's leisure. *Journal of Leisure Research* 26: 8–22.

Snyder, C. R. and Lopez, S. J. (2000) *Handbook of Positive Psychology*. Oxford: Oxford University Press.

Stebbins, R. A. (1992) *Amateurs, Professionals and Serious Leisure*. Montreal and Kingston, ON: McGill-Queen's University Press.

Stebbins, R. A. (1997) Serious leisure and wellbeing. In J. T. Haworth (ed.) *Work, Leisure and Wellbeing*. London: Routledge.

Taylor, R. (2001) The Future of Work–Life Balance. ESRC Future of Work Programme Seminar Series, Economic and Social Research Council, Polaris House, Swindon.

Taylor, R. (2002) Britain's World of Work-Myths and Realities. ESRC Future of Work Programme Seminar Series, Economic and Social Research Council, Polaris House, Swindon.

Uleman, J. S. and Bargh, J. A. (eds) (1989) *Unintended Thought*. London: Guilford Press.

Varela, F. J., Thompson, E. and Rosch, E. (1991) *The Embodied Mind: Cognitive Science and Human Experience*. Cambridge, MA: MIT Press.

Warr, P. (1987) *Work, Unemployment and Mental Health*. Oxford: Clarendon Press.

Warr, P. (1990) The measurement of well-being and other aspects of mental health. *Journal of Occupational Psychology* 63: 193–210.

Warr, P. (1999) Well-being and the workplace. In D. Kahneman, E. Deiner and N. Schwartz (eds) *Well-being: The Foundations of Hedonic Psychology*. New York: Springer-Verlag.

Warr, P. (2001) Employment, work and well-being. ESRC seminar series 'Wellbeing: situational and individual determinants' 2001–2002 www.wellbeing-esrc.com. Work, employment, leisure and wellbeing.

Warr, P., Cook, J. and Wall, T. (1979) Scales for the measurement of some work attitudes and aspects of psychological well-being. *Journal of Occupational Psychology* 52: 129–48.

Watson, D. and Tellegen, A. (1985) Toward a consensual structure of mood. *Psychological Bulletin* 96: 219–35.

# Chapter 10

# Leisure and Health

*Seppo E. Iso-Ahola and Roger C. Mannell*

## Introduction

Health is the most valued commodity, and it is shown in many ways, as in New Year greetings in which people wish their friends and relatives health and happiness. One often hears people saying that nothing matters more than health, and they proclaim you cannot buy health and happiness. In addition, claiming to have good health is often a psychological safety valve, a compensation mechanism for disappointments and failures in other spheres of life, such as finances: 'I don't have a lot of money and cannot do the things rich people do, but I am healthy'. Given this perceived importance of health, what do people do to achieve or maintain it? An answer seems to be: very little. For example, while the health benefits of exercise are well documented and widely trumpeted in the mass media, 78% of Americans are sedentary (Blair 1993). In other words, by not exercising regularly, Americans are significantly increasing their risk of premature mortality due to heart disease, stroke and cancer. Similarly, about 25% of people smoke even though the health hazards of smoking are well established and known. Further, many people drink alcohol excessively and have poor diets. In fact, experts now attribute the epidemic of diabetes to the typical American diet: soft drinks, white rice, white bread, and french fries.

Why this contradiction of knowing about the importance of health on one hand and doing little for it or even engaging in at-risk health behaviours on the other? While there is no unequivocal answer to this question, there seem to be two ironies with respect to this issue. First, people take health for granted, even as an entitlement. Because 97% of people are born healthy, they may view health as a birthright and pay attention to it only when reminded about it, for example, when falling ill or when seeing friends struggle with various illnesses. The second irony is that health is largely controllable, determined mainly by our own actions and behaviours, in other words, how we live our daily lives. It is estimated that over 80% of the factors determining health have nothing to do with medical treatment. For some years now, of the ten leading causes of death before age 65, lifestyle is estimated to account for

53%, more than twice the second most important cause, environment (21.8%) (Powell 1988). Most remarkably, if all types of cancer were eliminated, human life expectancy would increase by only two years, but if good health behaviours (i.e. good nutrition, exercise, non-smoking and moderate alcohol use) were practised the average life expectancy would go up a whopping seven years (Ornstein & Erlich 1989). In short, health is determined much more by environment than genetics, with lifestyle playing a critical role. Lifestyle, of course, is directly and individually controllable and modifiable, but as we will see, herein lies the main psychological problem.

Much of what is controllable about lifestyle is leisure-related. Most people's work lifestyle is determined for them, whereas leisure choices, in general, are under their own control. This, then, raises an important question about the relationship between leisure and health. In this chapter, we explore the relationship from a psychological perspective, first analysing the psychological obstacles for adoption of active and healthy leisure lifestyles, then examining leisure's health benefits, and finally reviewing the latest research on stress, leisure and health.

## Psychological obstacles

In theory, a person can be either proactive or reactive in relation to health. Being proactive means that he/she believes health is controllable and consequently engages actively in heath-promoting behaviours. Being reactive, on the other hand, refers to the absence of such behaviours, suggesting that one is involved in health-promoting behaviours mostly after encountering health problems. Proactive individuals have active lifestyles, are enthusiastic about various activities, and derive a lot of enjoyment from them. Reactive individuals, in contrast, tend to lead passive and sedentary lifestyles, viewing leisure as time to be killed rather than seeing it as an opportunity to engage in exciting and meaningful activities.

There seems to be little doubt that most people are reactive in their approach to health. For example, it has been shown that once people have had major illnesses, such as a heart attack, they are then more likely to adhere to their exercise programmes than when they have not had such health problems (Oldridge 1982; Dishman 1990). It takes a heart attack to get people exercising! Other evidence of people's reactive rather than proactive approach to health is seen in the amount of time devoted to watching TV: on average almost four hours per day in the United States. Yet in survey after survey, people cite lack of time as the biggest barrier to their failure to exercise. Given that it takes only 30 minutes of brisk walking three times a week to maintain one's physical health (Surgeon General's Report 1996), the lack of time appears to be nothing but an excuse. There can hardly be anything so important on TV that one cannot take 30 minutes out of four hours of TV watching time and go for a brisk walk. Thus, it appears that health is taken for granted and health maintenance is not a priority for most people. Those who spend weekends fixing their cars but not exercising are in essence saying that their car's health is more important than their own.

What, then, leads people to become more reactive than proactive in relation to health? An important reason is based on Festinger's (1957) idea of cognitive dissonance. In this case, cognitive dissonance exists because of two conflicting cognitions: knowing that exercise and not smoking etc. are good for one's health on one hand, and not engaging in such behaviours on the other. Festinger showed that people cannot exist in such a dissonant state of mind and therefore are motivated to achieve consonance by changing either their behaviour or cognitions. Since most people do not begin exercising or cannot stop smoking, their only option is to change the cognition. So, they say: 'Winston Churchill smoked cigars and lived for over 90 years'. Or, 'my granddad never exercised and was healthy all of his long life'. This kind of cognitive compensation allows people to maintain their sanity while not engaging in healthy behaviours. Unfortunately, it also makes them reactive in relation to health: smokers stop smoking after a diagnosis of lung cancer and couch potatoes start exercising after their first heart attack.

Another culprit is today's typical lifestyle. Many people's lives are stressful because of financial difficulties and the dominance of work. They live from payday to payday and push themselves to the brink of financial disaster because of credit-card debt. They have a work–spend–work–spend mentality (Schor 1991; Swift 2002): they work hard so that they can spend more, and the more they spend, the harder they have to work to maintain their lifestyle. They are stressed out about their work and their ability to pay the bills, and are mentally and physically tired after a day's work. This way of life trivialises leisure and promotes passiveness and sedentary leisure (Iso-Ahola 1997). Leisure is used for recuperation for and from work. Work and finances, not personal health, dominate their lives and leave little chance to 'discover' leisure. In this kind of lifestyle and context, leisure becomes synonymous with guilt rather than health. Because of their guilt feelings, people, especially women, are afraid of even asking: 'What about my leisure'? (Shank 1986). The net result is a passive leisure lifestyle and reactive approach to personal health.

Our consumer society clearly leads to people being more passive than active in their leisure. This happens mainly by commercial efforts to make home a better and bigger centre of entertainment. Of course, one occasionally hears and sees commercials promoting such active forms of leisure as belonging to health clubs, but they are rare compared to the constant bombardment of information on the latest devices geared to enhance TV-watching and movie-going at home. In the 1980s and 90s it was the video recorder, bigger TV screens and satellite dishes. Now it is DVD (digital video disc players). Of course, it does not stop at the DVD. The marketers are trying to convince people that with DVD, they need special speakers and a digital amplifier to create the surround sound so that they can fully appreciate the movie-going experience at home. And the experience would not be complete without an even bigger and wider-screen TV. This promotion of passive lifestyles is done to maintain a healthy economy and in that sense is unintentional, but it is nevertheless a powerful and invisible conspiracy against the more active and healthier lifestyle. It makes people increasingly more reactive to and dependent on stimuli than creators of their own action. Herein lies an answer to the question: 'If we are so rich, why aren't we happy'? (Csikszentmihaly 1999).

The promotion of passive home entertainment by the private sector is successful for several psychological reasons. First, people have a universal tendency to always take the path of least resistance in terms of time, money and effort. If they can have a good TV-watching or movie-going experience at home, they will opt for it rather than go to a local theatre or cinema because of savings in time, money and effort. Thus, they will acquire the latest device that will make choosing the path of least resistance easier. Second, two trends about living in today's society make people ripe for the passive using of home entertainment. One, continuous stress due to work, commuting and personal finances make people mentally exhausted and thus ready for passive home entertainment. Two, today's society emphasizes family and family togetherness rather than a personal and individualistic lifestyle. It is socially more acceptable to find things to do together as a family than individually. This, coupled with the overall importance of the Protestant work ethic, is likely to evoke feelings of guilt if one contemplates involvement in personal leisure activity. Thus, home entertainment is an easy and convenient solution for a joint family activity. As a result, all of these factors become a powerful psychological force that pushes people toward a passive and sedentary lifestyle.

## Motivation for leisure

If the way we live our lives is the main determinant of our health, lifestyle becomes critical for prevention of health problems. There is plenty of evidence in the literature (for reviews of research, see Iso-Ahola 1994, 1997) that an active leisure lifestyle is health-promoting. Adoption of such a lifestyle, however, requires a proactive approach to health, but as discussed, most people tend to be reactive in relation to health and consequently passive and sedentary in their leisure. As one person said: 'Why exercise because you're going to die anyway?' Perhaps most sedentary people are not that cynical and depressive, but they may not be too far from this way of thinking either. Such thinking obviously misses the point about health and quality of life and raises a major question about motivational foundations for leisure.

Why are some people active in and 'serious' (Stebbins 1992; Stebbins 2001) about their leisure while others do little or nothing in their free time? It is well documented that intrinsic motivation and a sense of freedom or self-determination or autonomy is at the heart of leisure (Iso-Ahola 1980; Mannell & Kleiber 1997). It is also known that these psychological factors are important for human health and mortality (e.g., Langer & Rodin 1976; Rodin & Langer 1977; Schulz 1976). So, motivation for leisure becomes synonymous with motivation for health. Figure 10.1 shows the motivational foundations of leisure behaviour. It demonstrates two things about motivation. First, there are 'ultimate' (biological predispositions and early socialization), 'distal' (knowledge and values/attitudes) and 'proximal' (constraints and facilitators) determinants of motivation.

Second, motivation for leisure can be both permanent and temporary, permanent in the sense that people have a stable predisposition toward intrinsic motivation for leisure and temporary in the sense that motivation can fluctuate as a function of situational constraints and facilitators.

As for the 'ultimate' determinants, Deci and Ryan (1991) have argued that infants are born with the 'innate' needs for autonomy, competence and relatedness. They state that 'from the time of birth, human beings are oriented toward the active exercise of their capacities and interests. They seek out optimal challenges, and they attempt to master and integrate new experiences' (Deci and Ryan 1991: 238–9). If so, everyone possesses in early

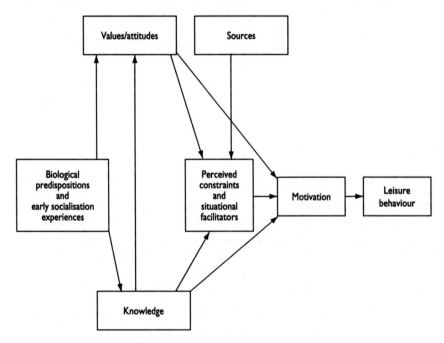

*Figure 10.1* A path-analytic model of motivational determinants of leisure behaviour

*Source:* adapted from Iso-Ahola and St. Clair 2000

childhood a tendency toward intrinsic motivation and active lifestyle. This tendency, however, can be easily stifled by a restrictive home environment, and as Iso-Ahola (1999) has argued, it is severely undermined by the school system that strips children of their sense of self-determination or autonomy and makes them dependent on extrinsic rewards and contingencies (e.g. grades). It is further derailed after young people adopt the values of the consumer society with its work–spend–work–spend mentality. All of this suggests that the adoption of an active leisure lifestyle becomes a psychological struggle as people get older. Again, this pattern is due to the fact their basic human tendency to explore, be curious, try new things, and master challenges is discouraged and undermined by the social system and environment. Early exposures to various activities and practices are critical in the sense that they determine what kinds of experiences and knowledge people accumulate in their formative years. These practices along with cumulative knowledge help in forming early values and attitudes toward activeness in general and certain types of activities in particular.

Some people succeed in acquiring knowledge and values/attitudes that are conducive to intrinsic motivation for leisure. They become cognitively aware not only of the importance of leisure but also about their capacity and skills to engage in various leisure activities. It further means that they are aware of opportunities and places where leisure activities can be pursued. Such knowledge, attitudes and values toward leisure can be effective in countering the prevailing emphasis on extrinsic motivation and thus in helping rediscover one's innate predisposition toward intrinsically rewarding activities.

Both knowledge and attitudes (and values) are 'distal' causes of leisure motivation, and their influence is mediated by more 'proximal' factors, such as situational constraints and facilitators. For example, constraints have less effect on those people's leisure motivation whose attitudes toward leisure are positive. On the other hand, constraints are more readily accepted as excuses for non-participation by those who do not value leisure or think they have no leisure skills. Similarly, the influence of such facilitators as friends calling and asking to participate in an activity depends in part on a person's underlying knowledge and attitudes. It should also be noted that those who have a permanent predisposition toward intrinsic motivation are less affected by these kinds of constraints and facilitating conditions (Iwasaki & Mannell 1999).

In the long term, it is possible to maintain motivation for leisure activities (and thus for health) only if one's participation is self-determined and intrinsically rewarding. Such involvement is marked by fun, enjoyment, excitement and enthusiasm. When a person is full of excitement and cannot wait to participate in an activity, it is a clear indication that behaviour is determined by intrinsic motivation. On the other hand, behaviour can be controlled by external factors or 'intrapsychic' pressures as well, but then the long-term maintenance of the behaviour becomes a major problem. This seems to be a key for understanding why 50% of people quit their exercise programmes within six months. Most of them participate because they have been told or have read that they 'should' do so. They do not like exercise or have not found an enjoyable form of exercise for themselves. Most people start exercising for instrumental reasons and extrinsic rewards (e.g. losing weight) and fail to turn it into a more self-determined activity (Iso-Ahola & St. Clair 2000). When one adds to this the fact that exercise has some costs (e.g. fatigue, muscle soreness), is often negatively reinforced or discouraged by the immediate social environment (e.g., an unsupportive spouse), is physically challenging, and is perceived to be demanding in terms of time and preparation, it is no wonder that 50% of exercisers quit within six months (Iso-Ahola 1999).

With its potential for freedom and autonomy, leisure can also be motivationally insidious. Recalling that the need for autonomy is a primary human need, a question then is 'how can it be minimally satisfied?' Leisure or free time choices offer an excellent opportunity for the experience of autonomy. That is, when a person comes home from obligatory work, she/he is free, free perhaps for the first time during the day, free from work. When people choose not to do anything in this situation, they feel freedom and are therefore able to fulfil the basic human need for autonomy. The next step, of course, would be to do something that they want to do, but psychologically it is not necessary to take such a step to find a sense of freedom. Thus, this need can be at least partially fulfilled by choosing to exercise, not to exercise, or do nothing. This ironic and insidious effect of leisure may also explain in part why people watch so much TV every day (Iso-Ahola 1999). They first choose to watch TV and in doing so find further freedom in the multitude of channels from which to choose. However, the irony is that choosing more challenging and effortful activity such as exercising has been shown to make people feel better in the long run (Mannell, Zuzanek & Larson 1988).

All of this means that health behaviours to be practised in one's leisure face a motivational uphill battle. First, today's society is clearly biased toward promotion of passive and sedentary lifestyle, especially in the form of home entertainment. Second, many people have lost their early childhood predisposition toward intrinsic motivation. Third, many health-behaviours are started for wrong (extrinsic) motives, and are perceived to be obligatory in nature. Fourth, by choosing to do nothing or to engage in passive home entertainment in his/her leisure a person is able to fulfil the basic human need for autonomy and self-determination. Taken together, then, it should not be surprising that passive and sedentary lifestyles are common in present-day society.

## Health benefits of leisure

As the previous discussion has shown, adoption of an active and healthy lifestyle is difficult for a variety of psychological reasons. However, there are many people who are able to overcome the psychological obstacles and consequently reap considerable health benefits from being physically and mentally active in leisure. The first benefit concerns the effects of physically active leisure on health. It has been shown that exercise reduces mortality rates by almost 50% among those who move from being totally sedentary to being moderately active (Blair & Connelly 1996). What about other types of leisure activities in this regard? A study by Glass et al. (1999) examined the association between social, productive and physical leisure activity and survival rates among older people. The results showed that social activities (e.g. spectator sports and playing cards) and productive activities (e.g. gardening and preparing meals) involving little or no enhancement of physical fitness lowered the risk of all causes of mortality as much as fitness activities. The authors suggested that these survival benefits may occur through 'psychosocial pathways', such that social contacts may reduce the adverse effects of psychological stress through the enhancement of both cellular and humoral immune response. Also, social and productive activity is likely to enhance social support and social networks and to facilitate the performance of meaningful social roles, all of which promote a sense of purpose in life and of self-efficacy that has been linked to important health outcomes in later life.

Although these findings are provocative, it would be premature to conclude that one can abandon physical activity and replace it by more social activity. However, as Glass et al. (1999) suggested, the findings call for a broader range of activity options for older people as a complement to exercise programmes. This is consistent with Roberts et al.'s (1989) findings that people with 'impoverished leisure' were the least healthy group while those with a 'rich leisure' lifestyle (i.e., more varied and frequent involvement than the average for the sample) were the healthiest people. The main reason why one cannot abandon physical activity is the well-documented significant effects of exercise on the reduction of risk in heart disease, stroke, colon cancer, diabetes, obesity and osteoporosis (e.g., Blair 1993; Nelson et al. 1994).

As for the mental health benefits of leisure, participation in both physical and non-physical leisure activities has been shown to reduce depression and anxiety, produce positive moods, enhance self-esteem and self-concept, facilitate social interaction, increase general psychological well-being and life satisfaction, and even improve cognitive functioning (for a review of research, see Iso-Ahola 1997). The fact that these mental health benefits are obtained from physical exercise activity and non-physical leisure activity alike is important. It demonstrates that the positive effects of exercise on mental health do not depend on significant increases in aerobic and anaerobic fitness and other physiological changes.

Another mental health benefit of leisure is prevention and alleviation of burnout. There is little doubt that today's stressful work environments are pushing people to their psychological limits (Time Out 1995). Society has become a paradox because we praise people who want balance in their lives, but reward those who work themselves to death (Breaking point 1995). As a result, some people's idea of vacation is a trip to the dentist's office where they can lie back in the chair and relax. Failure to find balance between work and leisure is therefore an important reason why an increasing number of people are falling victims to burnout. Burnout is 'an individual stress experience', a psychological syndrome of emotional exhaustion, depersonalisation, and reduced personal accomplishment (Maslach & Goldberg 1998).

Stanton-Rich and Iso-Ahola (1998) reported an empirical study on the relationship between burnout and leisure. They found that actual leisure behaviour and leisure satisfaction were inversely related to burnout, while leisure attitude had no significant relationship to burnout. Results indicated that the more active people's leisure and the higher their leisure satisfaction, the lower their emotional exhaustion and depersonalisation and the higher their personal accomplishments. It was further found that the higher a person's level of self-determination, the lower he/she was on depersonalisation and the higher on personal accomplishment. It is interesting that a person's leisure attitude did not contribute significantly to burnout and any of its components. This suggests that having a positive attitude toward leisure is not sufficient; one has to actively participate in leisure activities, and it helps even more if the person is satisfied with his/her leisure. From the prevention standpoint, the best combination seems to be an individual who has a personality predisposition toward self-determination and who actively engages in leisure behaviours and is satisfied with such a leisure lifestyle.

A question still remains as to whether burnout can be prevented and significantly alleviated by any kind of leisure behaviour, that is, by active as well as passive leisure lifestyles. Although this study did not directly address this question, there is a reason to believe that simply taking 'time-out' through any leisure activity is important in the reduction of burnout, at least in the short run. This view is based on the finding that leisure behaviour's contribution to the reduction of the 'emotional exhaustion' component of burnout was much greater than to the other two components. When one is emotionally overextended and depleted of his/her emotional resources, lacking energy to face another day or another person, time-out even in the form of passive activities can be helpful on the temporary basis. On the other hand, the fact that leisure behaviour contributed positively to the 'personal accomplishment' component suggests that this increased sense of self-efficacy can be obtained only through leisure activities that match challenges with personal skills. In fact, it has been shown ( Haworth 1993; Haworth & Evans 1995) that people rate psychologically as best those leisure experiences that offer challenge, require the use of personal skills, and provide a sense of personal control. In contrast, they rate as worst those leisure experiences (e.g. TV-watching) that rank low on these psychological dimensions (Csikszentmihalyi et al. 1977). It then appears that such passive leisure activities as TV-watching can at best be a temporary solution to burnout, whereas a sense of personal accomplishment and self-efficacy is derived from mentally and physically challenging leisure activities and can therefore provide permanent protection against burnout. Csikszentmihalyi (1990) argues that optimal or 'flow' experiences (i.e. mentally and physically challenging experiences) are critical to meaningful human existence and can be found equally well in work and leisure activities.

## Leisure, stress and health

As we have seen, burnout is a health problem resulting from specific types of stressors, that is, those that are job-related. There are, of course, many other sources and types of stress in contemporary life that can threaten health. Today, people report being inundated by time pressure and stressful events in all areas of their lives. They struggle with the stress of managing daily hassles (e.g. financial concerns), role strain (e.g. competing demands parenthood and unemployment), chronic life problems (e.g. long-term disability), life transitions (e.g. retirement), and life crises (e.g. divorce) (Zuzanek 1998). However, though stress has been linked to a variety of physical (e.g. fatigue, heart disease) and mental health (e.g. depression, eating disorders) problems, not everyone even under prolonged stress becomes ill. Some people are able to resist stress or 'cope' better than others. Researchers have been looking for the source of these differences in coping ability, hoping that if they were better understood, people could be taught to handle stress more effectively, and social arrangements could be improved to facilitate coping (Zeidner & Endler 1996; Salmon 2001).

Though stress and coping have been studied by social scientists for some time, interest in leisure as a potential coping resource is more recent. Coleman and Iso-Ahola (1993) stimulated thinking and research about leisure as a coping resource by formally proposing the *leisure buffer model*. Leisure serves as a coping resource by strengthening people's beliefs about being self-determined and having the social support of others. Both of these beliefs have been shown to be important resources for coping with stress. Since leisure is typically highly social in nature, leisure participation can facilitate the development of companionship and friendship, and consequently, strengthen beliefs about the availability of social support. Also, given that leisure is often the domain of life over which people have the greatest control, leisure by allowing the exercise of choice and control strengthens self-determination beliefs. These leisure-enhanced beliefs serve to buffer the negative effects of stress on health when stress levels are high. When stress levels are lower, leisure may have less impact on health and well-being.

In addition to buffering, there are other ways that coping resources may protect health from stress (see Ensel & Lin 1991; Wheaton 1985), and this is true of leisure as a coping resource as well (Iwasaki & Mannell 2000a; Kleiber et al. 2002). One such alternative occurs when stressful circumstances set in motion two opposing forces – a direct negative influence of stress on health and a positive influence that results when the stress triggers the operation of leisure-coping resources which in turn positively influence health. In this *counteractive model*, the stressors people encounter in their lives are in a see-saw battle with leisure and other coping resources for our wellbeing. For example, the stress of balancing work, family and financial concerns may have a negative effect on health, but this stress may also cause people to change their lifestyles and leisure behaviour to help with psychological and physical recovery.

Coping resources have also been thought to reduce the impact of stress on health without directly influencing health itself. One such model is the *stress reduction model*. The availability of coping resources may reduce the likelihood that an event will be perceived as a stressor or as highly stressful. For example, if I am a person who has a proactive problem-solving approach to life and I generally choose leisure to provide challenges, I would be more likely to experience a change in technology in my workplace, a potentially stressful event, as a challenge to be relished and surmounted rather than as an unwelcome and negative event.

What evidence is there for these different views of the way in which leisure helps people cope with stress? Some evidence has been found for the buffering influence of leisure on health. For example, among a group of people experiencing higher levels of stress, those who reported experiencing a high degree of freedom and control in their leisure also reported significantly lower levels of illness compared to those people who perceived low levels of freedom (Coleman, 1993). However, Coleman found no evidence for the buffering influence of leisure-based social support. On the other hand, Iso-Ahola and Park (1996) found that people who reported that their leisure participation enhanced their friendship networks and enjoyment of shared activities were less depressed and had fewer physical illness symptoms when under stress. Conversely, they found no evidence that leisure-based beliefs of self-determination buffered the effects of stress on health. Interestingly, they also found that those study participants with stronger social support and self-determination beliefs reported fewer illness symptoms regardless of the level of stress present in their lives. These findings suggest that these leisure beliefs, under some circumstances, not only buffer stress, but have a direct positive effect on health regardless of the level of stress encountered.

In a study in which the daily stress experienced by university students was assessed, Iwasaki and Mannell (2000a) also found that the belief that leisure provided a sense of autonomy and fostered friendships positively influenced well-being and health. Some evidence was found for the *buffer* effect of these leisure-coping resources, but there was also evidence that the students' leisure beliefs functioned to both *counteract* and *reduce* the experience of stress and consequently ill-health. These latter findings are consistent with those of social scientists who have studied general coping processes (Lazarus 1995), and suggest that the conditions that determine whether leisure-coping resources will act to buffer, counteract or reduce stress need to be further clarified (Iwasaki 2002).

It might also be useful to distinguish between leisure-coping *beliefs* and leisure-coping *strategies* (Iwasaki & Mannell 2000b). As we have seen, leisure-coping beliefs refer to people's relatively enduring generalized beliefs that their leisure helps them cope with stress in a variety of ways. It seems likely that these beliefs develop gradually over time as part of the socialization process and are maintained through relevant and positive leisure experiences. Leisure-coping strategies, however, can be conceptualized as actual leisure behaviours and experiences that may help people cope with or resist stressful circumstances. In some cases, people may intentionally choose specific leisure behaviours or experiences to help them cope with stress. At other times, they may find that what they do in their leisure has helped them manage stress even though they chose to participate for other reasons. Leisure-coping strategies, then, are more situation-specific and intentional than leisure-coping beliefs, and their use and effectiveness are assumed to vary depending on the specific stressors encountered by the individual. Although there are likely links between people's belief-based coping resources and the situation-specific coping strategies they use, research on general coping processes has shown that the two types of coping resources are not identical and likely do not operate in the same manner (Endler & Parker 1994).

Using leisure activities and experiences for *temporary escape, companionship* and *mood enhancement* appear to be common leisure-coping strategies (Iwasaki & Mannell 2000b). For example, stressful work responsibilities may encourage workers to engage in escape-oriented coping behaviour (palliative coping) in order to temporarily forget about the demands and conflicts they have encountered earlier in the day at work. Becoming engrossed in a favorite music CD or playing a game of squash may allow the individual to take a break from his problems and psychologically 'regroup' to gain renewed perspective. Sharpe and Mannell (cited in Mannell & Kleiber 1997) found that recently widowed women who were more active in their leisure experienced less guilt, depression and sadness, and greater happiness during their daily lives. These women reported consciously trying to keep busy with leisure activities to temporarily escape or distract themselves from intrusive thoughts about their deceased spouses and the resulting emotional distress. A comparison group of non-stressed married women were much more likely to engage in leisure for enjoyment and personal development than for temporary escape. In another study, emergency response workers (e.g. police, paramedics) who used some of their leisure for mood enhancement and palliative coping were found to be coping with job-related stress more effectively, even after the influence of general non-leisure coping strategies was accounted for (Iwasaki et al. 2001).

Before leisure is seen as a panacea for dealing with stress in contemporary life, however, it should be noted that these coping strategies do not always work nor are they necessarily appropriate for dealing with all types of stressors. Iwasaki and Mannell (2000a) assessed the amount of academic stress university students encountered in their daily life for a two week period. The students also reported on how they used leisure to cope with this stress during the two weeks. Students who experienced higher levels of academic stress were more likely to use leisure to escape thinking about this stressor, enhance their mood and seek companionship. Interestingly, not all of these strategies had the desired effect of improving coping and psychological well-being. Though the leisure coping strategies of temporary escape and mood enhancement did counteract the effects of academic stress to some extent and contributed to well-being, greater use of leisure companionship actually resulted in lower levels of well-being. Attempting to cope with academic stress, particularly the stress resulting from pending assignments, by using leisure companionship, may have diverted the students' energy from meeting those deadlines, and consequently, actually increased the stress experienced. While more work needs to be done to understand the operation of leisure as a coping resource, it seems promising to consider the use of leisure coping strategies as part of a process by which stressful events trigger the use of certain types of leisure coping strategies which in turn can influence health. Leisure-stress coping like other types of coping would appear to be a dynamic process that is influenced by changing transactions between people's coping resources (beliefs and coping strategies) and specific contexts and stressors over time. These transactional processes need to be examined if we are to understand not only general coping processes (Lazarus 1995), but also leisure as a coping resource (Iwasaki & Mannell 2000b).

While evidence is mounting that an active leisure lifestyle may be an effective coping resource (e.g. Iwasaki et al. 2001; Mannell et al. 2003), we have much to learn. It is also clear that strategies aimed at improving health through changes in leisure lifestyle should not focus solely on levels of participation. The coping potential of specific leisure pursuits needs to be considered. Also, leisure is not automatically a 'force for good health.' The choices people make can be completely benign in their influence on health or in some cases these choices can be quite destructive as with activities involving substance abuse and other forms of destructive behaviour. In fact, recent analyses of national U.S. and Canadian data suggest that participating in so-called beneficial leisure activities, including exercise, can even have negative consequences (Zuzanek & Mannell 1998). For example, if people who are experiencing heavy demands from work and family try to pack too much activity into their leisure in an effort to cope with stress, stress levels may actually be exacerbated rather than buffered. Having a physically active leisure lifestyle was found to be more strongly related to physical and mental health among older retired adults who have less demands on their time than other life-cycle groups (Zuzanek & Mannell 1999). In developing leisure interventions to enhance health, the individual's life circumstances must be taken into account.

## References and further reading

Blair, S. (1993) 'Physical activity, physical fitness, and health'. *Research Quarterly for Exercise and Sport*, 64: 365–76.

Blair, S. and Connelly, J. (1996) 'How much physical activity should we do? The case for moderate amounts and intensities of physical activity'. *Research Quarterly for Exercise and Sport*, 67: 193–205.

'Breaking point' (1995) *Newsweek*, March 6: 56–61.

Coleman, D. (1993) 'Leisure based social support, leisure dispositions and health'. *Journal of Leisure Research*, 25: 350–61.

Coleman, D. and Iso-Ahola, S. E. (1993) 'Leisure and health: The role of social support and self-determination'. *Journal of Leisure Research*, 25: 111–28.

Csikszentmihalyi, M. (1990) *Flow: The Psychology of Optimal Experience*. New York: Harper & Row.

Csikszentmihalyi, M. (1999) 'If we are so rich, why aren't we happy?' *American Psychologist*, 54: 821–27.

Csikszentmihalyi, M., Larson, R. and Prescott, S. (1977) 'The ecology of adolescent activity and experience'. *Journal of Youth and Adolescence*, 6: 281–94.

Deci, E. and Ryan, M. (1991) 'A motivational approach to self: Integration in personality'. *Nebraska Symposium on Motivation*. 38: 237–88.

Dishman, R. (1990) 'Determinants of participation in physical activity'. In C. Bouchard, R. Shephard, T. Stephens, J. Sutton and B. McPherson (eds), *Exercise, Fitness, and Health*. Champaign, IL: Human Kinetics.

Endler, N. S. and Parker, J. D. A. (1994) 'Assessment of multidimensional coping: Task, emotion, and avoidance strategies'. *Psychological Assessment*, 6: 50–60.

Ensel, W. M. and Lin, N. (1991) 'The life-stress paradigm and psychological distress'. *Journal of Health and Social Behaviour*, 32: 321–41.

Festinger, L. (1957) *A Theory of Cognitive Dissonance*. Stanford, CA: Stanford University Press.

Glass, T., DeLeon, C., Marottoli, R. and Berkman, L. (1999) 'Population based study of social and productive activities as predictors of survival among elderly Americans'. *British Medical Journal*, 319: 478–483.

Haworth, J. (1993) 'Skill–challenge relationships and psychological well-being in everyday life'. *Society and Leisure*, 16: 115–28.

Haworth, J. and Evans, S. (1995) 'Challenge, skill and positive subjective states in the daily life of a sample of YTS students'. *Journal of Occupational and Organizational Psychology*, 68: 109–21.

Iso-Ahola, S. (1980) *The Social Psychology of Leisure and Recreation*. Dubuque, IA: Wm C. Brown.

Iso-Ahola, S. (1994) 'Leisure lifestyles and health'. In D. Compton and S. Iso-Ahola (eds), *Leisure and Mental Health*. Park City, UT: Family Development Resources.

Iso-Ahola, S. (1997) 'A psychological analysis of leisure and health'. In J. Haworth (ed), *Work, Leisure and Well-Being*. London: Routledge.

Iso-Ahola, S. (1999) 'Motivational foundations of leisure'. In E. Jackson and T. Burton (eds), *Leisure Studies: Prospects for the Twenty-First Century*. State College, PA: Venture.

Iso-Ahola, S. and Park, C. J. (1996) 'Leisure-related social support and self-determination as buffers of stress–illness relationship'. *Journal of Leisure Research*, 28: 169–87.

Iso-Ahola, S. and St. Clair, B. (2000) 'Toward a theory of exercise motivation'. *Quest*, 52: 131–47.

Iwasaki, Y. (2002) 'Testing independent and buffer models of the influence of leisure participation on stress-coping and adaptational outcomes'. *Journal of Park and Recreation Administration*, 20: 90–129.

Iwasaki, Y. and Mannell. R. C. (1999) 'Situational and personality influences on intrinsically motivated leisure behaviour: Interaction effects and cognitive processes'. *Leisure Sciences*, 21: 287–306.

Iwasaki, Y. and Mannell, R. C. (2000a) 'Hierarchical dimensions of leisure stress coping'. *Leisure Sciences*, 22: 163–81.

Iwasaki, Y. and Mannell, R. C. (2000b) 'The effects of leisure beliefs and coping strategies on stress-health relationships: A field study'. *Leisure/Loisir*, 24: 3–57.

Iwasaki, Y., Mannell, R. C., Smale, B. J. A. and Butcher, J. (2002) 'A short-term longitudinal analysis of leisure coping used by police and emergency response service workers'. *Journal of Leisure Research*, 34: 311–39.

Iwasaki, Y., Zuzanek, J. and Mannell, R. C. (2001) 'The effects of physically active leisure on stress-health relationships'. *Canadian Journal of Public Health*, 92: 214–18.

Kleiber, D. A., Hutchinson, S. L. and Williams, R. (2002) 'Leisure as a resource in transcending negative life events: Self-protection, self-restoration, and personal transformation'. *Leisure Sciences*, 24: 219–35.

Langer, E. and Rodin, J. (1976) 'The effects of choice and enhanced personal responsibility for the aged: A field experiment in an institutional setting'. *Journal of Personality and Social Psychology*, 34: 191–98.

Lazarus, R. S. (1995) 'Theoretical perspectives in occupational stress research'. In R. Crandall and P. L. Perrewe (eds), *Occupational Stress: A Handbook*, Washington, DC: Taylor & Francis.

Mannell, R. and Kleiber, D. (1997) *A Social Psychology of Leisure*. State College, PA: Venture.

Mannell, R. C., Salmoni, A. W. and Martin, L. (2003) 'Older adults caring for older adults: Physically active leisure lifestyles as a coping resource for the health of caregivers.' *Society and Leisure*, 25: 397–420.

Mannell, R., Zuzanek, J. and Larson, R. (1988) 'Leisure states and "Flow" experiences: Testing perceived freedom and intrinsic motivation hypotheses'. *Journal of Leisure Research*, 20: 289–304.

Maslach, C. and Goldberg, J. (1998) 'Prevention of burnout: New perspectives'. *Applied and Preventive Psychology*, 7: 63–74.

Nelson, M., Fiatarone, M., Morganti, C., Trice, I., Greenberg, R. and Evans, W. (1994) 'Effects of high-intensity strength training on multiple risk factors for osteoporotic fractures'. *Journal of American Medical Association*, 272: 1909–14.

Oldridge, N. (1982) 'Compliance and exercise in primary and secondary prevention of coronary heart disease: A review'. *Preventive Medicine*, 11: 56–70.

Orstein, R. and Erlich, P. (1989) *New World–New Mind: Moving toward Conscious Evolution*. New York: Doubleday.

Powell, K. (1988) 'Habitual exercise and public health: An epidemiological review'. In R. Dishman (ed), *Exercise Adherence*. Champaign, IL: Human Kinetics.

Roberts, K., Lamb, K., Dench, S. and Brodie, D. (1989) 'Leisure patterns, health status and employment status'. *Leisure Studies*, 8: 229–35.

Rodin, J. and Langer, E. (1977) 'Long-term effects of a control-relevant intervention with the institutionalized aged'. *Journal of Personality and Social Psychology*, 35: 897–902.

Salmon, P. (2001) 'Effects of physical exercise on anxiety, depression, and sensitivity to stress: A unifying theory'. *Clinical Psychology Review*, 21: 33–61.

Schor, J. (1991) *The Overworked American: The Unexpected Decline of Leisure*. New York: Basis Books.

Schulz, R. (1976) 'Effects of control and predictability on the physical and psychological well-being of the institutionalized aged'. *Journal of Personality and Social Psychology*, 33: 563–73.

Shank, J. (1986) 'An exploration of leisure in the lives of dual career women'. *Journal of Leisure Research*, 18: 300–19.

Stanton-Rich, M. and Iso-Ahola, S. (1998) 'Burnout and leisure'. *Journal of Applied Social Psychology*, 28: 1931–50.

Stebbins, R. A. (1992) *Amateurs, Professionals, and Serious Leisure*. Montreal: McGill-Queen's University Press.

Stebbins, R. A. (2001) *New Directions in the Theory and Research of Serious Leisure*. Lampeter, Ceredigion, Wales: The Edwin Mellen Press.

Surgeon General's Report (1996) *Physical Activity and Health*. Washington, DC: US Department of Health and Human Services.

Swift, R. (2002) 'Rush to nowhere'. *New Internationalist*, March: 9–13.

'Time Out' (1995) *US News & World Report*, December 11: 85–96.

Wheaton, B. (1985) 'Models for the stress-buffering functions of coping resources'. *Journal of Health and Social Behaviour*, 26: 352–64.

Zeidner, M. and Endler, N. S. (1996) *Handbook of Coping: Theory, Research, Applications*. New York: John Wiley.

Zuzanek, J. (1998) 'Time use, time pressure, personal stress, mental health, and life satisfaction from a life cycle perspective'. *Journal of Occupational Science*, 5: 26–39.

Zuzanek, J. and Mannell, R. C. (1998) 'Life-cycle squeeze, time pressure, daily stress, and leisure participation: A Canadian perspective'. *Society and Leisure*, 21: 513–44.

# Chapter 11

# Serious leisure, volunteerism and quality of life

*Robert A. Stebbins*

## Introduction

Serious leisure and quality of life have an obvious affinity for one another; as suggested in the old popular song 'Love and Marriage', they go together like a horse and carriage. Consider the want-based approach to quality of life, the approach used in this chapter. It consists of four components:

> a sense of achievement in one's work, an appreciation of beauty in nature and the arts, a feeling of identification with one's community, a sense of fulfillment of one's potential.
>
> (Campbell et al. 1976: 1)

This, a subjective approach, contrasts with the objective social indicators approach (see Markides 1992); the former centres on people's perceptions, expectations, aspirations and achievements orientations (Mukherjee 1989: 44). Every serious leisure activity engenders at least three of the four components identified by Campbell and his colleagues, with the arts and outdoor activities producing all four. Career volunteering, the type of serious leisure that will be examined here for the quality of life it produces, can engender either three or four of these components, depending on the area of life in which the person in question decides to volunteer.

We first consider the idea of serious leisure and its counterpart, casual leisure. The concept of optimal leisure lifestyle is taken up next, which is then linked to that of quality of life. Precisely how career volunteering leads to optimal leisure lifestyle and quality of life is the subject of the final main section.

## Leisure: serious and casual

Serious leisure is the systematic pursuit of an amateur, hobbyist or volunteer activity that participants find so substantial and interesting that, in the typical case, they launch themselves on a career centred on acquiring and expressing its special skills, knowledge and experience (Stebbins 1992: 3). To sharpen understanding of it, serious leisure has often been contrasted with casual or unserious leisure, the immediately intrinsically rewarding, relatively short-lived pleasurable activity requiring little or no special training to enjoy it (Stebbins 1997). Its types include play (including dabbling), relaxation (e.g. sitting, napping, strolling), passive entertainment (e.g. TV, books, recorded music), active entertainment (e.g. games of chance, party games), sociable conversation, and sensory stimulation (e.g. sex, eating, drinking). It is considerably less substantial and offers no career of the sort just described for serious leisure. Casual leisure can also be defined residually as all leisure not classifiable as amateur, hobbyist or career volunteering.

Serious leisure is constituted of three types: amateurism, hobbyist activities and career volunteering. The amateurs are found in art, science, sport and entertainment, where they are inevitably linked in one way or another with professional counterparts who, with some exceptions, coalesce into a three-way system of relations and relationships involving the public whom the two groups share. The professionals are identified and defined according to sociological theory, a more exact procedure than the commonsense approach, which measures professionalism according to the criteria of more or less full-time employment for remuneration (Stebbins 1992: ch. 2).

Hobbyists lack the professional alter ego of amateurs, although they sometimes have commercial equivalents and often have small publics who take an interest in what they do. Hobbyists are classified according to five categories: collectors, makers and tinkerers, activity participants in non-competitive, rule-based, pursuits (e.g. hunting, mountain climbing, barbershop singing), players of sports and games in competitive, rule-based activities with no professional counterparts (e.g. field hockey, shuffleboard, badminton) and the enthusiasts of the liberal arts hobbies. The liberal arts hobbyists are enamoured of the systematic acquisition of knowledge for its own sake. Many of them accomplish this by reading voraciously in a field of art, sport, cuisine, language, culture, history, science, philosophy, politics or literature (Stebbins 1994). But some of them go beyond this to expand their knowledge still further through cultural travel, public lectures, documentary videos and the like.

Volunteering is voluntary individual or group action oriented toward helping oneself or others or both (Van Til 1988: 5–9). This definition alludes to the two principal motives of volunteering. One is helping others – volunteering as altruism; the other is helping oneself – volunteering as self-interestedness. Examples of the latter include working for a strongly felt cause or, as will become evident later, working to experience, as serious leisure enthusiasts do everywhere, the variety of social and personal rewards available in volunteering and the leisure career in which they are framed.

The taxonomy published in (Stebbins 1998a: 74–80), which consists of 16 types of organisational volunteering, shows the scope of career volunteering.

Career volunteers provide a great variety of services in education, science, civic affairs (advocacy projects, professional and labour organisations), spiritual development, health, economic development, religion, politics, government (programmes and services), human relationships, recreation and the arts. Some of these volunteers work in the fields of safety or the physical environment, while others prefer to provide necessities (e.g. food, clothing, shelter) or support services. Although much of career volunteering appears to be connected in one way or another with an organisation of some sort, the scope of this leisure is sometimes even broader, as when it includes the kinds of voluntary helping devoted individuals do for social movements or for neighbours and family. Still, the definition of serious leisure restricts attention everywhere to volunteering in which the participant can find a career, in which there is continuous and substantial helping, rather than one-time donations of money, organs, services and the like.

Serious leisure is further defined by six distinguishing qualities (Stebbins 1992: 6–8), qualities found among amateurs, hobbyists and volunteers alike. One is the occasional need to *persevere*, such as in confronting danger, managing stage fright or dealing with embarrassment. Yet, it is clear that positive feelings about the activity come, to some extent, from sticking with it through thick and thin, from conquering adversity. A second quality is, as already indicated, that of finding a *career* in the endeavour, shaped as it is by its own special contingencies, turning points and stages of achievement or involvement.

Careers in serious leisure commonly rest on a third quality: significant personal *effort* based on specially acquired *knowledge*, *training* or *skill*, and, indeed, all three at times. Examples include such characteristics as showmanship, athletic prowess, scientific knowledge and long experience in a role. Fourth, eight *durable benefits*, or broad outcomes, of serious leisure have so far been identified, mostly from research on amateurs: self-actualisation, self-enrichment, self-expression, regeneration or renewal of self, feelings of accomplishment, enhancement of self-image, social interaction and belongingness, and lasting physical products of the activity (e.g. a painting, scientific paper, piece of furniture). A further benefit – self-gratification, or the combination of superficial enjoyment and deep satisfaction – is also one of the main benefits of casual leisure, to the extent that the enjoyment part dominates.

A fifth quality of serious leisure is the *unique ethos* that grows up around each instance of it, a central component of which is a special social world where participants can pursue their free-time interests. Unruh (1980) developed the following definition:

A *social world* must be seen as a unit of social organization which is diffuse and amorphous in character. Generally larger than groups or organizations, social worlds are not necessarily defined by formal boundaries, membership lists, or spatial territory . . . A social world must be seen as an internally recognizable constellation of actors, organizations, events, and practices which have coalesced into a perceived sphere of interest and involvement for participants. Characteristically, a social world lacks a powerful centralized authority structure and is delimited by . . . effective communication and not territory nor formal group membership.

(Unruh 1980: 277)

In another paper Unruh added that the typical social world is characterised by voluntary identification, by a freedom to enter into and depart from it (Unruh 1979). Moreover, because it is so diffuse, ordinary members are only partly involved in the full range of its activities. After all, a social world may be local, regional, multiregional, national, even international. Third, people in complex societies such as Britain and the United States are often members of several social worlds. Finally, social worlds are held together, to an important degree, by semiformal, or mediated, communication. They are rarely heavily bureaucratised yet, due to their diffuseness, they are rarely characterised by intense face-to-face interaction. Rather, communication is typically mediated by newsletters, posted notices, telephone messages, mass mailings, Internet communications, radio and television announcements, and similar means, with the strong possibility that the Internet could become the most popular of these in the future.

The sixth quality revolves around the preceding five: participants in serious leisure tend to *identify* strongly with their chosen pursuits. In contrast, casual leisure, although hardly humiliating or despicable, is nonetheless too fleeting, mundane and commonplace for most people to find a distinctive identity there.

In addition, research on serious leisure has led to the discovery of a distinctive set of rewards for each activity examined (Stebbins 2001). In these studies the participant's leisure satisfaction has been found to stem from a constellation of particular rewards gained from the activity, be it boxing, barbershop singing or working with autistic children. Furthermore, the rewards are not only satisfying in themselves, but also satisfying as counterweights to the costs encountered in the activity. That is, every serious leisure activity contains its own combination of tensions, dislikes and disappointments, which each participant must confront in some way. For instance, an amateur football player may not always feel like attending the daily practices, occasionally be bested by more junior players when there, be required to sit on the sidelines from time to time while others get experience at his or her position, and still regard this activity as highly satisfying – as (serious) leisure – because it also offers certain powerful rewards.

Put more precisely, then, the drive to find satisfaction in serious leisure is the drive to experience the rewards of a given leisure activity, such that its costs are seen by the participant as more or less insignificant by comparison. This is at once the meaning of the activity for the participant and his or her motivation for engaging in it. It is this motivational sense of the concept of reward that distinguishes it from the idea of durable benefit set out earlier, an idea that emphasises outcomes rather than antecedent conditions. Nonetheless, the two ideas constitute two sides of the same social psychological coin. More on this later.

The rewards of a serious leisure pursuit are the more or less routine values that attract and hold its enthusiasts. Every serious leisure career both frames and is framed by the continuous search for these rewards, a search that takes months, and in many activities, years before the participant consistently finds deep satisfaction in his or her amateur, hobbyist or volunteer role. The ten rewards presented below emerged in the course of various exploratory studies of amateurs, hobbyists and career volunteers (for summary of these studies, see Stebbins 1998a, 2001). As the following list shows, the rewards of serious leisure are predominantly personal.

Personal rewards

1   Personal enrichment (cherished experiences)
2   Self-actualisation (developing skills, abilities, knowledge)
3   Self-expression (expressing skills, abilities, knowledge already developed)
4   Self-image (known to others as a particular kind of serious leisure participant)
5   Self-gratification (combination of superficial enjoyment and deep satisfaction – flow, fun)
6   Re-creation (regeneration) of oneself through serious leisure after a day's work
7   Financial return (from a serious leisure activity)

Social rewards

8   Social attraction (associating with other serious leisure participants, with clients as a volunteer, participating in the social world of the activity)
9   Group accomplishment (group effort in accomplishing a serious leisure project; senses of helping, being needed, being altruistic)
10  Contribution to the maintenance and development of the group (including senses of helping, being needed, being altruistic in making the contribution)

Furthermore, the rewards were not only satisfying in themselves, but also satisfying as counterweights to the costs encountered in the activity. That is, every serious leisure activity contains its own combination of tensions, dislikes and disappointments, which each participant must confront in some way. For instance, a volunteer board member may not always feel like attending board meetings, occasionally have his or her ideas rejected when there, be asked to perform a disagreeable task from time to time, and still regard this activity as highly satisfying – as (serious) leisure – because it also offers certain powerful rewards.

## Optimal leisure lifestyle

An optimal leisure lifestyle is the deeply satisfying pursuit during free time of one or more substantial, absorbing forms of serious leisure, complemented by a judicious amount of casual leisure (Stebbins 2000). A person finds an optimal leisure lifestyle by engaging in leisure activities that individually and in combination realise human potential and enhance quality of life. Given the multitude of effects of the Information Age in which many people now live, one of them being to reduce the significance of their paid employment (Rifkin 1995), they now have to confront, often for the first time, what they really want to do in their free time. Casual leisure, as respite, was the most common trade-off when work dominated their lives. But, now, with fewer hours on the job and less interesting and more stressful work to do while there, these people could well become interested in searching for more substantial leisure than they had heretofore. Certainly they have reached a point in life where pursuing an optimal leisure lifestyle is a realistic option, where they can take charge of enhancing their own personal well-being.

People searching for an optimal leisure lifestyle strive to get the best return they can from use of their free time. What is considered 'best' is, of course, a matter of personal definition; a quality of optimal leisure lifestyle predicated on the person's awareness of the great range of potentially available leisure possibilities. Thus people know they have an optimal leisure lifestyle when, from their own reasonably wide knowledge of feasible serious and casual leisure activities and associated costs and rewards, they can say they have enhanced their well-being by finding the best combination of the two types.

People enjoying an optimal leisure lifestyle are thus aware of other appealing casual and serious activities, but nonetheless sufficiently satisfied with their present constellation of activities to resist abandoning them or adopting others. Still, this could change in the future, as an activity loses its appeal, the person loses his or her ability to engage in it, or new activities gain attractiveness. From what I have observed in my own research, people with optimal leisure lifestyles seem to sense that, at a given point in time, if they try to do too much, they will force a hectic routine on themselves, risk diluting their leisure, and soon become unable to participate fully in what they have chosen.

Optimal leisure lifestyle is a new concept in the study of leisure. Its strength is that it examines, not leisure activities – the usual approach in leisure studies – but leisured individuals who pursue casual and serious leisure activities within one or more social worlds and combine these activities to their advantage and satisfaction over a typical day, week, month, season, year, and stage in their life cycle. Looking at annual combinations, for example, my own research indicates that many amateurs in Canadian football find such a combination, in part, by playing rugby during the off-season and, for some, going in for ice hockey during the winter (Stebbins 1992). Moreover, the mix of activities changes over each person's life course, varying with factors like age, sex, and health as well as occupational demand, socio-economic status, and place of residence. Yet, here, emphasis is always on individuals and personal agency, as they shape and reshape their optimal leisure lifestyles, draw on available social, educational, and monetary resources; and in serious leisure, find careers and participate in social worlds.

It is expected that, in the twenty-first century, optimal leisure lifestyle will vary more than ever across the life course, primarily because the ebb and flow of occupational responsibilities (e.g. oscillation between part-time and full-time work, temporary unemployment, early retirement) will be more unpredictable and, for a significant part of the population, because the availability of interesting work will decline accompanied by a rise in stressful work (Aronowitz and DiFazio 1994: 334–42; Rifkin 1995: ch. 12; Castells 1996: 264). For these reasons, too, leisure, compared with work, will assume ever greater importance, an attitude sure to elevate the importance of optimal leisure lifestyle. Much like when people once tried to maximise the benefits they could derive from work, they will increasingly try to do this with leisure, finding as they succeed certain benefits common to both spheres.

## Quality of life

Where does quality of life fit in all this? Applying to leisure the first component – sense of achievement – it is evident from what was said earlier about the rewards of personal enrichment, self-expression, group accomplishment and contribution to the maintenance and development of the group as well as the characteristics of career, effort, benefits and perseverance that people can routinely find that sense here, and not just in paid work. The second component, which refers to appreciation of beauty in nature and the arts, is as noted in the introduction, met in such serious leisure forms as the outdoor activities and artistic pursuits, including backpacking, cross-country skiing, sculpting and string quartet playing. Third, all serious leisure has links with the wider community, if in no other way, than through the social worlds of its participants. Additionally however, many serious leisure activities relate directly to the larger community, as through artistic performances by amateurs, interesting displays by hobbyists (of, for example, stamps, model trains, show dogs) and needed services by volunteers. Sense of fulfilment of potential – the fourth component – comes primarily from experiencing the reward of self-actualisation, but also, to a certain extent, from the serious leisure characteristics of finding a career in the activity and having to occasionally persevere at following it.

This close fit of serious leisure and quality of life gives substance to Neulinger's (1981) observation that

> leisure is not just a component of the quality of life, but the very essence of it. It is not a neutral state of mind, but a positive, highly desirable one, and an important value. Leisure in my opinion is the guideline needed for any decision relating to the quality of life.
>
> (Neulinger 1981: 66)

In other words, people find quality of life, in part or in whole, through leisure experiences.

But in this regard, not just any leisure activity or set of activities will do the job, as the idea of optimal leisure lifestyle demonstrates only too well. The highest quality of life comes with developing an optimal leisure lifestyle, as understood in all the detail just presented. That is, the highest quality comes with a satisfying balance of serious *and* casual leisure, as defined by the person whose leisure life is being considered.

Quality of leisure life is influenced by, among other factors, the people with whom leisure participants pursue their leisure (Csikszentmihalyi 1997: 13–14) and even by the number and intensity – the quantity – of rewarding experiences found in this sphere of life (Neulinger 1981: 66–8). Csikszentmihalyi found that most people spend roughly equal amounts of time in three social contexts, and depending on how satisfying life is there, they too, influence quality of life. The first is composed of strangers, coworkers, coparticipants in leisure and the like. The second is made up of one's family – parents, siblings, spouse (or partner), children, and so on. The third context is solitude, the absence of other people. It is quite possible that, since these three contexts are often settings for leisure activity, research will someday show that optimal leisure lifestyle, too, is influenced by how satisfying life is in them.

## Volunteering

Career volunteering, it was noted in a preceding section, can engender three and sometimes all four of the components of qualilty of life, depending on the area of community living in which the person in question chooses to volunteer. Of the 16 areas of organisational volunteering noted earlier, recreation, the arts and the physical environment offer obvious and consistent opportunity for expression of the second component of quality of life. Here volunteers can find all elements comprising the quality of life equation.

But what about the costs of serious leisure, in particular those associated with career volunteering? For part of quality of life consists of finding a sense of achievement and realising one's potential, which means, in practical terms, also coming to grips with these costs, in a word, conquering adversity. A study of key volunteers in two minority francophone communities in Calgary and Edmonton, Canada (Stebbins 1998b), the only study so far to examine costs in career volunteering, revealed a variety of tensions and dislikes, but no significant disappointments. Key volunteers are highly committed community servants, working in one or two enduring, official, responsible posts within one or more grassroots groups or organisations. Key volunteers are distinguished from other types of volunteers by at least four criteria. First, presidents, treasurers and the like have complex, extensive responsibilities whose execution affects in important ways the functioning of their group or organisation. Second, such positions are enduring. Officers are usually elected for a year, and chairs and directors may serve even longer. Third, the success of the groups and organisations in which they serve contributes significantly to the maintenance and development of the local community of like-minded people (e.g. of the same ethnic group, leisure interest, environmental stance, self-help concern). Fourth, key volunteers have a high degree of commitment to their collectivities and through them, the study clearly showed, to these two community goals.

According to the study, many tensions relate in one way or another to the volunteer's family life, where the presence of school-age children can be especially problematic. One tension – the *temporal tension* – centres on the need for constant planning and scheduling, the two principal ways of making most efficient use of scarce time. The temporal tension was felt mostly during the working week, since respondents with children tended to avoid volunteering at weekends, whose daytime hours they reserved for family-related activities and domestic obligations.

Furthermore, *relational tension* can occur, the friction that sometimes emerges between spouse and volunteer or children and volunteer when the latter privileges a volunteer engagement over demands of one or both of the former. Respondents who experienced this tension uniformly qualified it as a main cost of volunteering, and through constant planning, tried their utmost to avoid it, proclaiming in the face of their occasional failure that, nevertheless, 'family comes first over volunteering'.

I labelled *obligative tension* the stress arising from an inability to meet various domestic requirements when faced with volunteer commitments of higher priority. Several respondents mentioned feeling guilty for failing to perform certain repair, maintenance and housekeeping duties. This tension can also be relational when failure to do a chore or do it satisfactorily irritates another member of the family.

An especially thorny variant of the obligative tension revolves around the question of who makes evening meals when both parents volunteer. To make matters worse, solving this tension tends to beget another temporal tension, since responsibility for a particular weekday dinner must be set well in advance for the parent at home that afternoon or evening. When both parents have to be away from home the same evening with one doing volunteer work, their children, if young, become the focus of a special obligative tension. That is, a babysitter must be engaged (more advanced planning), a necessity made more complicated in linguistically endogamous households where this person must meet not only the usual moral standards for this responsibility but also the language requirement of speaking passable French. Such people can be difficult to find in Canada's urban francophone communities, and when found, may live at some distance from the volunteer's home.

Finally, some respondents experienced a *leisure tension*, which unlike the preceding tensions, is mainly positive. That is, committed to certain volunteer roles (leisure), they then discovered how little time they had for other leisure activities they were also fond of. The volunteers in this study nearly always resolved this tension by favouring volunteering, though often not without disquieting recognition that they were missing something interesting and satisfying. On this note, a handful of respondents said they had no leisure, or at least no other leisure. Schedule conflicts among volunteer commitments constituted for several interviewees an especially annoying variant of the leisure tension. Missing, for example, a meeting of the board of directors of the theatre society, of which one is secretary, to attend a meeting of the parish council, of which one is chair, would be most bothersome for these interviewees, in part, because they believe effective coordination of community volunteer activities is possible.

When I asked the respondents in this study to discuss their dislikes apropos their pursuits, I indicated my interest lay in more serious matters than pet peeves. Dislikes are problems requiring the volunteer to adjust significantly, possibly even to leave the volunteer role. It turned out that in these two francophone communities, as most everywhere else in life, annoyances were prevalent, whereas deeper dislikes were much rarer. On the one hand, all but three respondents could describe at least one substantially disagreeable aspect of key volunteering. On the other hand, very few could describe more than two.

The two most prominent dislikes were behaviour of *difficult persons* and shortage of *reliable volunteers*. The first are infamous for their propensity to complain excessively about all sorts of issues and be exceptionally critical of others. Fortunately, difficult persons are uncommon in these two communities, though this makes their presence even more conspicuous. The problem of a shortage of reliable volunteers baffled leaders of both communities, since many francophones live there who could do volunteer work.

The remaining dislikes, each mentioned less often than these two, are for the most part related to one of the tensions just described. Thus some respondents disliked the *temporal tension*, particularly their occasional lack of control over events, volunteer and otherwise, that engender it. Although lack of control is only sporadic, it is still aggravating when it occurs, as when the president calls an emergency meeting of the board of directors of a club or an association. The sudden new obligation may uproot carefully made plans involving family responsibilities of the volunteer and certain activities of its members. It also happens from time to time that community events (e.g., a talk, concert, reception, open house), many of which key volunteers feel they ought to attend even when the events are not directly related to their group or organisation, are mounted on short notice or broadly publicised only at the last minute. Again, family plans can be thrown into turmoil as parent-volunteers scramble to fill several roles at once. Citing excessive temporal tension as its main cause, a handful of interviewees also classified *fatigue* as a dislike, a dispiriting weariness that can sometimes develop, signalling impending burnout.

In the same vein, weekend volunteer commitments – usually for Saturday – though rare and scheduled at that time chiefly because the organiser has little choice, are nevertheless disliked by some key volunteers. They lament that such commitments can extend the temporal tension yet another day, while belying the claim and promise that weekends are for family. Of note here was my nearly total lack of success (one exception) in obtaining Saturday interviews, even though I offered every respondent the opportunity for one.

## Conclusion

Quality of life, whether achieved through volunteering or through another form of serious leisure, is a state of mind that, to the extent people are concerned with personal well-being, must be pursued with notable diligence. (Did we not speak earlier of career and perseverance?) Quality of life does not just 'fall into one's lap', as it were, but requires desire, planning, and patience, as well as a capacity to seek deep satisfaction through experimentation with serious and casual leisure activities that hold the possibility of becoming solid elements in an optimal leisure lifestyle. Personal agency is the watchword here. Leisure educators, leisure counsellors among them, can advise and inform about various leisure activities that hold strong potential for quality of life, but it is the individual who must become motivated to pursue them and develop a plan for doing so.

Spector and Cohen-Gewerc (2000) write in this same vein about the process of 'initiation', a sort of self-directed personal actualisation. A person who has free time

> is at a crossroads, in which he has been given the opportunity to make good use of the time which has now been 'freed-up' in the timetable of his personal life, by investing in his own self. This is an incredible opportunity, however its fulfillment is entirely his own responsibility.
>
> (Spector and Cohen-Gewerc 2000: 3)

Initiation, they hold, is individual attention, a process of supporting change leading ultimately to growth of the initiate's uniqueness.

In this matter, then, there is no shortcut. The route to initiation and the good life, though hardly a two-rut, rock-filled mountain road, is certainly not, however, a limited-access, four-lane highway. It always has plenty of hills, curves and bumps, but is nonetheless well worth travelling.

## References

Aronowitz, S. and DiFazio, W. (1994) *The Jobless Future: Sci-Tech and the Dogma of Work*. Minneapolis, MN: University of Minnesota Press.

Campbell, A., Converse, P. and Rogers, W. L. (1976) *The Quality of American Life: Perceptions, Evaluations, and Satisfactions*. New York: Russell Sage Foundation.

Castells, M. (1996) *The Information Age: Economy, Society, and Culture, Volume 1: The Rise of the Network Society*. Oxford: Blackwell.

Csikszentmihalyi, M. (1997) *Finding Flow: The Psychology of Engagement with Everyday Life*. New York: Basic Books.

Markides, K. (1992) Quality of life. In E. F. Borgatta and M. L. Borgatta (eds) *Encyclopedia of Sociology*, Volume 3. New York: Macmillan.

Mukherjee, R. (1989) *The Quality of Life Valuation in Social Research*. New Delhi: Sage.

Neulinger, J. (1981) *To Leisure: An Introduction*. Boston, MA: Allyn and Bacon.

Rifkin, J. (1995) *The End of Work: The Decline of the Global Labor Force and the Dawn of the Post-market Era*. New York: G. P. Putnam's Sons.

Spector, C. and Cohen-Gewerc, E. (2000) From education to initiation: leisure as a second chance. Paper presented to the Sixth World Leisure Congress, World Leisure and Recreation Association, Bilbao, Spain, July.

Stebbins, R. A. (1992) *Amateurs, Professionals, and Serious Leisure*. Montreal, PQ and Kingston, ON: McGill-Queen's University Press.

Stebbins, R. A. (1994) The liberal arts hobbies: a neglected subtype of serious leisure. *Loisir et Société/Society and Leisure* 16: 173–86.

Stebbins, R. A. (1997) Casual leisure: a conceptual statement. *Leisure Studies* 16: 17–25.

Stebbins, R. A. (1998a) *After Work: The Search for an Optimal Leisure Lifestyle*. Calgary, AB: Detselig.

Stebbins, R. A. (1998b) *The Urban Francophone Volunteer: Searching for Personal Meaning and Community Growth in a Linguistic Minority*, volume 3, no. 2 (New Scholars-New Visions in Canadian Studies quarterly monographs series). Seattle, WA: University of Washington, Canadian Studies Centre.

Stebbins, R. A. (2000) Optimal leisure lifestyle: combining serious and casual leisure for personal well-being. In M. C. Cabeza (ed.) *Leisure and Human Development: Proposals for the Sixth World Leisure Congress*. Bilbao, Spain: University of Deusto.

Stebbins, R. A. (2001) *New Directions in the Theory and Research of Serious Leisure*. Lewiston, NY: Edwin Mellen Press.

Unruh, D. R. (1979) Characteristics and types of participation in social worlds. *Symbolic Interaction* 2: 115–30.

Unruh, D. R. (1980) The nature of social worlds. *Pacific Sociological Review* 23: 271–96.
Van Til, J. (1988) *Mapping the Third Sector: Voluntarism in a Changing Political Economy*. New York: Foundation Center.

# Chapter 12

# Work and leisure

## Themes and issues

*John T. Haworth and A. J. Veal*

## A leisure society, or a society with more leisure

It is always foolhardy to attempt to predict the future, but we are continually driven to do so. In the area of work and leisure we should be doubly cautious, in light of some ignominious past attempts, particularly predictions of the coming of a leisure society. The fallibility of such predictions is a persistent theme of a number of chapters in this book. The leisure society, as envisaged by various commentators, from the 1920s to the 1960s, was to be brought about as a result of the process of technological advances making human labour increasingly unnecessary. Goods would be produced in greater and greater abundance by automated processes, such that human society would be able to satisfy its needs with less and less expenditure of labour. As many of the chapters in this book suggest, such a future is no longer seen as imminent. Technology has certainly produced immeasurably more material wealth in the West, but the anticipated leisure society has not emerged – at least, not yet. Despite gains in leisure time achieved during the course of the twentieth century, paid and unpaid work is perceived as the dominant activity in most adults' lives. And in recent years it appears to have become more rather than less dominant.

It can be argued that considerable progress has been made towards a 'society with more leisure' in the past 150 years. As indicated in Chapter 1, the average full-time paid 'working year' is half what it was at the height of the industrial revolution and, due to the higher school-leaving age and prolonged life expectancy in the developed economies, the amount of a person's total waking lifetime spent in leisure is now greater than the amount spent in paid work (Veal 1987: 16). However, as indicated in a number of chapters in this book, progress towards even a 'society with more leisure' appears to have stalled in Western societies, and perhaps gone into reverse, since the late 1970s.

## History

Chapter 1 indicated that one of the most obvious, but neglected, messages of such a history is the realisation of the scale and nature of the change that would be involved in any shift to a significantly more leisured society: it would constitute a social and economic revolution. From the time of the Enlightenment and the Reformation, work in the West has been seen as not only necessary but also *virtuous*, the means by which all might fulfil their duty of contributing to the maintenance and improvement of society. Any change to the fundamental balance between work and leisure would therefore involve moral and cultural as well as economic and social change.

In Clarke and Critcher's (1985) book, *The Devil Makes Work*, the implication was that, without a programme of socialist political activism and reform, any change in the balance of work and leisure, as in other aspects of life in capitalist Britain, would come about only if it was in the interests of capital. The message of Chas Critcher and Peter Bramham, outlined in Chapter 2, is that this remains the case two decades later. In Britain, despite 'all the real changes, especially in the cultural and leisure industries, the basic contours of daily life – of work, family and leisure – have remained remarkably recognisable' (p. 49). The implication is that this will continue as long as British society remains 'basically a capitalist one'.

The history of Western capitalism over the past 200 years has, however, been one of continual, often radical, social change. Many changes which have appeared inimical to the interests of capital, and which have been resisted at the time, have proved advantageous for capitalism in the long term. Examples are the development of the welfare state, which was, and is, resisted by capitalist interests, but which has in practice provided a benign social and political climate in which capital can flourish, and the advent of the eight-hour day and holidays with pay, which helped create the consumer market. As recently as the 1950s and 1960s, significant reductions in working hours were gained, in time, as it happened, to deliver audiences for commercial television as it was being introduced. Further, extended holidays with pay were gained at a time when the possibility of mass car-ownership was emerging, together with the need for customers for large passenger jet aircraft and the growth of tourism.

More recently, as noted in the introduction to the book, there are signs of some individuals adopting a 'counterculture' which rejects total involvement in work as not only undesirable but also as counter-productive (see, for example, Lewis and Smithson 2001). In the United Kingdom, the government, companies and trade unions are increasingly concerned with work-life balance. Family-friendly work patterns, including flexitime, term-time working and job-sharing, became common in the 1990s, due particularly to campaigns by women workers. It is now officially recognised that family-friendly work patterns can lead to economic benefits for business. The capitalist system therefore faces an empirical question: what balance of work and leisure maximises consumption and hence profits?

### Consumer culture: 'work and spend'

Schor (1991, 2000) sees no end to Americans' capacity to desire – and work for – material goods, and hence no prospect of a more leisured society. While Clarke and Critcher (1985) prescribed socialist measures to counter the power of the market – and possibly to produce a more leisured society – Schor (2000) calls for a 'new politics of consumption' – a sort of non-materialist consumer movement Such a call is seen as politically naive by a number of commentators contributing to the volume edited by Cohen and Rogers (2000) and would seem to fly in the face of the basic driving mechanism of the capitalist system. Even if most people might ultimately be capable of reaching a level of material satisfaction in absolute terms – and hence might be in a position to embrace the idea of more leisure rather than working for more material wealth – this seems elusive while significant social and economic inequalities remain, with a wealthy elite parading the pleasures of ever-increasing material prosperity. Capitalism is driven by the principle of high material rewards as incentives for those who take risks and can offer sought-after, marketable skills. Efforts by those lower down the scale to achieve greater equality seem to be continually matched by the efforts of those at the top to stay ahead.

As Fred Hirsch pointed out in 1977, many of the goods and services which people seek as they become more affluent are *positional* goods – such as the house in a sought-after location or a place in a top school or university. While such a scenario might suggest a striving after non-material goals, it also suggests a competitive drive for resources to achieve those goals. In the 1970s, the 'catching up' process was compared with a 'marching column' and termed the 'Principle of Stratified Diffusion' by Young and Willmott (1973). This was seen as a relatively benign phenomenon, by which those further back in the 'column' eventually enjoyed the same goods and services as those at the front. But if the head of the column keeps moving indefinitely, a more leisured society will remain for ever out of reach. One part of society constantly trying to catch up, while the other part is constantly trying to stay ahead, hardly seems to be a recipe for a leisured existence. The 'catching up' syndrome is of course extolled in various mass media, in advertising and editorial content, but is also reinforced by unions and professional groups who frequently use comparators with other groups, rather than absolute measures of income, to support claims for pay increases on the grounds that they are 'falling behind', such claims being laced with anxiety-inducing expressions of concern about loss of status and unfair treatment. This process is then replicated internationally by the efforts of countries at the top of the international income league table to stay there and of those lower down to catch up. The importance of economic growth as an indicator of political effectiveness, in rich and poor countries alike, is evidence of this. Thus, nationally and internationally, the desire of some to catch up and of others to stay ahead creates a drive for more work rather than more leisure. This orthodoxy is beginning to be challenged. Layard (2003) has reviewed evidence showing that above a certain level, economic growth (GDP) does not increase overall societal wellbeing, as people evaluate their income in relation to changing standards. He argues that the good society is the one where people are happiest. And the right action is the one which produces the greatest happiness.

## Technology

Technology also plays its part in the work drive. It has not only provided the means to produce *more* goods and services, but also produced a mass of *new* products, and with it the 'revolution of rising expectations'. And there is no end in sight. Technological innovation is now in-built into industrial economies, with billions of dollars being spent annually on innovation and development of new products. Such is the vigour of the innovative and competitive market process, that the new possibilities for consumption laid before the consumer frequently appear to outstrip any increase in wealth arising from increased labour productivity. This leads to a desire for more and more income to secure access to the increasing range of goods and services on offer. The evidence of the United States suggests that there is virtually no limit to the capacity of humans to demand and consume material wealth. Juliet Schor's (1991, 2000) exposition of this phenomenon, as the 'work-and-spend' syndrome, is portrayed as a sort of moral failing on the part of the American people, but it can be seen as an almost inevitable outcome of the structure of late capitalism. Without it, the very goals of Western political economies would seem futile.

## Post-industrialisation

The changing nature of Western economies also affects consumption and work patterns. A post-industrial economy is characterised by the growing importance of *services* and the declining relative importance of primary (agriculture and extractive) and secondary (manufacturing) industry. This is matched by increasing consumer expenditure on services. But, while material goods become relatively cheaper in real terms, as a result of technologically based efficiencies, services tend to remain relatively expensive, since they generally cannot benefit from technological efficiencies to the same extent. Typically, therefore, contemporary Western households spend increasing amounts on services such as health and education. There is an established literature on the ways in which this process plays out in the leisure service context. While leisure *goods* benefit from technological advance and become cheaper, the provision of leisure *services*, whether by leisure service organisations or by individuals making use of their purchased leisure goods, takes as much *time* as it ever did. In 1970 Stafan Linder coined the term 'harried leisure class' to describe relatively wealthy individuals seeking to pack more and more leisure consumption into a fixed – or reducing – amount of time (Linder 1970). Ironically, considerable levels of stress can be generated by the process of organising the 'weekend away', the 'night out', or even the 'quiet night in' or finding time to make use of the newly acquired boat, golf clubs or home entertainment centre. The balance of effort in acquiring and paying for the second home, boat or golf-club membership, as against the reward, in terms of the amount of enjoyment received from their very limited usage, is frequently questioned.

## The distribution of work and leisure

### Gender

Critcher and Bramham (Chapter 2 in this volume) discuss recent trends in work, family and leisure in the United Kingdom. They consider that the 'common experience of those selling labour power has been the actual intensification of work' and that ours has become a more work-centred society. They note that three-quarters of women aged 25–44 are now in paid employment, and that 80 per cent of part-time workers are women. Leete (2000) in *Working Time* states that much work by women, including childrearing, was done in the home, but that consumerism now drives women out to work and still do childrearing. Gershuny (2000), analysing time-use statistics in the United Kingdom, states that where wives move from being nonemployed to take full-time jobs, they reduce their housework by about ten hours per week, and their husbands increase theirs by about four hours per week. The total amount of paid labour in Western society has increased. The increased hours of paid work done by the average household is one of the contributors to the perceived increases in levels of stress experienced by contemporary families, as outlined by Zuzanek and by Schneider et al. in Chapters 7 and 8 of this book. In Chapter 4 on gender, Judy White draws attention to continued inequality between men and women in the distribution of work and leisure, indicating the need for more research to track the effects of recent change, and political and cultural action to achieve the goals of equality to which many aspire.

Paid work, whether full-time or part-time, can, of course, be beneficial financially and psychologically to women and to the family. Roberts (1999) notes that

Having money and, just as important, earning money, are important for the spending power that is conferred and for additional reasons. Going out to work widens people's social networks beyond their kin and immediate neighbours. Moreover, individuals who are earning are likely to feel, and to be regarded by others, as having earned the right to spend on their own pleasures.

(Roberts 1999: 93–4)

He considers that leisure equality is more likely in conditions of economic equality. He recognises, however, that with the arrival of children, it is still nearly always the mother who interrupts her career.

The Future of Work Programme has produced a report on the 'Future of Work–Life Balance' (Taylor 2001). This notes that the current focus in Britain on the relationship between paid work and parenting and caring reflects the dramatic growth in the proportion of women of adult working age who are in paid employment. While recognising that this is important, the report argues that it should be part of a much more comprehensive strategy that addresses work pressures and dissatisfactions experienced by both men and women in paid employment. The report notes significant class differences in access to basic minimum rights for time off, and that differences in the distribution of income and wealth, as well as power and authority within the workplace, have not gone away, and may even have increased. However, it is recognised that many small companies face genuine difficulties in providing basic rights for time off. Nevertheless, the report advocates that generous and sensible policies that reconcile work with responsibilities outside the paid job might become one of the company's commitment to wider social obligations and part of the definition of what constitutes the good firm. A UK government report on *Life Satisfaction: The State of Knowledge and Implications for Government* (Donovan et al. 2002) cited strong links between work satisfaction and overall life satisfaction, and also between active leisure activities and overall satisfaction. It noted the case for government intervention to boost life satisfaction, by encouraging a more leisured work-life balance.

Full-time dual-earner families are on the increase in the United Kingdom and in several countries in Europe. Gender plays a key role in patterns of work and leisure. Lewis (2003) discusses the integration of paid work and the rest of life, and raises the question: 'Is post-industrial work the new leisure, viewed as an activity of choice and a source of enjoyment?' Lewis notes that paid work is increasingly dominating people's lives. For many people, work is what they apparently choose to spend their time on and enjoy doing, though excessive workloads can be experienced as oppressive. Lewis also notes that the boundaries between work and non-work are, for many, becoming fuzzier and may be crowding out time and energy for personal life and leisure. The study by Lewis and colleagues of accountants indicated that the dominance of work over other activities was often seen as a life-choice, particularly among males where intense work involvement may be linked to professional identity. Yet her article gives a fascinating insight into the complex interplay between social norms, the attribution of choice, and the perception of satisfaction and enjoyment. Lewis points out that occupational identity is constructed within a given social context, and that there is a danger that explanations of the dominance of paid work in people's lives which focus on the individual tend to underestimate the constraints under which choices and identities are constructed. In accountancy, working long hours to please the client becomes identity affirming. But, Lewis argues, this is a highly gendered view that promotes work patterns based on assumptions of traditional male provider families and excludes substantial involvement in family care or other activities. Equally, she notes that women often feel less 'free' to choose to work long hours because of family commitments. Male-gendered views of work also lead to the assumption of inevitability, so that the possibility of working in other ways, which may be equally professional and identity affirming but less all encompassing, is not explored.

Lewis considers that people often talk about choice and working long hours because they enjoy the work, due to the vision of other choices being limited. Equally, 'choice' may be an illusion when working harder and longer is an inevitable consequence of changes in work and organisations. Lewis recognises that some people do gain a sense of enjoyment from intense work, but considers that post-industrial work cannot be unproblematically regarded as the new leisure. Further, that if work is taking over from leisure and other personal activities on a wide scale, we need to examine the broader and long-term effects on individual well-being, families and communities.

Lewis points out that growing awareness of such issues heralded the development of what become known as family-friendly employment policies, or more recently work-life policies, implemented ostensibly to enhance well-being and equal opportunities, but, in reality, largely driven by business concerns such as recruitment and retention. These policies included support for childcare and other family responsibilities as well as flexible working arrangements (the opportunity to vary where and when work is accomplished). They also include opportunities for working less, including part-time or reduced hours. However, take-up of opportunities to work reduced hours tends to be low, particularly among men and especially in white-collar work where to do so is frequently perceived to be career limiting (Perlow 1998; Lewis et al. 2002).

Greenhaus and Parasuraman (1999) reviewing research on work, family and gender indicate that while work and family can be in conflict, having negative effects on each other, they can also be integrated, having reciprocal positive effects. For example, positive attitudes and experiences in one domain may spill over to the other domain permitting fuller and more enjoyable participation in that role. They note that 'Stressful, rigid work environments that demand extended commitments can interfere with family life, whereas, flexible work environments that provide opportunities for self control can enrich family life' (Greenhaus and Parasuraman 1999: 409). Yet, they also note that

> family experiences can also constrain opportunities for involvement in work, and it is in this regard that gender differences are most pronounced. Women's family responsibilities can severely limit their careers in ways that do not generally affect men. Women tend to choose occupations that are compatible with their family's needs. They also limit their aspirations for career advancement.
>
> (Greenhaus and Parasuraman 1999: 409)

Greenhaus and Parasuraman call for the adoption of a life-stage perspective in research, and more research into dual-earner families.

Rapoport et al. (2002) argue from a series of action research projects in organisations, conducted primarily in the United States, that it is possible to advance gender equity and increase workplace performance; the so-called 'Dual Agenda'. They argue that only by investigating the link between current work practices and gendered assumptions about the role and organisation of work will it be possible to identify major leverage points for significant, constructive change. They note that the US Corporate Model is spreading internationally as part of globalisation, and that from the perspective of working men and women the model has serious defects as well as significant advantages. They see gender equity as a fair allocation of opportunities and constraints for men and women in all spheres, in distinction to focusing on equality which can lead to sameness and unfair outcomes. They consider that looking at work through a lens of gender equity or work–personal life integration can bring into focus obstacles to effectiveness that usually remain hidden because they are unquestioned.

Focusing on organisations does not, of course, supplant the role that state policies play in gender equity. Kay (2002) argues that state policies combine a direct practical impact with an ideological message. Part-time employment may confirm the female role as one of service to the household unit. She notes that lack of state childcare provision appears to be of considerable importance in constraining the labour market potential of mothers and households in the least affluent sectors of society.

Kay (2001) argues that gendered leisure and non-employment obligations should also be part of the equation in work-life balance. Within households, the capacity of male and female partners to individually exercise choice she sees as highly contingent upon explicit or implicit negotiation between them. Many studies have shown that, even when both partners are working, women still make a significantly greater contribution to domestic tasks. Kay draws on research which highlights key differences between men's ability to preserve personal leisure time, and the much more limited capacity of women to do so, replicating traditional gender ideologies, indicating a divide in men and women's approaches to reconciling the interests of 'self' with those of 'family'. As individuals, men and women appear to give different priority to the work, family, leisure domains of their collective life, while simultaneously striving to achieve a mutually satisfying joint lifestyle, which may hinder the integration of work and non-work activities. Kay argues that leisure is a significant domain of relative freedom and a primary site in which men and women can actively construct responses to social change. She considers that the recognition of this can contribute, at both a conceptual and empirical level, to a holistic understanding of contemporary lived experience; but that it raises the question about the extent to which we can realistically talk of families, collectively, being equipped to resolve the work-life dilemma.

Ferdman (1999) calls for increased attention to race, ethnicity and culture as key variables in the study of gender in organisations. Ferdman argues that research into gender is predominantly into the experience of white people, who can be blind to the priviliges carried by a white person in a white-dominated society. He notes, for example, that in the United States the increase in the proportion of working mothers is primarily a white phenomenon, because large numbers of black women have always worked outside the home. In a similar vein, it is noted that the financial advantage that white males have over females is not as evident for men of colour. Ferdman points to a growing literature documenting how the meaning and experience of gender is culturally defined in the context of particular societies, social settings and ethnicities. He considers that gender, as a set of beliefs and practices for structuring human experience, is relatively meaningless outside a particular cultural context; highlighting the problems inherent in attempting to generalise about all women and men.

A false universalism has also been identified in sport and leisure. Jarvie and Reed (1997) are critical of European intellectual constructions of racism, which they claim have often been applied in a devastating manner. They argue that black feminist thought has yielded a radical critique of both the sociology of sport and white European feminism (Plowden 1995).

These views on gender, work and leisure echo Judy White's call in Chapter 4 for the need to listen to many voices; arguing against trends to establish a 'grand' theory, which can 'travel' across academic disciplines. She calls for a return to feminist scholarship as research and writing grounded in people's experience, which does not claim to be universal, but which, nevertheless, is not purely individual, but has relevance for policy in leisure and work.

### Class, employment, leisure and income

While individuals from a range of social classes may consider the hours they work to be excessive, a greater proportion of manual workers than managers and professionals consider these to be necessary in order to earn enough money to live. And in a 'culture of consumption' both money and time are desired. But the uneven distribution of power and authority in the workplace, crucial to negotiation, may have increased in recent years in many cases. Yet, as Chapter 10 by Iso-Ahola and Mannell indicates, understanding of the link between active leisure and health and well-being is necessary to inform individual and collective choice and societal policy on work-life balance. Similarly, type of work is relevant, as Jiri Zuzanek shows in Chapter 7. While feelings of 'time crunch' can have a negative impact on well-being, people can work long hours without feeling 'time crunched' if they have freely chosen their work and are interested in it – though, in families, this may be drawing on 'collective social capital' to sustain long hours of work.

In developed countries increases in inequalities in income are associated with increases in mortality (Wilkinson 1996, 2000, 2002). As inequalities increase, Wilkinson argues, the level of trust within the community decreases and the quality of social relations deteriorate with a shift occurring from more affiliative social strategies based on equity and inclusion (friendship relations) towards social strategies based on dominance hierarchies with increased competition for resources, increasing levels of chronic stress. Low social status can mean increased subordination and exclusion, and a decreased willingness to participate in the community. Insecurities from early life can also exacerbate the insecurities and stresses that go with low social status. Studies indicate that wellness is achieved by the simultaneous and balanced satisfaction of personal, interpersonal and collective needs (Prilleltensky 2001). As Zuzanek notes in Chapter 7, individual coping strategies and lifestyle modifications alone are not sufficient to offset the negative impact of psychological stress on health. He indicates that most pressures faced by people in modern societies are social or structural. They are embedded in the competitive demands of globalised economies, changing workplace environments, and value orientations emphasising rapid material gains and conformity with standardised and fast forms of expression prevalent in popular culture. Pahl (2000, 2001) argues that the way societies are organised has a direct effect on the quality of social relationships, which will influence health and well-being. He considers that a more ruthless commitment to market principles and the development of a more low-trust society through multifarious controls can undermine the friend-rich nature of society and decrease well-being.

### Retirement and age

There is one sense in which a more leisured society has arrived – namely in retirement. A large proportion of the population of the West can now expect to live as much as one-third of their lives in retirement. Increasingly, they expect to do so at a standard of living well above the poverty level. While this yields a substantial period of leisure at the end of life, ensuring financial security during this period requires additional work in earlier years to pay superannuation contributions or other forms of saving. A worker needs to put aside about 15 per cent of his or her income to secure an acceptable level of income in retirement – that is, they must work 15 per cent longer than they would if an extended period of retirement did not exist.

The gerontologist, Tom Kirkwood (2001), in the BBC Reith Lectures 2001 *The End of Age*, argues that life expectancy will go on increasing in developed economies, and that we need equitable solutions that will meet our needs at all future stages of our life cycle. He considers that

> Market forces, particularly in the area of employment, will very soon wake up to the fact that there is going to be a shortage in the work force that can only be filled by recruiting and retraining older workers. Work patterns will have to become more flexible and attractive in order to retain older staff. Jobs and the workplace will require redesign. It is ironic to realise that in all probability it will be profit that will drive the attention to well-being of body and mind in old age that could so easily have been perceived as a priority with less-blinkered eyes.
>
> (Kirkwood 2001: 71)

He believes that diet and physical and mental exercise are crucial to ageing and quality of life, that a positive mental attitude is important, and that one is never too old to take up a new challenge or learn a new skill. He argues that the freedom to make choices is perhaps the greatest single index of well-being, but that choice tends to be limited by age much more than is really necessary either through negative expectations or just poor planning.

There is now considerable debate in the United Kingdom about raising the age for retirement. This may in part be driven by the 'pensions crisis': the need to have money for longer years in retirement. It is strongly argued that many people would not want to choose to work beyond the age of 65 years, particularly if their job is physically demanding. Equally, it is argued that many people would wish to continue working on a full or part-time basis up to the age of 70 years or beyond. Flexibility of working patterns seems crucial to the age of retirement.

Warr (2001) in a review of age and work behaviour notes that in many occupations, employees move out of physically demanding roles as they become older, but that it may be possible to retain them for longer periods than is currently the case by ergonomic adjustments and job redesign. While age differences occur in certain complex cognitive activities, Warr notes that in many cases they are likely to be unrelated to job performance because the abilities in question are not relevant to the task requirements. Some aspects of some jobs may pose difficulties for older employees when fast information processing is important, or rapid learning, though these requirements can be reduced. It has been found that undertaking substantively complex work gives rise to higher level intellectual functioning, especially among older employees. In many cases job performance may be better in older workers through greater experience, though learning and development initiatives should be available to older workers and not just younger workers. Personality traits have been found to differ by age; one possibility is that older individuals will tend to outperform younger ones in roles requiring good interpersonal relationships and dependable attention to detail and deadlines. Modifications of working conditions may also serve to harness older persons' motives. Older people may be less interested in a high level of job demands and higher salary. Some may be particularly effective if they were permitted to work on a part-time or intermittent basis. Warr (2001) notes that in order to reduce unfair discrimination against older individuals the focus should be on job-relevant attributes rather than stereotyped judgements about older people as a whole.

In 'A Positive Approach to Older Workers' in the What is? series produced by the Institute of Work Psychology at Sheffield University, Peter Warr states that 'Without changes in the culture of an organization explicitly valuing people irrespective of their age, improvements will not be sustained'. He also advocates that it is important for individuals to review their own approach to positive ageing, which would include a concern for employability as circumstances change, and the maintenance of learning motivation and confidence, which may not always be easy as workers become increasingly divorced from new learning as they grow older.

## Processes of change

Individuals make lifestyle choices within constraints imposed by the wider social system. The question arises as to the extent to which the social system is open to change by conscious collective action.

Issues of participation in society are now on the research agenda in the United Kingdom and Europe in relation to issues of governance. Ian Gibson (2002), Chair of the UK Parliamentary Select Committee on Science and Technology, considers that many controversies about new technologies, health risks and democracy reduce to questions of good governance. He stresses that we need to design processes, institutions and rules in a way that allows concerns to be voiced, heard and acted upon, and thus contribute to the creation of trust. Onora O'Neil (2002), in the BBC Reith Lectures 2002 *A Question of Trust*, considers that some of the regimes of accountability and transparency, developed in the United Kingdom since the mid-1980s or so, may damage rather than reinforce trust. She considers that we need intelligent accountability; to focus less on grandiose ideals of transparancy and rather more on limiting deception; and to provide assessable reasons for trusting and mistrusting, particularly in the mass media. The ESRC Democracy and Participation Programme includes research into civic participation, trust and social capital (e.g. Halpern et al. 2002). The new European Commission

Framework Programme (FP6 2002–2006), has a dedicated social sciences research priority *Citizens and Governance in the Knowledge-based Society*. However, as was indicated in *Work and Leisure* (Haworth and Smith 1975), public participation in decision-making, though strongly advocated, is not without difficulties, including concerns for both the efficiency of the process and legitimacy of expression in social situations where there would be conflicting requirements. This applies just as much today. Perri 6 (2002) argues that there are inevitably different forms of social organisation in society, and that no single form of social organisation is unequivocally conducive to well-being, rather each form of organisation creates risks and undermines some kinds of well-being in the process of promoting others. He considers that well-being must be pursued through politics, as the practice of negotiation and restrained conduct of basic conflicts. His view of well-being is about what people will recognise, under particular institutions, as shared life well lived and worth living together.

### Global dimensions

It is becoming recognised that a global perspective on these issues is necessary. Concerns and events in other countries influence concerns for work, leisure and well-being in one country. With one-fifth of the world's population living in extreme poverty some politicians see gross inequality as the biggest moral challenge that we face and the greatest threat to the future safety and stability of the world (Short 2002). The 2002 *Annual Report of the World Bank* considers that it is vital to link together considerations of poverty, environmental sustainability and economic growth.

## Quality-of-life, well-being and lifestyle

While work and leisure account for most of the average individual's waking hours, studying just these two aspects of individual, social and economic life is limiting. Individual and collectively, human beings do not pursue a particular balance in work and leisure for its own sake, but as a means to an end – a satisfactory quality-of-life. While the concept of 'quality-of-life', as an alternative to narrower economic measures of human well-being, has been the focus of research and debate for many years, it has been addressed in only a desultory manner in relation to leisure. Leisure clearly makes a contribution to quality-of-life, but in most assessments it comes well down the list of key components, following such items as nutrition, housing, education, health and environmental quality (Marans and Mohai 1991: 354). This is exacerbated by the tendency for quality-of-life research to be conducted in relation to social and economic development, with a particular emphasis on developing countries. In Western society, where the above basic contributors to quality-of-life are generally available at a high standard, other matters, in

Maslovian style, come into play. When nutrition, housing, education, health and environmental quality are all at a relatively high standard, improvements in quality-of-life revolve around non-material, 'modern' issues, such as stress.

In recognition of these 'first world' concerns, research and policy have come to focus on *well-being*, as explored by John Haworth in Chapter 9. Well-being can be seen as being synonymous with quality-of-life, but in practice the two terms denote two traditions of research, quality-of-life being concerned with more objective and communal criteria and measures, and well-being being generally concerned with more subjective and individual criteria. Hence research on well-being connects directly with the emerging research on time-use, work and leisure, which has focused on 'harriedness', 'time crunch' and stress, with their implications for interpersonal relationships and individual psychological and physical health.

Social science inputs to issues of well-being, work, leisure and quality-of-life are important, even if in themselves they cannot provide definitive answers. Research findings are not universally applicable. In most cases they apply only to a limited number of situations similar to those in which the research is conducted, though they may provide potential insights into related situations, and bring into focus choices we should consider. Well-being is a concept that requires further delineation. While there are useful quantitative and qualitative measures of well-being, further development is needed. Different constructions are put on well-being by different groups in society. There are also questions of exclusion in relation to the social construction of well-being. Some voices are not heard. It is important to investigate how individual attributes interact with aspects of the social and physical environment to produce different states of well-being.

A consideration of well-being is now very much on the social science agenda. In the United Kingdom it is viewed as a trans-disciplinary issue. An ESRC seminar series on 'Well-being: Social and Individual Determinants' conducted in 2001–2002 aimed to generate research interest in the processes and circumstances that facilitate well-being (including positive mental and physical health) in individuals, groups, communities and societies.[1] The objective was not to replace, but provide an alternative to, and to complement, the overwhelming harm-based focus of much social scientific research into health. Well-being offers a paradigm that allows those in the academic, policy and user fields to focus on positive outcomes, and how best to realise them.

In addition, these seminars highlighted the fact that social institutions and environmental factors facilitate and constrain well-being, in interaction with characteristics of persons; and that enjoyment plays a pivotal role in this interaction. This is discussed in Chapter 9 by Haworth. Enjoyment in both work and leisure is important for well-being, and even in work it is not just an optional extra (Bryce and Haworth 2002). Delle Fave and Massimini (2003) note that creative activities in work, leisure and social interaction can give rise to 'flow' or 'optimal' experiences. These experiences foster individual development and an increase in skills in the lifelong cultivation of specific interests and activities. Delle Fave and Massimini (2003) report studies which show a relationship between optimal experience and quality of performance at work. They argue, in line with others, that these optimal experiences are important in shaping our future. In Chapter 11 Stebbins discusses serious leisure, volunteerism and quality of life. His research shows that extended engagement in absorbing leisure activities which require effort can provide a range of rewards. But there are also costs involved, which entails a commitment to the pursuit. Rewards and costs may be an integral part of the social world and identity associated with the pursuit, which would require the confidence and social skills necessary to participate in community activity.

### Social capital

Social capital has been viewed as the notional commodity of community engagement and cohesion which can be associated with better health and well-being. Yet preliminary studies are beginning to show that social ties have the potential to both improve and constrain health and well-being; and that an emphasis on increasing social capital has the potential to exclude those who are different (Sixsmith et al. 2001; Sixsmith 2002; Sixsmith and Boneham 2002; Sixsmith et al. 2002). Perri 6 (2002) considers that the general argument that we need more 'social capital' for well-being is misguided, since the concept lumps together too many forms of social organisation to be useful. He argues that, understood at the level of social networks, the theory enables one to reread with more exactitude the body of research that finds social networks, friendship and social support to be beneficial for a wide range of outcomes, to show that different kinds of networks benefit different practices of well-being. However, following his thesis on the different and conflicting forms of social organisation in societies, he advocates that policys-makers' thinking about the larger sets of interests need to sustain the requisite variety of all the types of friendship and acquaintance that are defined by different forms of social organisation.

## The question of policy

Changes in the balance of work and leisure in Western societies over the past 150 years have been brought about by a mixture of market forces (from both the demand and supply side), industrial action and government policy. In the past, governments have legislated in the area of working hours and holidays with pay largely on the basis of humanitarian concern for vulnerable groups in the labour market. Concerns about the overall balance between work, leisure and consumption in the economy and society have tended to be secondary. Recent campaigns by European trades unions to reduce working hours as a macro-economic policy have been successful only in France. 'Going it alone' was seen as extremely risky in a globally competitive environment, and the results to date appear not to have delivered the hoped-for reductions in unemployment.

Whether or not governments should intervene in this way is a political as well as social and economic issue. 'Labour market reform' in the current economic and political climate is generally seen as involving deregulation rather than imposition of, for example, controls on working hours. But as with labour market reforms in the past, what may appear immediately attractive to individual firms may not be beneficial to the market and society as a whole or in the long term. A pattern of work and leisure which leads to high levels of stress among some employees and underemployment, with its attendant social problems, among others, hardly seems ideal or in anyone's long-term interest. An informed consideration of issues surrounding well-being, individual and collective choices in work and leisure, is increasingly required, to which it is hoped this book will significantly contribute.

## Note

1   Papers relating to the seminars are on the website www.wellbeing-esrc.com. There are also key links to other sites concerned with well-being and Positive Psychology. The website will be available for interaction until 2006, and additional material can be emailed to haworthjt@yahoo.com. The series, and related publications, show the importance of considering societal, environmental and individual factors in considering well-being. Several of the points on well-being made in this chapter were discussed in the seminars and are summarised on the pages of the website.

## References

Bryce, J. and Haworth, J. T. (2002) Wellbeing and flow in a sample of male and female office workers. *Leisure Studies* 21: 249–63.

Clarke, J. and Critcher, C. (1985) *The Devil Makes Work: Leisure in Capitalist Britain.* London: Macmillan.

Cohen, J. and Rogers, J. (eds) (2000) *Do Americans Shop Too Much?* Boston, MA: Beacon Press.

Delle Fave, A. and Massimini, F. (2003) Optimal experience in work and leisure among techers and physicians: individual and bio-cultural implications. *Leisure Studies* 22(4): 323–42.

Donovan, N., Halpern, D. and Sargeant, R. (2002) *Life Satisfaction: The State of Knowledge and Implications for Government.* London: Cabinet Office.

Ferdman, B. M. (1999) The color and culture of gender in organizations: attending to race and ethnicity. In G. N. Powell (ed.) *Handbook of Gender and Work.* London: Sage.

Gershuny, J. (2000) *Changing Times: Work and Leisure in Postindustrial Society.* Oxford: Oxford University Press.

Gibson, I. (2002) *Social Sciences* (Economic and Social Research Council, London), 52 (September): 5.

Greenhaus, J. H. and Parasuraman, S. (1999) Research on work, family, and gender: current status and future directions. In G. N. Powell (ed.) *Handbook of Gender and Work*. London: Sage.

Halpern, D., John, P. and Morris, Z. (2002) Social Capital, Participation and the Causal Role of Socialisation ESRC seminar series 'Wellbeing: situational and individual determinants' 2001–2002 www.wellbeing-esrc.com Research and Policy for Wellbeing.

Haworth, J. T. and Smith, M. A. (eds) (1975) *Work and Leisure*. London: Lepus.

Hirsch, F. (1977) *The Social Limits to Growth*. London: Routledge and Kegan Paul.

Jarvie, G. and Reid, I. (1997) Race relations, sociology of sport and the new politics of race and racism. *Leisure Studies* 16: 211–19.

Kay, T. (2001) Leisure, Gender and Family: Challenges for work–life integration. ESRC seminar series 'Well-being: situational and individual determinants' 2001–2002 www.wellbeing-esrc.com Work, employment, leisure and wellbeing.

Kay, T. (2002) The sexist state: leisure, labour and the ideology of welfare policy. *Leisure Studies Association Newsletter* 61: 23–9.

Kirkwood, T. (2001) *The End of Age*. London: Profile.

Layard, R. (2003) *Happiness: Has Social Science a Clue?* Lionel Robins Memorial Lectures 2002–3, http://cep.ac.uk.

Leete, L. (2000) History and housework: implications for work hours and family policy in market economies. In L. Golden and M. Figart (eds) *Working Time: International Trends, Theory and Policy Perspectives*. London: Routledge.

Lewis, S. (2003) The integration of paid work and the rest of life: is post industrial work the new leisure? *Leisure Studies* 22(4): 343–55.

Lewis, S. and Smithson, J. (2001) Sense of entitlement to support for the reconciliation of employment and family life. *Human Relations* 55(11): 1455–82.

Lewis, S., Cooper, C., Smithson, J. and Dyer, J. (2002) *Flexible Futures: Flexible Working and Work–Life Integration*. Report on Phase Two. London: Institute of Chartered Accountants in England and Wales.

Linder, S. B. (1970) *The Harried Leisure Class*. New York: Columbia University Press.

Marans, R. W. and Mohai, P. (1991) Leisure resources, recreation activity and the quality of life. In B. L. Driver and G. L. Peterson (eds) *Benefits of Leisure*. State College, PA: Venture.

O'Neil, O. (2002) *A Question of Trust*. Cambridge: Cambridge University Press.

Pahl, R. E. (2000) *On Friendship*. Cambridge and Oxford: Polity.

Pahl, R. E. (2001) Social Support and Wellbeing. ESRC seminar series 'Wellbeing: situational and individual determinants' 2001–2002 www.wellbeing-esrc.com Work, employment, leisure and well-being.

Perlow, L. (1998) Boundary control: the social ordering of work and family in a high tech organisation. *Administrative Science Quarterly* 43: 328–57.

Perri 6 (2002) Sense and Solidarities: a neo-Durkheimian institutional theory of well-being and its implications for public policy. ESRC seminar series 'Well-being: situational and individual determinants' 2001–2002 www.wellbeing-esrc.com Research and Policy for Wellbeing.

Plowden, M. (1995) *Olympic Black Women*. Gretna: Pelican.

Prilleltensky, I. (2001) Personal, relational, and collective wellbeing: an integrative approach. ESRC seminar series 'Wellbeing: situational and individual determinants' 2001–2002 www.wellbeing-esrc.com Wellbeing: interaction between person and environment.

Rapaport, R., Bailyn, L., Fletcher, J. K. and Pruit, B. H. (2002) *Beyond Work–Family Balance: Advancing Gender Equity and Work Performance.* San Francisco, CA: Jossey-Bass.

Roberts, K. (1999) *Leisure in Contemporary Society.* Wallingford, UK: CAB International.

Schor, J. B. (1991) *The Overworked American: The Unexpected Decline of Leisure.* New York: Basic Books.

Schor, J. (2000) A new politics of consumption. In J. Cohen and J. Rogers (eds) *Do Americans Shop Too Much?* Boston, MA: Beacon Press.

Short, C. (2002) Secretary of State for International Development, UK Government, reported in *Guardian*, Monday 30 September.

Sixsmith, J. (2002) Health, Wellbeing and Social Capital. ESRC seminar series 'Wellbeing: situational and individual determinants' 2001–2002 www.wellbeing-esrc.com Research and Policy for Wellbeing.

Sixsmith, J. and Boneham, M. (2002) Men and masculinities: stories of health and social capital. In C. Swann and A. Morgan (eds) *Social Capital for Health: Insights from Qualitative Research.* London: Health Development Agency.

Sixsmith, J., Boneham, M. and Goldring, J. (2001) *The Relationship between Social Capital, Health and Gender: A Case Study of a Socially Deprived Community.* Final Report. London: Health Development Agency.

Sixsmith, J., Boneham, M., Goldring, J. and Griffiths, J. (2002) *Young Men's Health and Social Capital: An Exploratory Study of Participation in a Youth Community Project.* Final Report. London: Health Development Agency.

Taylor, R. (2001) The Future of Work–Life Balance. ESRC Future of Work Programme. Economic and Social Research Council, Polaris House, Swindon.

Taylor, R. (2002) Britain's World of Work-Myths and Realities. ESRC Future of Work Programme. Available from the ESRC (tel: 01793 413001).

Veal, A. J. (1987) *Leisure and the Future.* London: Allen and Unwin.

Warr, P. (2001) Age and work behaviour: physical attributes, cognitive abilities, knowledge, personality traits and motives. In C. L. Cooper and I. T. Robertson (eds) *International Review of Industrial and Organizational Psychology, Volume 16.* London: John Wiley.

Warr, P. (2002) *What is? A Positive Approach to Older Workers.* Sheffield: Institute of Work Psychology, Sheffield University.

Wilkinson, R. G. (1996) *Unhealthy Societies: The Afflictions of Inequality.* London: Routledge.

Wilkinson, R. G. (2000) *Mind the Gap: Hierarchies, Health and Human Evolution.* London: Weidenfeld and Nicolson.

Wilkinson, R. G. (2002) Social Capital: the impact of inequality. ESRC seminar series 'Wellbeing: situational and individual determinants' 2001–2002 www.wellbeing-esrc.com Research and Policy for Wellbeing.

The World Bank Annual Report (2002) Washington DC: The World Bank.

Young, M. and Willmott, P. (1973) *The Symmetrical Family.* London: Routledge.

# Author index

# Subject index